HEALING YOUR RELATIONSHIP WITH YOURSELF

End Inner Conflict by
Developing a Harmonious Inner Family

To Suzyn,
      Value yourself,
Don't sell out. Go
within so that you can
love yourself first.

By   Joel

Joel Brass

Order this book online at www.trafford.com/08-1065
or email orders@trafford.com

Most Trafford titles are also available at major online book retailers.

Cataloguing Data:

1. emotional healing 2. psychotherapy 3. self-help

Note for Librarians: A cataloguing record for this book is available from Library and Archives Canada at www.collectionscanada.ca/amicus/index-e.html

Printed in Victoria, BC, Canada.

ISBN: 978-1-4251-8559-6

We at Trafford believe that it is the responsibility of us all, as both individuals and corporations, to make choices that are environmentally and socially sound. You, in turn, are supporting this responsible conduct each time you purchase a Trafford book, or make use of our publishing services. To find out how you are helping, please visit www.trafford.com/responsiblepublishing.html

Our mission is to efficiently provide the world's finest, most comprehensive book publishing service, enabling every author to experience success. To find out how to publish your book, your way, and have it available worldwide, visit us online at www.trafford.com/10510

www.trafford.com

North America & international
toll-free: 1 888 232 4444 (USA & Canada)
phone: 250 383 6864 ♦ fax: 250 383 6804
email: info@trafford.com

The United Kingdom & Europe
phone: +44 (0)1865 487 395 ♦ local rate: 0845 230 9601
facsimile: +44 (0)1865 481 507 ♦ email: info.uk@trafford.com

10 9 8 7 6 5 4 3

Acknowledgements

To Marim, my wife: You waited for me to do my healing work so that I could join you in a beautiful, loving relationship. You are *my* Universe of Love. To Adam and Simon, my sons: You are my lights and teachers. As children, and now as young men, you have shown me a pure and unlimited love. It humbles and motivates me to match it. To my late parents, Abe and Rose Brass: You gave your all to D. and me. You demonstrated the complete extension of self that love is. To my sister D. and brother-in-law Yale: With me always, in spirit and support, from the first draft to the final product.

To my mentors: Ed Allen, Joseph Goodman, Leonard Shaw, and Sheldon Kopp—brilliant, compassionate, and wise men—psychotherapy mavericks and pioneers.

To my editor, Richard Clark: Your belief in my work and your knowledge and stunning array of editing skills have moved and inspired me. You have gone the "extra mile".

To all of my clients and seminar participants: Through your courage, honesty, vulnerability, and humility you have demonstrated the individual healing that I write about in these pages. You are this book.

Respect and Dignity

Readers may encounter ideas they disagree with. My intent in writing this is to offer a path to healing that I have seen work with consistent success, not to generate disagreement or conflict. The opinions and observations I offer throughout this book are entirely my own, and for that, only I am responsible.

Table of Contents

"Furthermore, we have not even to risk the adventure alone, for the heroes of all time have gone before us. The labyrinth is thoroughly known. We have only to follow the thread of the hero path, and where we had thought to find an abomination, we shall find a god. And where we had thought to slay another, we shall slay ourselves. Where we had thought to travel outward, we will come to the center of our own existence. And where we had thought to be alone, we will be with all the world."

Joseph Campbell
The Power of Myth
With Bill Moyers;
Sue Fowler Editor
Doubleday, 1988, p. 123

Prologue

The Universe of Fear and The Universe of Love

There is a fear of which I am a part that passes all understanding, and there is a peace and love of which I am a part that passes all understanding. *Fear separates me from everything and love connects me to everything.*

I am afraid. I am more afraid than I know—more afraid than I can conceive of. On some very deep sub-conscious, level I am afraid of everybody and everything. I am afraid of almost every single human being. Even with those few people who are the blessed exceptions to this rule, I become afraid from time to time. I have found it embarrassing, and at times shameful, to admit that I am *so* afraid. To hide all this I have created many public faces. In attempting to control my fear, I have demanded of myself that I present myself to the world as unflappably strong, poised, and confident; or at the very least, to appear to others to be unflappably strong, poised, and confident. You might say that I have been too afraid to be afraid. This pretence of being fearless, as I now see it, has only driven my fear underground. This has caused my fear to splinter and refract into a multitude of expressions that affected literally every area of my life.

Over the years I have devoted considerable *conscious* attention and effort to intimately knowing and working through all of this fear. I have been able to track it, map it, and heal it, to the point where it does not have complete control over my life. I have come to know that it is a part of me; a twisted, pained and sometimes toxic part of me, but a part of me nonetheless. This part of me is in great need of attention, healing, and love. I have come to know that by embracing whatever fear I encounter, and following it to its origins in my consciousness, I can experience peace, safety, and sanity with more and more regularity.

There are occasions when my fear actually disappears completely. It is as if it has evaporated. It is at those times that I can touch and experience *a peace and connectedness that passes all understanding*. In my efforts to heal I have also devoted considerable attention and effort to knowing this peace and connectedness and following it to its origins in my consciousness.

Presently, at this stage of my healing I have considerable

influence over whether I experience fear and conflict or peace and love. I know almost all the signals that tell me, as I will describe in this book, whether I am operating out of the Universe of Fear or the Universe of Love. I know when I have lost my peace. I know when I am operating lovelessly (meaning living in the Universe of Fear). Most importantly, using the approach I present in this book—that of creating an Inner Family living in harmony and working together—I experience an integration and healing of the inner conflicts and divisions that have predisposed me to my emotionally erratic ways.

By taking on the work of healing their Inner Family, I have witnessed many clients and seminar participants rid themselves of a vast array of debilitating symptoms and unwanted behaviour patterns by ending the conflicts and divisions raging inside of them. These people experience a transformative sense of self-integration, balance, and unity. The purpose of this book is to, hopefully, extend these possibilities to you.

The Story of the Little Plug

Once upon a time there was a plug, but not your ordinary garden-variety kind of plug. *This* little plug was produced by its manufacturer already connected to its socket. The plug and socket were so merged together it was impossible to see them as separate.

For curious and complex reasons, the people in power in the world did not trust the indivisible, invisible relationship between plugs and sockets. They believed the most important and necessary thing they could do to help little plugs survive in the world was to teach them to see themselves only as a plug among plugs. They taught the plugs to pull away from their sockets and be completely independent of them.

This brought much confusion and pain to the little plug because it is in the nature of plugs and sockets to be connected. One day it came to pass that it completely disconnected from its socket. From that day forward, strange as it may seem, the little plug learned to want no part of its socket. As a result, when it was thrust into the world, it never felt complete. And, just like the people in power, soon, it too, had forgotten it ever had a socket.

This left a deep, empty feeling and the little plug tried to discover what was missing. Because it was completely disconnected, and wanted no part of sockets (it learned its lessons well), the only thing it could do was to try to "hook up" with an ever-changing array of the other disconnected plugs. And, as you might imagine, there was quite a pile to choose from!

There was a faint, hopeful thought that by connecting to another disconnected plug it could find what it once had known with its socket. So it moved from one disconnected plug to another, yet it never found what it sensed it was missing. Most of its time in the world was spent in this way, only to create more confusion and pain than it had ever known before. Its solution was to try *even harder* to connect to another plug. Each new attempt always held great promise in the beginning—that connection with another disconnected plug would and could offer everything the socket used to. However, it would eventually show itself as nothing more than another disconnected plug (exactly like the little plug itself). At this point some plugs quickly or slowly, subtly or obviously, choose to fizzle out and die. Is this what the little plug should do too? Where could it turn? Oh, what to do, what to do?

It took many, many misconnections with other plugs, but the little plug finally realized the only thing the world of people in power could offer was another misconnection to another disconnected plug. It had enough of this confusion and pain. It decided it would rather fail and die looking for the connection to its socket than experience one more prong to prong misconnection. The little plug could not live the way it had one more minute. It decided to find and go down a different path in search of its original socket.

The journey of healing is to take ourselves down a different path; to take ourselves back to connect to the original socket of which we are an indivisible part.

The Map of Healing

We are conceived and born. In that, we are created equal and each arrive in this world being conscious—awake and aware. In early infancy, while living and growing, there are two operating consciousnesses. These I call a *natural child consciousness* and a *spiritual consciousness*. These are true and authentic conscious-nesses that "should" guide us through life. I often refer to these together, so it may appear like they are the same thing. They aren't. In my view, a *spiritual consciousness* is our connection to the universe and to all things in Life—that which some of us symbolize in using words like "God" or "Universal Love" or "Spirit"—the universal nature of our personal existence. The *natural child consciousness* is like the representative of that spiritual conscious-ness here, in this life, on earth.

For many reasons—the way our parents were raised, traditional parenting practices of the era we were born, trauma, illness, oppressive religions, politics—for many reasons, our care-givers and the authority figures in our infancy and childhood unconsciously moulded our spontaneous, natural, and spiritual loving characters. This caused each of us to unknowingly create an altered personality that adapted to the rules and demands of our environ-ment. This became our *adaptive child consciousness* and allowed us to cope with and "survive" the emotional pain and fear that was imposed upon us. The *adaptive child consciousness* is a reflexive response to hide and protect the *natural child consciousness* and the *spiritual consciousness*. Creating the *adaptive child consciousness* to survive these non-loving, repressive, or overtly abusive environ-ments is something we *all* had to do (granted, in varying degrees).

As we were continuously forced to deny our true natural and spiritual natures, the pain persisted and increased. It became overwhelming and our minds then went to the next level of survival. Out of the *adaptive child consciousness* we unknowingly created an *aggressive/defensive ego consciousness*. This was for emotional and often physical survival.

The *aggressive/defensive ego consciousness* manifests in a thousand different ways in each of us; we are each incredibly unique in how this controls our personality and harms ourselves and others. And, *at the same time*, this ego convinces us we don't have one (an aggressive defensive ego) and we are each innocent or justified in how we conduct ourselves.

The *aggressive/defensive ego* is in such overwhelming control, in such a wide range of destructive and harmful (*un*loving) behaviours and attitudes, that it is quite impossible to list all its variations. Here are a few blatant examples that manifest "dysfunction": violence, crime, drug addiction, alcohol addiction, use of pornography, adultery, sex addiction, prostitution, greed, gross consumerism and *all* advertising, chronic illness, compulsive behaviour, road rage, blatant competitiveness, politics, racism, sexism (misogyny and male-bashing), religious righteousness.

Subtle and moderate examples of a controlling and harmful *aggressive/defensive ego* are: passive-aggressive behaviour, depresssion, punishing, over- or underachieving, belligerence, lying, irresponsible spending, unnecessary eating, passionate viewing of aggressive sports or films, most television viewing, weight issues, impatience or annoyance with drivers, gossiping, sarcastic humour, mental and verbal putdowns, being macho, excessive pleasing and helplessness, cheating on your taxes, spitefulness, cynicism, frequently interrupting others, creating social cliques, arrogance, struggling for control, any harsh criticisms of yourself or others, on-going or repetitive conflict (especially within families and relationships), sulking, bad moods, arguing, shouting, screaming, raising your voice. All of this, and *much more*, is evidence of having an *aggressive/defensive ego* in prominent control of your life.

Healing work first requires that we neutralize or reduce the viciousness of our *aggressive/defensive ego*. Then, we heal the pain carried by the *adaptive child consciousness*. These are accomplished through specific exercises, and the creation of what I call an *independent/aware adult consciousness*. These four different inner "consciousnesses" [(i) spiritual; (ii) natural child (and its adaptive side); (iii) aggressive/defensive ego; (iv) independent/aware adult], I collectively refer to as an Inner Family.

Through healing, once we have created harmony within ourselves, we can then (more often, but not always because the work is on-going) live in a Universe of Love. Experiencing love is the natural extension of the two consciousnesses you were born with: a *natural/child consciousness* and its connection to your *spiritual consciousness*.

That is what is explained in this book, and what you will experience in committing to this work.

Introduction

One belief this book, and the inner work described in it, is founded on, is the belief that your state of consciousness is the defining factor that determines the quality of your life. How you experience everything in life, for example, the weather, the day, your finances, your self-worth, your marriage, your family, other people (and their motives), and the world around you, is not determined by the external agents and circumstances you experience. It is determined by the state of consciousness that you are in when you experience them. Your state of consciousness actually gives rise to what you perceive, think, feel, say or do, and is responsible for the results you produce in yourself and others. Your state of consciousness determines the quality of your life.

Rain falls from the sky. It creates oceans, rivers, lakes, and streams which, in turn give rise to wells and reservoirs and the supply of your daily drinking water—a supply which must be clean and safe for your body to be nourished. The rivers, lakes, and drinking water reflect the purity or contamination of the rain.

So it is with your state of consciousness. Your state of consciousness gives rise to the oceans, rivers, lakes, and streams of your perceptions, thoughts, feelings, words, and behaviours. As such, these will be natural or unnatural, pure or contaminated, and healthy or destructive to yourself and your world.

A second belief on which this book is founded is that your "normal" state of consciousness is fear-based and survival-oriented; a consciousness I call the aggressive/defensive ego. This consciousness, if left unchecked and unhealed, produces and perpetuates an extremely dark vision of reality and inestimable hardship and damage for yourself and other human beings.

The good news, and a third belief upon which this book and approach to personal healing is built, is that there are other states of consciousnesses within you (which I call Inner Family members). If you can develop the desire and the skill to access them, they will offer you an entirely different way of interpreting and experiencing your reality. Through these other consciousnesses (ones I have named the *natural child consciousness/authentic self* and the *spiritual consciousness*) you are afforded a friendlier and safer version of the weather, the day, your finances, your self-worth, your marriage, your family, other people (and their motives), and the world around you—a version that is much lighter and brighter and considerably easier on yourself and everyone else. You gain access to these two consciousnesses by toning down or reducing the influence of your *aggressive/defensive ego* and by creating a fourth member of your Inner Family, the *independent/aware adult consciousness.*

This book will present a model for personal healing (creating inner harmony) and offer you an extremely significant choice—*a choice over your moment to moment state of consciousness and whether you are giving rise to a fear-based consciousness or a heart and spirit led consciousness.* If you decide to change, at first you will probably exercise this choice only occasionally, but with practice you can increasingly choose the state of consciousness you are in. The natural child and spiritual consciousnesses, guided by a responsible *independent/aware adult consciousness,* are so powerfully healing and restorative that even experiencing them one-half hour a day, or two minutes an hour, can make a tremendous difference in the quality of your life and the contribution you make to the world.

Fortunately, there are many ancient spiritual and more modern psychological paths that have been devised to assist human beings in the alleviation of their unhappiness and suffering. This book describes one more path. It is my hope that you find it effective and it brings you greater balance and harmony, inner freedom, and personal happiness.

With a smile, I offer this Warning:

To some people, the first four or five chapters are somewhat dry and intellectual. This is necessary because in the first part of the book I am presenting theory. We must understand *some* theory so that the practical exercises which follow make sense. In other words: The healing exercises and client stories offered in the last half of the book will provide you with more self-understanding and deeper insight after you reasonably understand the "more boring" theory. (But then some of you will quite enjoy the theory, too.)

Chapter 1

"The whole is greater than the sum of its parts."

What Is The Model of Inner Family Self-Healing?

The Inner Family Model of Self-Healing is both a spiritual and an emotional practice for transforming our ordinary state of consciousness. After twenty-five years experience of being a part of peoples' most intimate and tortured struggles for growth and healing, it is my belief that what we intuitively seek for our lives and relationships can only be obtained by means of a significant shift in our consciousness. Anything short of a major shift in our fundamental state of being; anything less than a spiritual and emotional redefinition of how we see ourselves as human beings, can, at best, offer only relief and symptom substitution. Without a fundamental and sustainable shift in the operating consciousness of the person suffering, their life will remain unhappy, their relationships return to being problematic and discordant, and symptoms will reinvent themselves in ever more imaginative and clever disguises. There will be no enhancement in the quality of their life.

If we do not learn how to take responsibility for our usual state of consciousness—that of the aggressive/defensive ego—and switch out of it when we need to, we can be compared to heavily burdened travelers carrying bulging suitcases in both hands through life. Our solution, to obtain relief, is one day to wearily drop our suitcases on the street, open them up, move the shirts to where the shoes were, switch the underwear and toiletries, shuffle the socks and pants around, and then pick up exactly the same luggage and plod on. Are the suitcases any lighter? No. Are we any freer? Is our journey any easier? No. Will we enjoy it any more? Obviously not.

I have often felt I was offering the people I worked with only insignificant changes and relief; however, I have always dedicated myself to discovering more effective therapeutic techniques that could offer them and me permanent and lasting shifts in the quality of our lives. I define a shift as something taking root so deeply in our emotional and spiritual natures such that *we can't return to the old ways of operating even if we want to*. After a shift has occurred we will see and react to our world in a noticeably different way. I believe that nothing less than a fundamental change in our basic operating consciousness can provide us with more than temporary relief. We must develop a new vision of what "healing" is. *Relief just isn't good enough.*

I have witnessed sincere and committed clients, in therapy and seminars, achieve *and maintain* shifts in their consciousness from the Inner Family Model of Self-Healing. Lives become happier; relationships transform and become reliable sources of consistent love, and self-destructive symptoms can be truly released rather than reinvented.

How does this self-healing occur? Regardless of the type of healing you seek (be that physical, mental, emotional or spiritual), **you must be patient with yourself and determined. You must also choose to be personally accountable for the quality of your life.** The signs that healing is taking place are:

- you consistently experience more moments of inner peace within than moments of fear;
- seemingly incompatible and even adversarial sides and forces in your make up as an individual find common ground and harmony;
- you no longer *unknowingly* bring the emotional pain and survival mechanisms of your past into the present;
- with every perception, thought, feeling and action, you have a clear and conscious choice over whether you are coming from and generating fear or love;
- you are grounded in a heart-based and spiritually-guided internal information system that will act as your personal leader through all of life's hardships and difficulties; and.
- Over the long term there will be fewer (much fewer!) painful symptoms and life difficulties.

I believe the Inner Family Model of Self-Healing described in this book is a reliable and proven practice that addresses and fosters the growth of all of these aspects. So, let's take one step at a time towards your personal healing. First I'll explain the most fundamental concept of this approach: The Inner Family.

What Is an Inner Family?

All of us are walking contradictions. Often we think one thing, feel another, say a third, and do a fourth. Though we use the pronoun "I" in our conversations when referring to ourselves, we presume there is only one of "me"; however, we are not the same "me" from moment to moment. We are a walking, talking set of multiple, and often conflicting personalities—a whole host of "I's". "I" may feel one way about a circumstance or person; yet another aspect of "I" may feel quite differently. "I" may hold a certain opinion or belief about something, while simultaneously another aspect of "I" holds a different (or even completely contrary) belief about that same thing.

Many of us are aware, at least superficially, that we are comprised of disparate parts. We even use the phrase "part of me" as a figure of speech. I used this expression just the other day when speaking with a client about the weather expected for the weekend. I mentioned I have two boys and that usually Saturday is a busy day running around to soccer games. She informed me she had heard the weather was supposed to be great, whereupon I said something like: "Part of me is happy about this because it makes watching the games so much more enjoyable." Then I added: "On the other hand, another part of me wishes we would get a thunderstorm, so the games would be cancelled and I could sleep in and relax for the rest of the day."

As simple as this example may be, it points to at least two different "I"s inside of me in regard to the weekend weather—one that would prefer it be sunny and warm, the other hoping for seriously bad weather. Aside from the fact that I live in Canada, and can routinely have both my wishes come true, a logical and reasonable interrogator wanting to press me might insist: "Well, which is it? What do you really want? Warm and dry or thunder and lighting?" My answer would be, "Yes!" This illustrates, in a very small way, the concept of a conflicted Inner Family.

On a more serious and tragic note, the contradictions and wars inside us tear us apart and make a mockery of our best intentions, especially in matters of relationships and love. A client who comes to mind was in the process of having his third marriage end amidst high drama and conflict. Sobbing, he said: "There is a part of me that wants only to love and be loved by someone. Yet there is another part of me who considers love to be dangerous and painful, and sooner or later, I run away. How do I run away? Sometimes with a bang; sometimes with a whimper." Clearly, even though he enters love relationships with good intentions, there are many conflicted parts inside this confused man.

Though we may be normal, "well-adjusted", effectively functioning human beings, we each carry many disparate parts or "I's. As seen in the frustrated man above, these "I's" can and often are conflicted, contradictory, and antagonistic.

In your mind there can be a raging war of "I's" taking place. A strongly developed "I" may be taking on a weaker "I" or may be going up against another strongly developed "I". A weaker developed "I" may be sabotaging a strongly developed "I", or may be turning in on itself. It's complex.

Conventional self-awareness thinking, which asserts that you are only one "I", is no match for this level of self-destructive, internal conflict. On a humorous note, it could be said that if taken to a vote, the "I"s would have it!

The Inner-Family Model of Self-Healing posits that there are essentially four primary "I's or consciousnesses within each of us. At the *beginning* of any healing journey there are these three:

- **a spiritual consciousness**: The only whole, complete and indivisible Inner Family member. [This is often suppressed by the *aggressive/defensive ego conscious-ness.*];

- **a child consciousness**: There are two aspects to this consciousness: (i) a **natural** or **free inner child**, which I will also call the **authentic self**; and (ii), an **adaptive** or **broken inner child**, created to cope with pain and trauma; and,

- **an aggressive/defensive ego consciousness** which is necessarily developed out of the *adaptive child con-sciousness*, and becomes the primary and controlling force of a person's life, suppressing all the other Inner Family members. [As the healing work progresses, the *aggressive/defensive* ego is modified so it becomes an *ego-in-service*, but more about this later.]

Through healing work. a fourth member of this inner family is created.

- **an independent/aware adult consciousness**: This consciousness doesn't exist in the Inner Family until the work of personal healing begins. This is because the unhealed person is almost totally identified with or controlled by their *aggressive/defensive ego consciousness* (mentioned above).

I realize this is complex. The list of the various players of your inner world may be difficult to understand at first. Let's take it slowly and begin our understanding of things by examining these four primary Inner Family members more closely. I'll define them, and show you how they comprise, for better or worse, your **Inner Family**.

Who's In My Inner Family Anyway?

Where The Healing Starts

Before I explain the four members of your Inner Family I wish to provide some information about two related items. These are the *Physical You* and the *Unaware Adult Person* (which is an ego-controlled person). Together, these comprise the state of affairs right now—"you", the person that right now lives from day to day; probably the person who is reading this book. The *Physical You* and the *Unaware Adult Person* are not members of your Inner Family; however, it is necessary to provide some information about them because it is from them that your healing begins.

The Physical You

No one can see, taste, touch, smell, or hear your spiritual, child, or ego consciousnesses (at least not with your usual senses). But there stands the physical person "you", indisputably tangible and real. It is what you see when you look at yourself in the mirror: height, weight, gender, age, hair color, skin tone, sexual orientation, profession, income bracket, culture, etc. It is your physical presence which is perceived and acknowledged by the world as "all that you are" *and* it is the basis for how you are defined. This is your physical reality.

All you have to do to be granted "adult" status by your community is to reach a certain physical age; the so-called legislated age of majority. And, depending on the country, era, and culture you were born into, this age can be different. Reaching the age of majority alone confers upon you the status of full-fledged adult, with the complete allotment of your rights, privileges, obligations, respon-sibilities, and freedoms. *But what exactly is required intellectually, emotionally, and spiritually to become a fully healed adult person? — a lot more than reaching the legislated age of majority.*

The Unaware Adult Person (an Ego-Controlled Person)

This is the state that most of us are in as we live our daily lives. It is the state of unknowingly being controlled by the aggressive/defensive ego consciousness. As such, it is the point where your healing begins.

Because you are perceived as an "adult", it is the unaware (ego-controlled) person that has the assigned task of navigating through the world each day. This unaware adult is ultimately held responsible for your actions and behaviours.

There are few courts in the land which will honour a defence based on the contention that: "My aggressive/defensive ego made me do it. I, the person standing in court, had nothing to do with it." The visible, physical "you" is deemed the agent of your behaviours, successes, and failures. As much as this is what happens in our culture, that is seldom the truth of the matter.

Here is one illustration of an *unaware* adult consciousness: I met with a man and his teenage son. The father, a star football player in his youth, had become so enraged with his child that he got into a physical altercation with him. According to the father, the presenting cause of this nightmare was his son. He, the son, did not want to play football anymore and was not going to try out for the school team. Of course, Dad loved his son and somehow knew there must be more going on than just "football". To the father's credit, he looked deeper into himself and saw how controlling he was with his son. He realized it was his previously unfelt emotional pain and fear from his own youth (where he needed football in order to feel "good enough"), that lay behind his extreme reactions to his son.

The father's aggressive/defensive ego consciousness, in the guise of a "responsible adult", certainly a well-intended *unaware* adult, was trying to dominate his son, believing his son needed to be "good enough" in exactly the same way he did as a youth. Near the end of the session, the father realized the issue was his alone and he was harming his son. He began to cry. At that point he had commenced healing himself and his relationship with his son.

Contrary to common thought most adults don't have egos, *most egos have unaware adults.* Only by bringing forth a new consciousness, that of an *independent/aware adult*, can a healing transformation occur. By doing this, which is one of the principle objectives of the Inner Family Model of Self-Healing, you (and most certainly I, as well) will live with a harmonious Inner Family led by an *independent/aware adult consciousness*, and we will more consistently become an integrated and loving adult.

*

Now follows a description of the four members of your Inner Family.

The Spiritual Consciousness

The spiritual consciousness of your Inner Family has been with you from the beginning of this lifetime (and some might say many lifetimes), and has its own quiet agenda for the unfolding of your greatest good. It has and conveys a unique and immeasurable love, wisdom, and compassion that is indispensable in the healing process. It is not in the least attached, in an egotistic way, to the survival of the Inner Family and can consequently guide you to a more loving and peaceful way of being.

I am not implying that the spiritual consciousness of the Inner Family is a god or the highest power. That is not my experience. I am, however, prepared to say it is a link or conduit to a higher power (by whatever name). Your spiritual consciousness could be described as a higher source of wisdom for the Inner Family and a unique, personalized guide for it.

Never forceful or judgmental, the spiritual consciousness, when invited in as a "family consultant", advocates for cooperation, integration and healing in the Inner Family. It holds a vision of a loving, united, egalitarian family in which each member has a unique and precious set of attributes and skills; where each can co-exist with and contribute to the welfare and comfort of the other members. This is a family in which the whole is far, far greater than the sum of its parts; a family in which no family member's gain is at another member's loss. Everyone flourishes.

The spiritual consciousness (unlike the other Inner Family members, whose perspectives of the events that have shaped your life have given rise to the conflicts and divisions within you) can put an individual's life, with its particular triumphs, tragedies, joys, and disappointments, into a larger universal context. This can, if pursued, offer the baffled and often disturbed adult some meaning and value to their suffering.

Instead of seeing ourselves as victims of a random, senseless, cruel universe, where calamity and destruction befall us in mysterious ways, it is possible to be aided by this spiritual consciousness to perceive things differently. Losses, failures, and setbacks can be understood as influences and factors that are much needed, moreover perhaps necessary, for a person to grow in the direction of their highest and greatest good. This will then meet the intentions of the spiritual consciousness for this lifetime.

Throughout history, whether explained by an enlightened leader, or heard within the deep recesses of our ordinary thoughts, the spiritual consciousness has had things to show us that confront, challenge, and deeply upset the overriding ego consciousnesses of the world. Ideas and sentiments which suggest that we are not as small or powerless in the scheme of things as the individual ego consciousness forcefully insists (and especially that we are co-creators of our own reality) have never been greeted with a great deal of receptivity or enthusiasm by ego-controlled adults.

The only variation in response to profound spiritual truths, with which the mass ego consciousness confronts these teachers, is whether to kill them by fire, stones, torture, poison, or bullets. This ages-old contempt of the truly spiritual life by powerful aggressive/defensive ego consciousnesses is played out every day in every culture and every generation.

To sum it up, while offering more insight as to how this works: It is easy for most of us to appreciate the spiritual consciousness when receiving gifts and abundance. However, loss and hardship are seen by most of us as unfair or cruel. This sets up yet another aspect of an inner, unconscious war—a "civil war" within. There will be more on this throughout the book. For now, I will just say that typically (even though it is the primary source of wisdom and love), the spiritual consciousness has a hard time finding a listening audience in a fractured Inner Family.

The Child Consciousness (In Two Aspects)

There are two aspects to the child consciousness: the natural child consciousness; and, the adaptive child consciousness.

The child consciousness could be said to be the heart dimension of our lives. This consciousness, in both its natural and adaptive forms, processes the circumstances, events, and people of your life emotionally. *It predates your intellectual, conceptual, and analytical thinking processes and predates your ability to put words to your feelings and experiences.*

One way to describe the child consciousness in its natural state is to view it as an emotional radar system that *constantly* tracks the exact and true nature of the emotional energies in its immediate world. When a child lives as **the natural child consciousness**, this child is innately in touch with its internal emotional and spiritual process. This child is not internally wounded and *experiences sufficient safety, acceptance, and support from its caregivers and environment.* As a result, this child is more or less uninterruptedly connected to their **authentic self**. For instance, when the child feels happy, sad or angry, it can safely have and express those feelings.

In a healthy family environment, the child does not have to worry about feeling too happy, sad, or angry. It can and will remain congruent with its experienced reality and know that it will always be loved and cared for. This child is the little plug connected to its socket.

If it is possible, think of yourself in your most real, natural, and undefended state—those times when you feel so absolutely safe with the people around you, that you can express your deepest and truest self. This will give you a glimpse of the presence and energy of the **natural child consciousness**. This child consciousness within you is a constant source of emotional peace, wisdom and clarity.

The other aspect of the child consciousness, and the one which is usually much more prominent in an unhealed adult is **the adaptive child consciousness.** *This is the child who was forced to adapt and conform to a childhood environment which did not foster (or actively crushed) the natural child consciousness.*

To the child, or the adult looking back at their childhood, sometimes they will never be able to understand why this happened. The **adaptive child** was forced to survive life rather than live it; forced to "fit in" rather than show itself to the world. Because its needs could not be met in any other way, *the adaptive child learned to be inauthentic* i.e.: controlling, manipulative, contrived, reactive, or hidden, in order to get their needs met. This adaptive child consciousness, I will later explain, is the antecedent and less harmful version of the full-blown **aggressive-defensive ego consciousness.**

If you are willing to access the child consciousness within, particularly the adaptive child, a great many personal issues and problems that have chronically baffled and sabotaged you as an adult, will begin to make perfect *emotional* sense. This is true for a wide range of personal difficulties, and no more true than in matters to do with your love-life, e.g. with whom you fall in love; what unfolds in your love relationships; and what lies behind the self-defeating patterns that keep repeating themselves.

I know that many readers, and possibly you, would protest that what has happened in your relationships and love life has made no sense at all and could not possibly make sense. This is true if you rely on a logical or rational point of view. Yet, by coming to understand the nature of your story, and above all the emotional pain and fear of your adaptive child consciousness, you will make emotional sense out of how you love and are loved. This is because this powerful (inner) child consciousness is pre-logical, pre-rational, and non-verbal. If you begin to use the emotional information provided by this child consciousness, and view your personal issues and problems through that perspective, you will begin to understand yourself from the inside-out, perhaps for the first time. With this new and deeper level of understanding will come healing and a permanent and lasting shift in the quality of your life.

In short: The natural child (consciousness) lives spontaneously; the adaptive child (consciousness) survives by manipulation.

The Ego Consciousness (In Two Aspects)

The two aspects of ego that I will explain are *the aggressive/defensive ego* and *an ego-in-service*. But first there is this:

In the Inner-Family Model of Self-healing, the ego can best be described as the consciousness you have developed and rely on for your survival in the world. This refers not only to your survival as a physical organism—doing whatever is necessary for the prolongation of your body's life in the face of the many dangers which might or do threaten it; but just as critical is your psychological and emotional survival in the world of other people—preserving the often fragile experience of being a good, worthwhile, lovable person in a sometimes emotionally unsafe world.

A strong and well-developed ego is indispensable for navigating through, and succeeding in, the world. A non-aggressive ego, which I call a **healthy ego-in-service** is vital to a sense of personal power and competence that brings with it qualities such as planning, discipline, self-restraint, being somewhat think-skinned, perseverance, ambition, drive, and sacrifice—all valuable assets in accomplishing your life's goals, ambitions, and dreams. This healthy side of the ego consciousness has made many wonderful contributions to humanity.

There is however, another side to the ego consciousness' passion for physical and psychological survival which is not nearly as beneficent. This is the **aggressive/defensive ego consciousness** and it cannot tell the difference between someone threatening your life with a knife or gun and someone else being rude to you. This other aspect of our ego, the **aggressive/defensive ego consciousness,** is responsible for our own minor irritations and annoyances in everyday life, for humanities most despicable horrors and atrocities, and everything in-between. I will explain how this consciousness is so obsessed with survival that it infringes upon other beings' rights to do the same. It could be described as a defender gone berserk, so lost in its dark, fearful perceptions, that it can rationalize and justify being a predator that attacks enemies and loved ones alike.

Where do its dark and fear-based perceptions come from? The aggressive/defensive ego consciousness was born inside you at approximately the same time that your natural child consciousness "died" or more accurately, was forced to disconnect and go underground—at the same time as the little plug was forced to pull out of its socket. The aggressive/defensive ego's origins are directly associated with an accumulation of emotional pain and fear which, at some time in your distant past, became too much for you to bear.

Rather than taking personal ownership of this emotional pain and fear, one of the signature features of the aggressive/defensive ego is its ability to blame. It's brilliant at externalizing the problem and seeing its (own) suffering as being caused by outside agents. Thus, this consciousness seldom lives in the present. To it, everyone in the present is the same as all the people who have hurt you in the past. Consequently, the aggressive/defensive ego is comprised of a vast and complex attack-and-defend system aimed at keeping these hostile outside forces from inflicting further damage on an already injured inner self.

Which aspect of the ego consciousness is operational—the healthy ego-in-service or the aggressive/defensive ego—will determine whether it improves or destroys your own or other people's well-being. This makes it the most confusing, complex, and double-edged member of the Inner Family.

For instance, the ego may cultivate power and position in society in order to protect its Inner Family. You may become rich, influential, or famous as a means of enhancing your survival. This will guarantee you will never be as hurt or defenceless again as when you were a child. This can be a positive contribution to yourself and others—extending material benefits and opportunities for many life choices to loved ones can bee seen as an act of service. Yet, if this same action is crafted by your aggressive/defensive ego consciousness it can turn into a narrow, self-serving, poisonous pursuit of money and power for its own sake and then used to harm and oppress others.

I will explain how the machinations of the aggressive/defensive ego consciousness are cunning, baffling, powerful, and patient, and employ a dizzying array of contradictory survival strategies. As an example, just as easily as making sure that you are the "smashing success" described above, it can mould you into a "born loser"; an abject personal failure and financial flop. As seen through the eyes of the aggressive/defensive ego, and as strange as it may seem, the born loser can be an equally effective way of safeguarding an imperilled Inner Family from the world.

The aggressive/defensive ego consciousness can also play "both ends against the middle"; it can get you coming and going. To truly understand its ways, as an essential component of personal healing, you will need to become adept at seeing and understanding contradiction and paradox. Regardless of "which end is up", it interprets its job description as doing *whatever is necessary* to ward off and control others.

In the aggressive/defensive ego's perception this avoids adding to the accumulated and filled-to-capacity reservoir of emotional pain and fear you carry. This aspect of ego consciousness, ironically and tragically, ends up perpetuating more lovelessness and pain in your life. The aggressive/defensive ego's trajectory in life is *from fear with fear to fear*. More than anything else, it is this fear which must be healed.

The fourth, and final member of your Inner Family is:

The Independent/Aware Adult Consciousness

I do not mean to be insulting or deliberately provocative to people by making the following distinction; however, even though most of us are "all grown up", we do not make adult choices regarding our state of consciousness. As a matter of fact, and generally speaking, we do not operate as if we have any choice at all over our state of consciousness, thereby harming ourselves, other people, and our planet.

In many of us, before healing, there is little or no *independent* aware adult consciousness. There is no observer or "internal witness", which I later explain, that is able to discern what state of consciousness is operating.

In the process of healing a new leader of the Inner Family is created. I refer to this as an *independent/aware adult consciousness*. This consciousness allows several things to happen. With it operating you can:

- choose to have a direct and positive (i.e. spiritual and loving) response to life;
- mediate and invite wise contributions from the other members of your Inner Family to resolve issues and make decisions; and,
- take compassionate and positive action to maintain Inner Family harmony.

*

Have you ever had a sincere conversation with your wiser, spiritual consciousness? When was the last time someone talked to you as if you are a child consciousness? Has anyone ever acknowledged your aggressive/defensive ego? Did you ever receive a compliment on your ego-in-service? What would it be like if you could speak with all members of your Inner Family and bring an abundance of love and harmony to you and your life?

You, as a fully-healed <u>aware</u> person will have an independent/aware adult consciousness. This gives you the ability to identify and choose what state of consciousness you are in—whether you present a fear-based and survival-oriented aggressive/defensive ego, or a healed, respectful and assertive ego-in-service. When you are led by an independent/aware adult consciousness you can choose to operate from the heart-and-love based natural child consciousness and the spiritual consciousness. These choices would be ever-present, regardless of circumstances, other people, or what you or they have done in the past.

What Does An Unhealed Inner Family Look Like?

The Civil War Within

Too many of us have come from a much-troubled or divided "outer" family, often referred to as our family of origin. The state of your unhealed Inner Family will reflect this, and be no healthier or happier. You are a house divided. The general state of affairs is tension and conflict. Inner Family members are separated and distant from each other. They do not understand each other, often perceiving each other as competitors and adversaries for scraps of emotional nurturing and support. In this emotional climate, there is a build-up of unexamined and unresolved emotional pain in the family. This is sometimes overtly, or more commonly, covertly directed towards others and often hardens into positions of distrust and hostility. Typically, the aggressive/defensive ego consciousness rules over the volatile Inner Family with an iron fist. It is so loud and powerful it dwarfs the child consciousness and the spiritual consciousness, and prevents the development of an independent/aware adult consciousness. Its near totalitarian grip is seldom contested and causes no end of destructive behaviour patterns.

This aggressive/defensive ego consciousness is fear-based

regarding its view of the outer world *and* the inner family. It is threatened by any influence granted (by the independent/aware adult consciousness; the inner family mediator so-to-speak) to the natural child consciousness/authentic self or to the spiritual consciousness. On the basis of its history and experience, it does not trust the presence, opinions, or wishes of your child or your spiritual consciousness. Only its own beliefs and opinions are in the best interests of the Inner Family's survival. [It actually believes the development of a love- or spiritually-based consciousness would make the Inner Family much more vulnerable and fragile, thus making it potentially a greater victim to the wide variety of threats and dangers posed by life, love, and other people.]

The aggressive/defensive ego consciousness trusts only itself. After all, you are alive so its system has worked, hasn't it? You and your Inner Family have survived some pretty threatening and nasty experiences. It needs no other proof to claim the validity and necessity of its system. And, it is *not* in favour of the growth and development of an independent/aware adult consciousness. Too many cooks spoil the broth; too many leaders produce anarchy. *The aggressive/defensive ego is ruthless in maintaining its power and control.*

As I said earlier, in the unhealed inner family there are more sources of discord other than just the relationship between the aggressive/defensive ego and the other subordinated family members. There are significant ruptures and tension in the relationship between other Inner Family members. Camps and alliances have formed which generate conflict and these have to be healed, too.

The *un*aware adult person is, for instance, often torn in their loyalty between siding with "the biggest kid on the block" (the aggressive ego), and wanting to stand up for "the little guy" (the natural child consciousness). This conflict is usually a constant source of strife and second-guessing that leads to paralysis. Sometimes expressed as the conflict between the head and the heart; between power and peace; between external and internal power, the conflicted adult can never seem to please everyone in their Inner Family no matter what decision it makes, and *very often,* hurts and causes trouble to itself and others.

If it moves in a direction "approved" by the aggressive/defensive ego consciousness (because it perceives "survival" is enhanced) the natural child consciousness is alienated. [The natural child doesn't just want to survive life, but to enjoy, feel, and deeply connect with others.] If this unaware "adult" sides with the softer, more vulnerable child consciousness, it runs the risk of alienating and infuriating the ego which believes that the world is hostile and being vulnerable is dangerous.

How Does An Inner Family Heal?

Though I will discuss the healing of each consciousness separately in later chapters, and describe how they come together as a cohesive and supportive unit, the steps in healing an Inner Family are remarkably similar to those required in healing any real life family. Of great importance is that each consciousness must be known to the others. Each must tell its story to the others.

Components of the story of each consciousness might include: What is its history in the Inner Family? What are the sources of its deepest psychological and emotional injuries? What place has it been given there? What distrust, conflict, and alienation exist between it and each of the other members? How can this be brought out for discussion and worked through for the mutual benefit of all? How has it covered up its injuries? How have these injuries been expressed indirectly or destructively to other family members? What does it most need from the rest of its family in order to heal? What will it take to make certain that the Inner Family does not become divided again?

Warring sides, with seemingly irreconcilable differences and histories, replete with misunderstandings and acrimony, can hopefully learn to surrender self-will and self-protection long enough to try a cardinal principle in healing any family, outer or inner: *There is a solution to this problem which can please everybody. And none of us have it alone.* Diversity needs to be found in the supportive context of unity.

There are built-in limitations to any single voice or point of view. An Inner Family which is united can incorporate and be guided by the input from each of its unique members. Any major decision made or action taken, could be moulded by the concerns, needs and wishes of each family member. In this way it is possible to ascertain whether all sides of your being are on board, or whether one particular Inner Family member might turn into a saboteur or renegade because its needs and wishes have not been included or respected.

Most importantly, an Inner Family heals by understanding, accepting, loving, and empowering all of its diverse members. This is the way to stop the civil war raging inside us. We can move through fear to harmony and peace.

Healing The Inner Family Produces A Shift In Consciousness

The premise of this healing work is that significant and lasting change in people's behaviours, relationships, and quality of life, can only take place if and when a real shift of consciousness takes place within them. *Transformation occurs when there is an authentic shift from a ego-centered, fear-based, survival-oriented consciousness to a spirit and heart-led one*. Within the pages of this book are the stories of people who have experienced diverse and positive changes in their lives by healing their Inner Families.

This is a shift in who we think we are. Instead of remaining in essentially the same survival consciousness throughout our lifetime, that we created to surmount the emotional and spiritual injuries of our formative years, we go beyond the "primal slime" of conditioning. ("primal slime" is taken from the Herman Hesse quote, cited at p. 122.)

The aggressive/defensive ego consciousness, and the fearful adaptive child consciousness from which it has arisen, is the consciousness which helped us at one time to survive. But now, as adults, it might be our quickest route to individual and global annihilation. This aggressive consciousness can be set aside with increasing regularity through a sincere effort by an adult conscious-ness that is no longer willing to abandon a blossoming emotional and spiritual connection with its inner family and the world at large.

The individual who comes to know they are more than their ego comes to realize that an aggressive ego consciousness has given them only one vision of life; only one version of reality—the darkest and loneliest. Trusting this consciousness, which has got them this far in life, is not going to provide anything other than more darkness and loneliness. *Continuing to trust the aggressive/defensive ego is not going to add one ounce more of quality to their life*. In fact, it is the source of significant problems in its own right; problems which will inevitably lead to more despair and self-destruction.

In contrast, and the good news is, **we can choose to live for more than survival.** Healing our Inner Family allows us to know and embrace ourselves at deeper and deeper levels. Perhaps the greatest gift may be that we learn we are more, *much* more, than the fear which has riddled our entire existence. We can live with a deep and abiding peace, of which we are a part, that passes all understanding.

If you have read this far, you have already begun your journey into healing. I will now explain more about our most developed consciousness, the one in which we spend most of our time here on earth—the aggressive/defensive ego consciousness.

Chapter 2

"Always, we are self-destroyers, and the spears we are forever aiming at imagined enemies are plunged into our own hearts. We live as though in a perpetual state of siege, equally afraid of the mines beneath and the artillery without. Life is so 'cluttered up with self-protective rubbish and greedy self-seeking' that we move as clumsily as any medieval knight in full armour. And our state of preparedness makes others prepare their defences against us (even animals attack those who are afraid and self-protecting). 'What the next man fears is my lust for possession' and that lust for possession is bred of our desire to protect ourselves against him. The other man has every right to suspect our intentions, since fear of him makes us aggressive."

Gai Easton
The Richest Vein:
Eastern Tradition and Modern Thought

The Ego Consciousness

What is this?

The aggressive/defensive ego is the term I will use to describe the entire physical, psychological, and emotional attack-and-defend system of a human being. This ego is comprised of the accumulated fear of a lifetime. Fear is the fundamental organizing principle of this ego. This creates the emotional environment you live in—the universe that surrounds your existence. Every decision made, and every action taken by this ego consciousness makes sense in the universe which it inhabits, a universe I call the Universe of Fear. The aggressive/defensive ego consciousness is a self-contained and self-perpetuating way of being that generates a Universe of Fear.

When we are controlled by the aggressive/defensive ego consciousness, we see ourselves as isolated and fragile objects, dangerously exposed to hostile elements everywhere. We are surrounded by enemies. It could be said that this ego consciousness is the war mentality of the human being. On a global scale, this mentality has resulted in the horrific murders, atrocities, and destruction that we have perpetrated on ourselves and the planet. On the scale of an individual life, this mentality is the principle agent behind the breakdown of relationships and the dissolution of marriages and families.

Though perhaps only slightly exaggerated, as a metaphor, when I speak about the unhealed or aggressive/defensive ego consciousness, imagine a blood-thirsty warrior swinging some weapon of destruction at anyone and anything in its path. Granted, the ego consciousness in the twenty-first century is a smoother operator than its blood-dripping ancestors, but its essence and ways of operating remain exactly the same. It is an attack-and-defend system.

How Have We All Come To Be Attila The Hun?

The principle concern and primary focus of the aggressive/defensive ego consciousness is survival. First and foremost, this means the sheer physical preservation of your life, and protection against all threats of bodily harm and pain of any kind. You were born tiny and helpless. As an infant and child there were literally thousands of things that could have injured or killed you. Even if you were blessed with well-meaning and attentive parents, they could only protect you from so much. In its original intent and design, *your ego consciousness is nature's equivalent of another full-time parent or guardian figure.* Just as you would not be alive today without your parents' care and intervention, you would likely not be alive today without your ego's presence in your life.

If the ego is the equivalent of a third parent in its original design and function, how does nature's parent turn into Attila the Hun? To answer this question, we must go deeper.

The preservation of your physical life is only one aspect of your ego's definition of survival. If your life is anything like mine, on any typical day, I do not encounter anyone who is trying to kill me. No one in the course of a usual day physically harms or hurts me. As far as I know (and maybe as they say, "what I don't know won't hurt me") no one out there has my injury, misfortune, or even disadvantage, as their conscious intent. Granted I might need an aggressive ego when I am being assaulted; but I, for one, have never in my life been assaulted.

If physical survival is the chief concern and pre-occupation of the ego, we could deduce that the aggressive/defensive ego consciousness, for most of us, would hardly ever be required in the course of day-to-day living. Yet, I suggest that, for most people, the ego consciousness is an *always-present, full-time, constantly-active aggressive/defensive system.* Many of us spend from cradle to grave in this survival-oriented, fear-based consciousness. We are completely controlled by it.

I will explain later that to heal and create inner harmony we need an independent/aware adult consciousness; however, for most of us, *there is no separated, independent/aware adult consciousness.* (Part of the work is to "create" this inner family member.) For now, at this stage, you don't have an ego your ego has you.

The aggressive aspect of "ego" does not only come into play to keep you physically alive and safe. It is just as concerned with your emotional and psychological survival as well. It defines your survival in terms of whether you live or die physically *and* whether you live or die ("suffer") emotionally in the world of other people. It equates any noticeable emotional pain as a kind of death, and does everything to avoid this.

We all want to believe we are good people. We want to feel we are respected, liked, wanted and important. We have a need to feel loved, most importantly by the people nearest and dearest to us. When you do not feel these, your ego perceives this as a direct threat and attack on your survival. It reacts exactly the same as if you were being killed. **To the ego, emotional pain is perceived as death.** Any emotional pain is interpreted as a threat to your survival. It will be registered by your aggressive ego as a death threat. *The ego has no tolerance for emotional pain.* It will attack and defend in the face of any kind of actual, perceived, or anticipated emotional pain.

Consequently, it will constantly struggle in a myriad of ways to control your (its) world to avoid pain. *Control of everything* is a primary focus of the aggressive/defensive ego.

The Denial Of Fear and Emotional Pain

Why is the aggressive/defensive ego deathly afraid of emotional pain? Why does the smallest bit of pain bring out the ego's entire attack-and-defence arsenal? This is because the ego consciousness in particular, and the Inner Family which it serves to protect and defend from any threat, is already full of emotional pain. Imagine a deeply buried reservoir of emotional pain inside you that is filled beyond its capacity. The reservoir of pain is over-flowing and *it cannot absorb one more drop.*

This is the precarious situation this ego consciousness faces on an hourly and daily basis, and one significant explanation for why it experiences emotional pain as a death threat. Put slightly differently, *any* experience of emotional pain, however temporary, adds to the already over-filled reservoir, and could spell the possible meltdown and disintegration of the Inner Family. Understandably, the overwhelmed aggressive/defensive ego will attempt to avoid *any* pain and therefore becomes significantly over-reactive when confronted with even the possibility of additional pain.

There is another critical factor in this ego's lack of tolerance for *any* emotional pain. This is its ardent denial it carries any pain or fear at all. It does not want to see (meaning become responsible) for the fear and emotional pain it already carries. Many of the people I work with, even though struggling with serious and occasionally dangerous symptoms or behaviour patterns, are initially surprised to realize that these self-harming ways are associated with fear and emotional pain they have buried deep inside themselves. Their initial reaction to our healing work is often: "Who me, afraid? Me, in pain? I think you're wrong!"

Why is that? Why does the ego-identified adult (a person controlled by their aggressive/defensive ego is ego-identified) live in such massive denial of their own accumulated fear and pain? Of course, we realize with some justification, it will not be particularly pleasant or easy to experience our fear and emotional pain, even if it may be the best and only way of lowering the incapacitating levels of our pain-filled reservoir. However, there is more to our denial and resistance than our strong preference to seek pleasure and avoid pain.

Deep down inside, we know that the ego and its images which we present to the world are ultimately a false self. We know, no matter how cleverly they have been crafted, they are a cover up; a contrived, artificial social fabrication we have employed all of our lives as a substitution for our authentic selves. Underneath the kaleidoscope of ego presentations we have used to ensure our survival in the world, we are ashamed of our more vulnerable self and the fear and emotional pain which are a part of it. We are humiliated by it and contemptuous of it. So, we hide it and deny it.

Besides avoiding pain and seeking pleasure, acknowledging our fear and pain is an affront to our way of seeing ourselves. It's a rebuke of the very self-images the ego consciousness has used, perfected, and presented to the world as who we really are.

Let me give you an example of one such self-image. Most of us, myself included, like to see ourselves as composed, collected, and capable adults. Always. Even if we do not experience ourselves to be on top of every situation; even if we sometimes feel terribly inadequate and have significant doubts about our competence, we like to see ourselves (and most certainly want other people to perceive that we are) always in charge of ourselves; that we always know what we are doing. The notion that we aren't "always in charge" and that we are very, very afraid, and a huge proportion of our lives is shaped and determined by fear, does not bolster this image. *The truth that we are afraid all of the time, and that we are afraid of practically everyone and everything, challenges this highly polished self-image of competency to its core.*

Many of our self-images, including the one of always being composed, collected and capable, would have to be surrendered if we are to own our fear and emotional pain. No wonder most people respond to the proposition that they are run by fear with something like this: "I am not really afraid at all in my life. Okay, things like public speaking and death might scare me a little; but I seldom think about them and they hardly bother me at all. I am *not* afraid all of the time, and I am *definitely* not afraid of just about everybody and everything." [This is the point of what is referred to in the Gai Easton quote, p. 32.]

Most people are too afraid to admit that we could possibly be afraid. Something inside of us would rather commit the atrocities of violence and war than admit to feeling afraid, and that something inside us is the aggressive/defensive ego. In manoeuvres akin to the slight-of-hand skills of the most talented magician, the same ego consciousness that is a depository and wellspring of practically unlimited fear and emotional pain, is also the same one which believes itself to be fearless. [Recall that at the beginning of the book, I wrote that a healed person must come to terms with their contradictions and paradoxes? This is a major one.]

Sources Of Fear And Emotional Pain Are Everywhere

In the context of our relationship with others, emotional pain can come in hundreds of forms. We can feel rejected, disliked, shamed, humiliated, hurt, offended, attacked, hated, patronized, distrusted, or manipulated. We can feel wronged, ridiculed, judged, criticized, tricked, insulted, forced, blamed, beaten up, picked on, or deprived whether they are anticipated, imagined, or real. The aggressive/defensive ego will mobilize itself in the face of any of these experiences. Furthermore, once they happen, the ego will dwell on them.

Any human being can cause pain. It can be either intentional or accidental; the other person doesn't always intend to be hurtful. Thus, in the aggressive/defensive ego's way of perceiving other human beings, no one is exempt from being a cause or potential cause of painful experiences. Everyone becomes dangerous.

In the universe of this ego, then, other people are a two-fold threat. First, they can physically kill you. Second, they can cause you emotional pain, which feels *as if* they are killing you. Because every human being out there has the potential to kill you or cause you emotional pain, the ego requires that every instant you must be on guard against them (because everyone is dangerous). Aside from being exhausting, this is truly being stuck between a rock and a hard place!

We yearn for soulful connection but our aggressive/defensive ego prohibits it. Strangers can most definitely kill or hurt you. At the same time, even those who are closest to you, like members of your own family or friends, can kill or hurt you too. It may have been the people closest to you who are associated with the most grievous emotional wounds you have ever known. Your ego remembers this. If so, they can be trusted no more than the stranger, and probably trusted less than strangers.

Because all forms of emotional pain are death to the ego, it lacks the ability to discriminate levels of threat. It cannot be bothered by (or trust in) fine distinctions. All pain and threats of pain equate to the threat of death. It mobilizes and reacts essentially the same way to anything which makes it afraid. This explains why, so often, the reactions of the aggressive/defensive ego consciousness to even slightly threatening or painful stimuli are so out of proportion to the actual offence or perceived danger.

For example, to an aggressive/defensive ego, there is not much difference between being cut off by a motorist in traffic and being invaded by an enemy's army. It has a hard time telling the difference between feeling the temporary withdrawal of a spouse's love and a valid life threatening condition. It can be just as quick to blame and attack another nation as to blame and attack a neighbour or friend. The ego lacks tools of discernment. Be it a physical or emotional threat, in the present or future, real or imagined, serious or incidental, originating from friend or foe, a threat is a threat. Like a blind gate-keeper at the castle entrance, it cannot separate out citizens and friends of the kingdom from dangerous and subversive enemies. The gate-keeper's solution: ***Keep Everybody Out!***

To the aggressive/defensive ego, "social" survival is the avoidance of the experience of any emotional pain. This propels the ego to expand its role from a seldom-needed chief physical protector and bodyguard to an always-present, always-vigilant bodyguard whenever other people are around.

Fear, Fear, and More Fear

One more way to perceive the aggressive/defensive ego consciousness and the Universe Of Fear which it generates, is to imagine that surrounding every human being is a gigantic ball of fear. The fear is impossible to distinguish because it is the universe we live in—the environment of our existence. It is largely invisible *because* it is so all-encompassing. This makes it the only thing we know. And, in my view, this description does not do justice to the magnitude of its size and dimensions. This fear is so immense and invisible it has no dimensions or contours that allow it to be seen.

For something to be seen it must have a beginning, a middle and an end. It is some visible or emotional definition (boundaries or limits) of some "thing" that allow it to be seen as separate from other "things". At this early stage we cannot be separated from fear, and therefore, without a dramatic shift in how we perceive ourselves, it cannot be seen or appreciated. Fear is so pervading, its energy affects the hearts and souls of (almost) all human beings. [The exception might be Gandhi or someone like him.] It becomes the environment in which we live our lives.

A fish doesn't know it is swimming in water. "Water" completely encloses *everything* about a fish's existence. In other words, a fish doesn't know that water exists (until it is exposed to something else—air). Our universe of fear is the same as the fish's universe of water. The aggressive/defensive ego's fear-based ways are the last thing that most humans discover. Why? Because we are in it all the time.

In the way our mind works: Anything within us which is denied has a life of its own. Like the presence of a thief who has bypassed the alarm system in a shop late at night, they can, at least until morning, do anything they want. Generally speaking, an independent/aware adult consciousness is (at this point) non-existent, and so, a person is not even aware of the fear that completely encloses them. Since there is nothing for comparison, there is nothing to act as a check-and-balance system against the fear.

It is in this manner that the aggressive/defensive ego consciousness progressively takes us over, and, promotes life in a universe of fear. For the most part, as we age, we become more and more afraid of life. We become more and more afraid of other people. We become more and more afraid of ourselves.

How Does the Ego Come to Be Our Dominant Consciousness?

The Birth of the Ego

Have you looked into the face of a child lately? I have the privilege of gazing into my two boys' faces every day and I have come to believe that children are born without egos. Their love for me is greater, fuller, and more steadfast than mine is for them. Occasionally they don't like me and may even be mad at me, but they never judge me. They do not possess enough fear-based ill will inside them to even formulate a negative judgement of me. They offer me an acceptance that humbles me and on occasion brings tears to my eyes; tears of appreciation and relief that my shortcomings and even my offences against them can be met with such love.

My children and I are very different. More accurately, we are exactly the same beings, human beings, identified with and operating out of markedly different states of consciousness. Over the course of my life, I have become more and more survival-oriented and fear-based. My own aggressive/defensive ego consciousness, as my principle guide and ruler, has motivated me to do whatever it takes to survive life, to survive love, and to survive other people.

On the other hand, my children (and all children) are born egoless. They are born with only "spiritual" and "authentic-self" consciousnesses; they are, first and foremost, emotional and spiritual beings. That is to say, they are governed completely by an entirely different consciousness than mine. *Children live out of their natural child and their spiritual consciousnesses.* They understand and react to the people and events of their lives by processing them through their innate emotional and spiritual sensibilities. They are not engulfed by the Universe Of Fear which governs the vast majority of their parent's perceptions, reactions, and behaviours. Surviving life, love and other people is not an issue for them. Surviving is essentially their parents' issue. As such, children are perhaps the most extraordinary spiritual teachers that I have met (or will ever meet).

I think that children are here to lovingly reshape their parents into their own image; to bring their parents back to their original emotional and spiritual selves. Unfortunately, most parents are already hidden behind and controlled by their ego-based images of themselves. They attempt to shape their children into similar "adult fear-based" images. An epic power struggle ensues.

This is not a power struggle in the conventional sense, however, where two forces exert power in competition for something they both want i.e.; fighting over property or money. Conventional conflict (i.e. contract negotiation or divorcing spouses fighting over plates and pictures) is rooted in both sides' aggressive/defensive ego posturing; hence: conflict mediation and negotiation.

Instead, this conflict is more like two entirely different values and belief systems (aggressive/defensive ego vs. natural child/spiritual consciousness) crashing into each other. The aggressive/defensive ego demands compliance because it is afraid; the natural child/spiritual consciousness simply resists by "not wanting to do it" because it is happy and safe the way it is. This is the substantial content of the conflict, which cannot be resolved in the conventional ways of conflict resolution. And of course, the adults always prevail because (a) their opinions are presented as indisputable fact; and (b) they have absolute power and control.

Without doubt, some of this parental shaping is necessary and kind. A child needs to be educated in life skills by the *healthy ego-in-service consciousness* of their adult caregivers: understanding and fulfilling personal responsibilities; treating others with politeness, consideration and respect; developing the intellect; developing the capacity to delay immediate gratification, to name but a few. Parents, having lived in the world a lot longer than their children, know how it works and what it takes to navigate success-fully through it. They are much more advanced in their knowledge of how to function effectively and productively by keeping to schedules, setting goals, and thereby achieving results. They can develop in their children many of the characteristics required to be competent and capable performers in the world. Yet, on a spiritual level, children (who are at least for a short time bereft of egos, especially the aggressive/defensive ego) are far ahead of their parents in matters of love and peace. The egoless members of the human race, as few and far between as they have been, have always been our most important teachers.

I do not intend to portray all parents as completely fear-based brutes. This is far from the case. From my observation the majority of adults are well meaning and have the best intentions for their families. It is just that adults are much, much more fear-based than children. They have come by this honestly. They have learned how to survive life. From time immemorial the primary responsibil-ity of all parents of a species, be it the human or animal kingdom, is the survival of their offspring. This is a primal, innate, genetically programmed responsibility. For the adult member of any species, no assignment is as critical to accomplish as the survival of their young.

Where this becomes a limitation rather than an asset is with adults who have unconsciously come to identify themselves with their egos (and who have no ability to separate themselves from it). They teach their children how to survive life in *exactly the same ways that they have survived life, by trusting only their fear consciousness.* Rather than having this as something to rely on in rare circumstances, it completely dominates their way of being, and that is what their children learn.

For instance, if their fear consciousness has told them that their chances of survival are substantially enhanced by living only amongst "their own kind", they will teach their children that it is dangerous to live anywhere else but amongst "their own kind". If their fear consciousness has told them that feeling and expressing their real feelings is a liability, they will teach their children not to feel and express their real feelings and, one way or another, will punish their children for violating this rule. Thus, the consciousness of fear and aggression is passed on from generation to generation.

This is how parents, identified with their aggres-sive/defensive ego consciousness, become teachers of fear for children who are born without this consciousness. In this way, parents could not be more different than children. And, human history shows us that fear-based people become progressively more irritated, threatened, and intolerant. Deep down, and largely beyond the light of their awareness, all parents who are identified with their fear-based, survival-oriented aggressive/defensive ego consciousness, feel irritated, threatened, and intolerant of many things, including their own young children who live from their natural child and spiritual consciousnesses.

What happens to the people without egos when, in a position of vulnerability and powerlessness, they are raised by adults who have, for the most part, become totally identified with aggressive/defensive egos? Before I answer that question, let's see if, even for a moment, we can experience what it might be like to be our children. Try and recollect what it was once like to live life from the *natural child consciousness* and *spiritual consciousness,* rather than *the aggressive/defensive ego consciousness.*

The Brief Experience Of Sufficiency and the Fall Into Ego

As children, though lacking the ability to conceptualize and articulate it, we knew that who we were, at our core, were emotional and spiritual beings. From somewhere deep within ourselves, we knew that we were whole and complete, special and loveable; perfect creations of a perfect creator. As children, what we needed most was for our perfect beauty and indisputable value to be affirmed by the adults around us.

We did not need to be shaped and conditioned into becoming persons who, one day, would have beauty and worth. Our innate worth and god-given beauty were already present and undeniably real to us. Our innate spiritual consciousness surrounded and protected us like a safe, friendly, protective bubble. We just needed a few grown-ups to see us for who we already were—beings of extraordinary emotional and spiritual depth and magnificence.

We wanted to be loved and accepted, rejoiced and celebrated over, and to be a source of spiritual instruction and loving guidance to our world. Every single child born needs and waits for a transcendent moment of parental affirmation; a moment in time when their parents do the equivalent of lifting them in the air high above their heads, praising the universe for who they are—the greatest of all miracles. Every child craves being a privilege and source of meaning to their parents. Sadly, most children are never seen or affirmed for who they are. Few adults see their children as holy and perfect beings who have already made it; children who do not need to do or achieve anything to be loveable and priceless. Instead, the adults and the culture and world around them tell children every day how they have to be "more, different or better than" who they are in order to be loveable and valuable.

To put it more starkly: you learned that you were not good enough just being born. You were not good enough just being here. Being innately perfect wasn't all that you needed to be good enough. Your spiritual and emotional resume needed constant upgrading and embellishment. What have you done lately? What have you done lately to be good enough? How can you improve? What must you do to be considered loveable, or valuable, or beautiful: Run faster? Read sooner? Look prettier? Be quiet? You were forced to become something new or better or different than who you naturally were if you were to receive love and acceptance in the world.

To not feel good enough is a threat to your survival: enter the ego consciousness. *It could be said that the ego consciousness is synonymous with, and born out of, the experience of not being good enough*. It is also synonymous with the loss of your god-given identity. In some childhoods, loss occurred in a sudden and cataclysmic painful event, perhaps associated with one particularly horrible or destructive relationship. In almost all childhoods the loss of the child's connection to their natural, emotional and spiritual process occurs because of acts of omission and neglect by adults; adults who come to be so identified with their fear-based, survival-oriented aggressive/defensive ego consciousness that *they do not know and cannot see who their children are*. This makes it very difficult (or impossible) for parents to meet their child's emotional and spiritual needs.

To the extent that a child's physical, emotional, and spiritual needs are respected and, within limits, met, as they grow they will not have the predisposition to develop a dominating aggressive/defensive ego consciousness. A fear-based, survival-oriented consciousness will not grow and override their natural child/authentic self and spiritual consciousness. However, to the exact extent that a child's physical survival was imperilled, or their emotional and spiritual nature was negated is the very extent to which they will become more and more identified with (and ruled by) their aggressive/defensive ego consciousness. It may take a little while for that ego to dominate the growing consciousness of the child or adolescent, but it is inevitable.

It happened to me and it happened to you, too. There was too much loneliness, or anger, or hurt, or fear, whatever... for the little plug that you were, to stay connected to the socket. The emotional pain and fear associated with all the authority figures in your life accumulated inside you and became too much to bear. Additionally, one aspect of your suffering which made it even more overwhelming and difficult to endure, was that it seemed to be caused by the very people who said they loved you and claimed to be looking out for your best interests. It was a pain that the people in power denied they were causing (because it was in "your" best interests), let alone acknowledged and took responsibility for.

The emotional pain and fear inside you grew but had nowhere to go. The natural connection you briefly enjoyed to your authentic emotional and spiritual self could only endure so much stress. A moment came when it was severed. In that instant the god-given identity you inherited at birth was lost to you and a new, man-made, fear-based one materialized—you became identified with the aggressive/defensive ego. Being identified with it means you viewed life through it, it defined your identity, and it controlled you.

Let's listen in on an allegorical conversation from your childhood between "you" and your ego. It has had enormous consequences. The first mind-chatter ever uttered by your ego might have gone something like this:

"Look kid, no one here knows you for who you really are. No one here even seems to be able to see you. You are invisible to them. They don't know what you feel or need or want. Worse yet, they don't even seem to care. They hurt you time and time and time again, and don't even notice they're doing it! That's tough, kid. Everything you do is unacceptable. See kid, everything they do to you is acceptable to them because they believe they are well-meaning and doing what they do "for our own good". They have all the power. You have none. You're insignificant.

"Life is just too damn lonely and painful like this. You're not going to make it, kid. Take it from me— you're just not going to

make it. There's no one to help you. No one's coming! If anything, when the grown-ups come they just cause more pain. I'm not even sure that they like you or even want you.

"Let me take charge. I'll save us. I'll save us from a lonely and painful death. If you let me be the boss I'll show you what to feel or think or say or do to survive this damn thing called life. We'll make it. As for love, I don't know it and I don't trust it. But if you come with me, at least I'll teach you how to survive it too."

"We'll make it any way we have to. Perhaps I'll show you what it takes to be powerful by becoming rich or important or beautiful or famous; or, I'll show you how to protect yourself by going the other way—by isolating and maintaining a low profile. Maybe I'll turn you into a failure, a loser, a loner, or maybe I'll show you how to be cunning and manipulative in your dealings with people. I'll make you exceptional in some way. We'll survive. Face it kid, exceptionally good or bad, it hardly matters. At least with me in charge you'll make it! You'll survive. This way we'll join them and beat them at their own game. They won't ever again be able to hurt you like they have. I'll see to that."

The unexamined and unhealed emotional pain and fear of one generation, meaning its aggressive/defensive ego consciousness, will automatically be passed on to the next generation. Over time the young inherit this legacy of fear, just as they will a legacy of love. **Transforming the fear you have inherited into higher and greater love is the essence of personal healing.**

Thrown into a world of fear-based and survival-oriented aggressive/defensive egos, you learned how to become one. Raised by other egos, you learned how to play the game. With insufficient protection and mentoring to keep it alive, your natural emotional and spiritual identity withered and died, like a flower that couldn't get enough exposure to the sun. The natural child consciousness/authentic self and spiritual consciousness within you acceded to the rule of the ego consciousness. The little plug disconnected from the socket and a false self was born. Life and relationships became a battleground; something to survive rather than something to trust and truly enjoy. You were cheated out of communing with the oneness of all living things.

The Upside of the Ego Consciousness: The Healthy, Ego-in-Service

Though it would be easy to typecast the entire ego consciousness as the "bad guy" of the Inner Family, whose removal from the scene would be a blessing to all, it would be both short-sighted and a terrible mistake to do so. Recall that there are two distinct aspects of this consciousness—the aggressive/defensive ego and (later in healing) the healthy ego-in-service. Many spiritual schools of thought have advocated for the slaying of the "whole" ego by one means or another. Attempts have been made to deny it, punish it, trick it, disavow it and, perhaps most commonly, transcend it, with seemingly dubious benefit. It is my experience that the aggressive/defensive ego consciousness, if in any way resisted or fought against, only gets more subtle and powerful. It sneaks up on you in ever more cunning and destructive ways.

In the Inner Family Model of Self-Healing, the aggressive/defensive ego is not the enemy. Though it is true that if left unhealed and unmodified by the adult consciousness, it is capable of producing substantial hurt and harm, its healing counterpart—the healthy, ego-in-service—is a vital and indispensable component of healthy functioning. Trying to banish a part of your humanity from your over-all make up, even an unattractive and unflattering part like your aggressive/defensive ego, does not heal it. This is the equivalent of trying to deny that a close relative is a part of your family because you don't like every facet of their personality. Not inviting them to a birthday or Christmas celebration may give the rest of the family a temporary sense of tranquility, but this is ultimately an illusion. It is a refusal to face and take responsibility for embedded family rifts and the emotional wounds which have precipitated them.

It is only by approaching and embracing your aggressive/defensive ego consciousness that it can be healed and lovingly guided into its transformed twin—a healthy ego-in-service. This is a critical aspect of personal healing and a major focus of this book. If you are willing to understand your fear-based, survival-oriented ego consciousness, take on its buried emotional pain and fear, and help it, it can abandon its place as the dominating ruler of the Inner Family. It will move into a role as a dedicated, extremely effective team player in the service of the greatest good for all.

In the next section I will examine some of the many benefits of having an ego consciousness in the first place. Why has nature designed it? What are nature's intentions for a healthy ego-in-service consciousness?

Design Functions of the Ego

A. Physical Survival

We are born tiny, helpless, and dependent. No other species takes as long as a human being to achieve independence from its parents. The preservation and continuation of life, is not a given. There are real dangers in life. An abundance of forces and circumstances could do real and significant injury to us. We must learn what they are.

We must have a consciousness that stores and recalls the things that can hurt us. We must know and remember that we cannot touch the hot element of a stove. Even something that we can chew on contentedly like a gum ball, can be swallowed whole, block our windpipe, and cause us to asphyxiate. We can drown in the same amount of water that we can play in. We must know what represent stupid, reckless and unnecessary risks that could cause harm to ourselves or others. The ego consciousness helps us safeguard our lives. It plays a critical role in helping us shape a life that lasts.

B. Earning Your Daily Bread

Ultimately none of us is a free and independent agent. In order to ensure our own physical survival and well-being we must accomplish things in life. We must obtain things from it so that we can feed, shelter, and clothe ourselves and have some measure of security and comfort when we are old and frail. Here again, it is the ego consciousness which leads the way. It can lead in an aggressive/defensive way or in a more cooperative/assertive way.

Relying on the ego and its attributes such as drive, determination, perseverance, delaying gratification, toughness, and tenacity, have allowed us to succeed at long-term and difficult undertakings. Obtaining an education, developing a set of marketable skills, persevering in an profession or career, or honing an ability or talent, cannot be achieved without a strong and durable ego.

Generally speaking, we earn our daily bread on the basis of our professional or occupational ego in action. While a fortunate few may be paid directly for using their hearts and souls in the workplace, the majority of us are evaluated and rewarded (or demoted) for the performance of our egos and the skills which it utilizes. So, "having an ego" is not necessarily a pejorative term. A strong and finely developed ego serves many adaptive and life-enhancing purposes. There are many benefits and a certain beauty that is associated with a healthy and mature ego.

C. Getting Things Done

A healthy, ego-in-service is an absolutely essential component of our psychological make-up. *It is the consciousness in charge of the executive function of our lives.* An integral requirement in the survival of every human life is getting things done. We cannot always live in our hearts or be in touch with our spirituality and still get things done. We need to function in the world.

A lot of "doing" goes into the preservation of any life form. Whether these things are cooking a meal, building a business, paying a mortgage, or keeping an appointment, an ego-in-service supports us in accomplishing and obtaining things. We cannot cope with the full impact of everything around us and get where we need to go. The ego consciousness lies behind the smooth and efficient functioning of our lives. It prevents us from being immobilized by our own feelings and reactions to the multitude of invasive stimuli which bombard us from all directions every day.

Life is full of challenges. Some of these challenges we choose to take on. Choosing our most precious goals, ambitions, and dreams, and accomplishing them, gives us a tremendous sense of our strengths and resources, and an experience of personal pride and fulfillment in a job well done. Some of life's challenges we do not choose. They are forced upon us. Unwanted or adverse circumstances not of our making, unsupportive people not of our choosing, and illnesses and physical conditions not of our wanting, bring challenges of another kind. A healthy and functional ego is an indispensable element in meeting these. It is a fundamental component of any person's source of personal power. A healthy ego-in-service is what we fall back on as a source of help in times of struggle. The solid and grounded nature of an ego-in-service, like the deep root system of a tree, gives us a much needed sense of grounding and security in the face of life's constant trials.

Task orientation, projects, and goal setting are some of the ego's specialties. It can amount to a highly sophisticated, state of the art, "doing" machine. Give it a job to do, point it in the right direction, and watch it go! If we need to get things done (and who doesn't?), the healthy, ego-in-service is unmatched as an Inner Family member in its ability to achieve these aims. Under its tutelage we accomplish great things.

Today, for instance, I had several errands to run in the ninety minute break I take for my lunch. Among the decisions I had to make to achieve my goals was calculating the flow of traffic and the quickest, least congested routes I needed to take. Of course, I had to drive my car safely and conscientiously, at a speed within the legal limit, but also at a speed at which I couldn't dally either. I had to prioritize the importance of my errands and purchases, and spend my ninety minutes in a way that reflected these priorities. With each business interaction, I determined the amount of banter I engaged in, when to get to the matter at hand, and even what questions I could put to the people assisting me in the time I had (per errand) at my disposal. "Ordinary life" is complex. All of my errands were satisfyingly, if not fully completed in those ninety minutes, and the ones that I might have to return to or touch up at some point in the future were duly noted.

It was my healthy ego-in-service consciousness that carried out this complicated operation in a smooth and streamlined fashion. It planned, created strategies, juggled, and delivered what had been asked of it: "these things" accomplished in "this" amount of time. Productive? Yes. Efficient? Yes. Single-minded and focused on the goal? Yes. For performance, achievement and successfully navigating through an absurdly complicated world, one often fraught with obstructions, the ego-in-service consciousness is without peer.

Yet, at the same time, doesn't this sound a lot like a car commercial? I must be clear that while executing its timed tasks during my lunch time today, my ego was not at all concerned about whether I (or anyone else) derived an ounce of enjoyment from the experience. As a matter of fact, the ego that "I" was during this, did not even see what I was doing as an experience at all. It was simply a chore; a project; something like a tactical exercise in efficiency.

My ego had little interest in the gorgeous yellows and reds in the autumn leaves, or the sensual pleasure of the warm sunshine on my arm out the car window. My ego-in-service had no interest in any kind of pleasant exchange, much less "feeling" connected with the salespeople in the stores. "Getting the job done" was its only concern. I could even hear a critical voice inside my head when I decided to divert from the tasks at hand for a few minutes, pick up a latte, and take a moment to savour it's flavour. I didn't really notice the pleasant music coming through my car's CD player, and certainly didn't want to feel any of the diverse feelings and memories that some songs provoked.

My ego consciousness was appropriately and exclusively concerned with the job at hand and getting these errands done. This is what it valued. At the end of the day, it measures its progress and value by what it has accomplished and completed. In the "doing" of life, the ego-in-service excels.

Yet for me to experience the "feeling and being" dimensions of life, other Inner Family members are required. It is next to impossible for the aggressive/defensive ego to understand, moreover support the need and value for presence, enjoyment, peace and connection. To it, the emotional quality of my life is irrelevant. Getting to the finish line, and the apparent rewards that await me when I do, is all that counts. Of course, what immediately follows, is the requirement to cross the next finish line... and the next, and the next, and so on.

The unhealed ego is completely oblivious to the idea that life is the journey, not the destination. The inner process of turning from a healthy ego-in-service to its aggressive/defensive counterpart is what I will discuss in the next chapter.

D. The Implementation of a Social Code Of Conduct–
Protection of the Rights Of Self and Others

Living in a world with other people, we must learn how to get along if peace or serenity are to prevail. We must come to realize that we can hurt other people's feelings, ignore their rights, and offend their pride and dignity. Learning about and offering respect and dignity are integral to the sanctity and happiness of all beings. It is the healthy ego-in-service which accomplishes this.

The egos of our parents, teachers, and authority figures are what shape and mould our values, social behaviour, and etiquette. True, we may have been admonished one-too-many times in our childhood when we refused to share a favourite toy; or, we may have been harshly scolded when we hit a brother or sister, but there was a point to our authority figures' (egos') interventions and prohibitions. They, for the most part, tried to turn us into their version of good citizens—for the most part, a possibly flawed but well-intentioned attempt to make the world a better and safer place.

At the same time, we also needed to learn to stand up for ourselves and preserve our inviolable human rights. A strong and healthy ego is a great defender and formidable ally to have in the face of personal mistreatment or injustice. There are occasions in life when we need to say "Don't mess with me!", or at least: "I will not allow you to treat me this way." It is the healthy ego-in-service consciousness which carries out this function brilliantly. There is presently a need in all governments for a Department of Defence. However, when the Department of Defence becomes the only function of government, or when it takes over the leadership of the government, bloody events ensue. This is often the legacy the aggressive/defensive ego leaves behind.

Like so many things in life, the ego consciousness can be a blessing or a curse. It can be an effective contribution to the health and well-being of the individual and human race (ego-in-service), or a cause of immeasurable sorrow, hardship and harm (aggressive/defensive ego).

E. The Warding Off Of Emotional Pain

One of the most staggering realizations clients of mine regularly have is the timelessness, magnitude, and ongoing after-effects of the emotional pain they did not know they were carrying. Many are shocked by the discovery of a huge vault of feelings— some of them as fresh and raw as the day the events that caused them took place. It can be a humbling experience for people to become aware that events that they had believed to be over and done with are still alive, powerful, and influential in determining many things in the present. Once that vault has been opened, it becomes apparent the pain, hurt, anger, and sadness of the past haven't gone anywhere except underground (have been cleverly concealed from you).

In the middle of this experience, an individual may wonder incredulously how they have survived at all. How could they have emerged from these experiences as a rational, coherent and even sane adult, operating relatively effectively in the world? How could they have succeeded to the extent they have? How have they achieved even a semblance of the love, good-will, and happiness they have come to know in their relationships to date?

When I am asked about this, my answer may sound a bit contradictory and perplexing: they should feel extremely indebted to their ego consciousness. Without it, they would likely not have survived, or survived as well as they have. However in the same breath, I also tell them that they should feel eternally grateful for the other consciousnesses within them that are not, and never will be, "ego". Without these other Inner Family members, they would have never sampled a smidgen of the real love or peace they have known.

The part of us that is our ego consciousness has helped us enormously in dealing with the emotional pain of our lives. It has done this by devising a multitude of approaches, tactics, strategies, and philosophies for *not* dealing with the pain. A *critical* aspect of the ego's job description is the warding off or concealing of emotional pain. It is nothing short of brilliant in doing this.

Remember that to the ego consciousness, *emotional pain of any kind is death*. The individual ego and our culture at large (a culture ruled by egos) have devised and rigorously enforce a belief system and set of practices aimed at not feeling anything unpleasant or painful. Conventional thinking in these matters is designed to not allow ourselves to actually *have* the experience of emotional pain. Feeling pain, even fleetingly, it is argued, accomplishes nothing good; it only adds to the burdens and difficulties which a person has to endure.

With this way of thinking, there is something very dangerous about approaching our emotional pain and fear. If we're not careful, it could become a multi-headed monster with far reaching tentacles, holding us in its clutches, and squeezing all remaining life from us. There must be something wrong with us if we want to experience it. An aggressively ego-centered culture is so compulsively extroverted, seeking pleasure and avoiding pain, that it perceives there is something wrong with those who feel badly. If emotional pain is death we don't want to get near it or anything resembling it. The unhealed ego goes to *extreme* lengths to eradicate as much of it as possible from our awareness. This can offer significant benefits to us in some circumstances; however, if it goes unchecked and unbalanced, causes very harmful consequences.

Where the Costly Drawbacks Begin

The Aggressive/Defensive Ego

A knife can be used to butter your bread or kill your neighbour. Such is the case with the Inner Family member known as the ego consciousness. The same consciousness that we have employed to survive the most grievous physical and emotional threats and wounds of our lives; that we have developed in order to be able to stand up and protect ourselves; and whose attributes we have relied on to master skills which have allowed us to obtain gainful employment and thus feed, shelter, and clothe ourselves and our loved ones, has turned in on itself.

The aggressive/defensive ego consciousness has become one of the most significant threats to our health, relationships, and the future of our planet. It has turned into a compulsive, aggressive, and defensive ruler of human affairs. Originally designed to be a loyal and trusted foot soldier in the service of the Inner Family, it has become a tyrannical and megalomaniac general, a menace, endangering that very survival. Like a cancer that is eating away at the physical body which has produced it, the unhealed ego is entirely capable of bringing harm and death to the very same individual it is supposed to keep alive.

I'd like to reiterate that though it may be tempting to see this side of ourselves as bad and wrong; to vilify it and eliminate it, such an approach will only fragment our already broken inner selves even further. Remember: the only purpose for us doing this work is to help us heal. Healing, if it is to be true and real and lasting only occurs with the reconciliation, not the obliteration, of seeming opposites. It occurs in the experience of integration and harmony; in finding unity in diversity and diversity in unity.

The model described herein is called the Inner Family Model Of Self-Healing in the hopes of conveying that *all* members of that Inner Family, just like all members of our nuclear family (and all members of the family of mankind) ***must be included*** if the healing is to amount to the shift in consciousness that we seek. Please keep this in mind as we delve into the most dark and tortured elements of the aggressive/defensive ego consciousness—we are here to heal it, not to slay it.

Chapter III

> *"Nor certitude, nor peace, nor help from pain;*
> *And we are here as on a darkling plain*
> *Swept with confused alarms of struggle and flight*
> *Where ignorant armies clash by night."*
>
> Mathew Arnold
> Dover Beach

The Aggressive/Defensive Ego

The aggressive/defensive (unhealed) ego is an extremely complex and confusing consciousness. It is both contradictory and paradoxical in nature. Its codes of conduct and rules to live by are not rational, logical, reasonable, and are most of the time unkind. *We must remember that the aggressive/defensive ego consciousness is founded upon a life lived in a universe of fear.* Physically, psychologically, and emotionally, it has done whatever it deemed necessary to survive in that universe. It has been shrewd and cunning. It has been wounded, and when seen as necessary, has wounded others—a warrior stumbling on in an interminable battle against unknown enemies. It "knows and believes" that people and life are dangerous.

Taking our instructions from the aggressive/defensive ego consciousness is like following the bizarre edicts of an insane and paranoid king. Yet, for many of us, living under a dictatorial regime is considered preferable to the rudderless chaos of uncertainty and change. At least we have survived; we have made it this far. How can we be sure we will survive any other way? Why adopt some new and untested way of being? In our healing we must awaken to the tyranny of this aggressive/defensive ego.

The Aggressive/Defensive Ego Has Many Faces

Of the principle Inner Family members or consciousnesses the aggressive/defensive ego consciousness is the most baffling and the hardest to pin down. In its desperate efforts to survive life and love, it has developed a stunning array of different faces which can be contradictory and evasive. It uses defence and attack as the ways to survive in the world.

The aggressive/defensive ego, years before, experienced the natural child consciousness/authentic self as not welcomed or safe. The natural child had at some point realized, "I cannot be who I am and be loved. I do not have enough value just being who I am. Then who must I be? Who must I be? Who must I be?" The aggressive/defensive ego offered a solution: "Try this face or try this one, or that one. Try a hundred faces and see if you feel more loved and valued." And so, guided by the ego, as eloquently captured by the poet T.S. Elliot, *"We put on faces to meet the faces that we meet,"* (from his poem J. Alfred Prufrock).

The aggressive/defensive ego has many faces. This is one reason why it is such a confusing and elusive state of consciousness. It can dress itself up in a stunning and unsettling array of characters in the play of life and remain the mastermind operating behind all of them. Let's look at how deft and varied it can be in order to accomplish its principle mandate of survival.

For one person, this consciousness and its tenets may drive them relentlessly to become nothing less than president of the company. The person may be prepared to sacrifice their health, well-being, and even family and integrity to get there. Another person may sink into an addictive spiral of substance abuse in the back alley behind the company offices. They, too, are sacrificing their health, well-being, and family (their integrity), in order to meet the agenda of survival.

The addict and the corporate president, seeming opposites in so many ways, are tightly gripped by their aggressive/defensive ego consciousness. One in a compulsive need for corporate ascent, is likely driven to achieve fabulous success, prosperity, and power as a means of avoiding their well-concealed emotional pain and fear. In the process of avoiding, they become addictively consumed by an organization and a work schedule. The other person, the "street" addict, finds their inner world just as intolerable and unmanageable, and finds their needed distraction in "street" addictions. Then there is the largest group of addicts that are middle-income and deny their pain and fear by addictions to television, pornography, food, adrenalin, shiny things, relationships, religion, recovery, gambling, romance, religion, sex, exercise, righteousness, shopping... and many more.

The aggressive/defensive ego consciousness lies behind all of these seemingly disparate lives. Sadly, many of them are culturally endorsed and applauded; but the "street addict" meets with social repugnance and disdain. Yet, the divide between any of them, may be much, much narrower than appearances would lead us to believe, or (maybe more importantly) than society would have us believe.

Someone who is a social "wallflower" or the "life of the party", again seeming opposites, may both be very frightened of real intimacy with others. They may be compelled to take on these roles because of unexamined issues and fears that reside in their unhealed ego consciousness. Each of the actor's scripts, on one level, may produce markedly different reactions in others. One is likely to be perceived as a social misfit, the other as popular and blessed with a "winning" personality. On another and deeper level however, the consequences for the life of either actor may be much more similar than different. In both situations the authentic or natural self is not brought forward and shared. If this is the case, deep within both people will be painful states of loneliness and alienation. Denying these states, or otherwise attempting to cover them up, will only embed these ego scripts and presentations even more.

Expert at wearing any cloak, the aggressive/defensive ego can use absolutely *anything* to hide behind in its efforts to bolster a sense of (always elusive) safety, loveable-ness, or worth. I have known clients who have developed strong ego attachments to the very symptoms, illnesses, and wounds that they have come to therapy ostensibly to heal. For all intents and purposes they do not "have" these symptoms, rather they **are** their symptoms, illnesses, and wounds. Feeling victimized or persecuted, and positioning themselves as the hopeless and innocent target of malevolent forces, gives them a very real and significant ego-identity, which they cling to. In a certain sense, these love- or value-starved individuals, whose natural child consciousness/authentic self has been long ago lost or submerged, become "larger than life". They become important or exceptional; possibly a *cause celebre* with their illness or victim-hood, if to no one else, at least to themselves.

By the same token, I have met other clients in therapy who **are** their income brackets, their successes, their beauty, their humour, their expertise, their intellect, and even their spiritual enlightenment.

Their ego has become just as attached to these faces or identities as their own particular *cause celebre*. Seemingly polar opposites to the "ill" people described above, these individuals do not see or present themselves as having symptoms or illnesses but as having extraordinary attributes and successes. The price for their mark of distinction, as it is wont to be, is excessively high emotionally and spiritually. These impressive character features are symptoms of a deeper imbalance and represent unexplored emotional pain and fear.

Contradictory, hypocritical, and seemingly opposite ego presentations, such as the ones described above, can exist side by side in the same person. The apparent contradictions within our own make-up can baffle, amuse, and regularly sabotage us for sure. We can be kind or mean, dominating or submissive, outgoing or wanting to run away and hide. We can enjoy supporting someone's success and, if we are willing to admit it, enjoy someone's disgrace and ruin. We can feel good about ourselves one hour and like the world's biggest loser the next. In comparing ourselves to others, who cannot feel inadequate and inferior one minute and righteously superior the next?

Twelve step literature describes the nature and power of addictions and the addictive process as "cunning, baffling, powerful, and patient". These same adjectives best describe the aggressive/defensive ego consciousness. Its tirades can be heard in the mind of the student who demands nothing less than an "A+" average or similarly the student who seems to enjoy the position of being bad and failing. It can play both ends against the middle and, as the saying goes, speak out of both sides of its mouth simultaneously. To understand the nature of the aggressive/defensive ego consciousness and the universe it inhabits, we will have to enter realms which are irrational, illogical and unreasonable—a world which is upside down and inside out.

By studying this ego consciousness, you can discover a thinking process and way of reacting to the world, which explains your destructive behaviour, *if you can remember that the aggressive/defensive ego is afraid of practically everybody and everything.* In this dimly lit chamber of mirrors, its objective is to survive love and life by not being authentic. Your ego will do this by forcing you to do anything but be your true self. Trying to attain the experience of being safe, loved, and valued through a myriad of indirect and convoluted routes, your aggressive/defensive ego consciousness forces you down a path that conceals who you really are.

Now, of course, not every contradiction in your nature or presentation to the world can be attributed to the operations of this consciousness. As I have already mentioned, separate from the ego's many and varied faces, there are other conflicted Inner Family members with competing interests who may also be responsible for the contradictions and hypocritical traits in your personality. Yet, most often, it is your unknown fear-based, survival-oriented aggressive/defensive ego acting alone which is responsible for this.

Behind the Apparent Contradictions: The Need for Power and Control over Others

Though riddled with contradictions and inconsistencies, and being cunning, baffling, powerful, and patient, there is an important unifying element underneath the aggressive/defensive ego consciousnesses' mysterious and chaotic ways. Once this is understood, we can begin to make perfect emotional sense of its ways of operating and its presentations to the world. *Underneath the many different attributes, manoeuvres, and public faces of the aggressive/defensive ego is its need to wield and maintain power and control over others.* That is its primary focus.

Recall that this ego consciousness both arises from (and perpetuates) a Universe Of Fear. In that universe, it is never, repeat *never*, certain of its survival. It never relaxes. It never takes a day off. The threats to our survival early in our lives, be they physical or psychological, were sufficiently terrifying for the aggressive/ defensive ego consciousness to appoint itself Chief Knight and Protector of the castle (of you). Back and forth it marches, relentlessly back and forth, protecting the well-being and the very life of the natural child consciousness/authentic self. Hostile forces, and real or imagined enemies lurk everywhere. The gallant, self-appointed knight can never rest. One moment of no vigilance; one instant of dozing off; one incident of admitting the wrong person, could mean serious additional harm or even death.

The best, the surest, and perhaps the only way of accomplishing its aims, is establishing and maintaining power and control over others. No matter how varied and contradictory the public presentation, the aggressive/defensive ego seeks external power and control. This gives it the ability to safeguard itself against others' actions, words, and feelings, and of course against other people's desire to wield power and control.

Both the corporate executive driven to achieve spectacular success, and the drug addict sprawled in the street, seek power and control over others. The "wallflower" and the "life of the party", while taking up very dissimilar social roles at the same party, are using very different means to the same end—power and control over other people. Even apparent contradictions in the behaviour patterns of people such as being kind or mean, dominating or submissive, social or anti-social, can all be viewed as changeable ego strategies for establishing and exerting power and control over others.

People who have become completely identified with their work, physical beauty, wit or charm, intelligence, income bracket, sense of humour, or sexiness, generally use that identity as a way of seeking power and control over others. The same dynamic applies on the opposite end of the scale of social acceptability: people who identify themselves as "less than"; as perpetual losers or failures; as unfairly treated "innocent" victims of people or circumstances; or as being *only* the illness they possess, are usually seeking external power and control. The formula for attaining it in this case could be called winning by losing.

Even the thought system generated by the aggressive/defensive ego, the negative judgements and critical opinions, beliefs and generalizations which constantly swirl around in our minds often without our awareness—are the mental correlates of the need for power and control over others. The power of thought in shaping our reality and determining the quality of our lives cannot be overestimated. Let's take a deeper look at the thought processes by and through which the aggressive/defensive ego views its world.

The Aggressive/Defensive Ego Is a Judgement and Generalization Machine

The aggressive/defensive ego employs countless tactics designed to survive a world which long ago it concluded was threatening and dangerous. In addition to hiding behind a kaleidoscope of public faces and identities (which will be the central theme of Chapter IV), the ego navigates through the Universe of Fear. It inhabits and survives in this universe by taking control of our thought processes.

How does the aggressive/defensive ego consciousness think? First and foremost, by grouping incidents, circumstances, and people (which have been associated with emotional pain and fear) into a classification system of massive generalities. In the ego's thinking, *everything is the same as everything else (dangerous!) until proven otherwise.*

What does this mean? As an example, if you've experienced being badly hurt by one particular man or woman in your past, your ego concludes that *all* men or women, sooner or later, will hurt you. Or if, when a child, you were bicycling down the street, watching the boughs of the trees overhead, feeling the sunshine on your face, and smelling the delicious scent of apple pie coming from a neighbour's kitchen, and a bad accident happened, your aggressive/defensive ego consciousness may interpret riding a bicycle, the sight of tall tree branches swaying in the wind, the sensations of the sun on your face, or even the scent of apple pie, as dangerous. At the core of its thinking, it *is a massive judgement and generalization machine*. It will perpetually scan its environment seeking objects that are in any way similar to past sources of emotional pain and fear. When finding even the most remote similarity, it will react to them as if they were the originals.

I will, in due course, explain the origins and purpose of this massive judgement and generalization machine. Firstly though, let's look further into our daily lives for common and concrete examples of the aggressive/defensive ego's judgements and generalizations at work.

There is a voice in your head full of judgements, criticisms, and attack thoughts for yourself and others. It can sometimes appear to come out of nowhere. It is usually not fair, kind, or necessarily accurate; though it believes itself not only to be accurate, but a definitive authority and final truth on all things. It can harshly judge you or others for anything under the sun. It can put you or others down in the blink of an eye. No distinguishing personal feature, trait or characteristic in yourself or others is too small (or big) to be exempt from its consistently scathing assessments. The voice of your aggressive/defensive ego, whether a whisper or a shout, has a tremendously negative impact on the quality of your life.

"My nose is too big!" "My breasts are too small." "My arms are too thin." "I'm such a loser!" "I'm so stupid!" "I'm not good enough!" "There's something wrong with me." "Nobody finds me attractive." "What do I matter?" The litany of abusive judgements and criticisms can be endless.

Or, it may take its wrath out on others. The disparaging voice may insist that: "He's such a jerk!" "She's such a bitch!" "Look at the missing teeth in that man's mouth; how disgusting!" "She is so fat." "The way he wears his hair makes him look like such a freak!" Or groups of human beings: "Homosexuals are sick people." "Left-wing liberals are the real problem!" "All Arabs are _____." "All Jews are _____." "All Chinese are _____." "All Americans are _____." "Politicians are _____." "Authors are _____." "Doctors are _____." "Lawyers are _____." "People on welfare are _____." Fill in your ego's judgement.

The aggressive/defensive ego is a judgement machine. It just never stops. It is righteously attached to judgements and generalizations that it creates on the basis of the flimsiest information or the most singular of experiences. Because its devious patterns are not rational, logical, reasonable, or linear many of the judgements it forms contradict and undermine themselves. This hardly seems to matter to the aggressive/defensive ego as it rushes on in a steady stream of judging, condemning, evaluating, comparing, criticizing, blaming, and "measuring" us against them and them against us.

"Am I better than they are? Well of course I am!" (or) "Am I as good as they are? Yes! (or No.) Most certainly, yes! or no!. (or) "Am I absolutely right about everything I believe in and do? Yes, I am, most certainly, yes!" (or) "Could I be wrong about everything I believe in and do? Yes, I'm sure I'm wrong. No! I'm sure I'm not!"

Remember the development of the aggressive/defensive ego consciousness is based upon the belief that who you naturally are is not enough, so, the faces and identities that your ego has adopted to help you feel safe, loveable, and valued may come under harsh scrutiny. "Is my beauty enough?" "Have I succeeded enough?" "Am I intelligent enough?" "Do I have enough money?" "Am I famous enough?" "Am I likeable enough?" If the aggressive/defensive ego is the only Inner Family Member that you listen to for the answer to these questions, it will unswervingly leave you in a perpetual state of emotional insecurity.

At the risk of being repetitious, I must stress that the aggressive/defensive ego consciousness is cunning, baffling, powerful, and patient. It can speak out of both sides of its mouth at the same time. It can make two contradictory and incompatible demands simultaneously. For example, if you are reticent to participate or speak in the company of others, it may scream: "DON'T BE SO QUIET AND SHY! SPEAK UP! YOU'RE SUCH A LOSER!" Yet, one minute later when you do participate and speak up, it can just as likely shout: "YOU'RE BEING TOO FORWARD! YOU'RE TAKING UP TOO MUCH TIME! WHO DO YOU THINK YOU ARE?" Your aggressive/defensive ego can judge and find fault with yourself and others for anything and everything. And the opposite of anything and everything!

An Example From My Own Life

One of the faces (or identities) that my aggressive/defensive ego has employed over the course of my adult life, to obtain the sense of being loveable and worthwhile is: "I am Joel, the therapist, the teacher, the guide to others."

As I discussed earlier in the section <u>Design Functions of the Ego</u>, not all of this is a bad thing. Just because my ego has become extremely attached to this identity does not mean that it is entirely bad or false. This ego consciousness has also pushed me to achieve success in my chosen profession. It has helped me to be disciplined, focused, perseverant, and ambitious in meeting a host of academic and professional standards and challenges that have helped me to become the best psychotherapist that I can be. With my ego's pushing and prodding, I have made a very good living, and I'm able to provide and care for myself and my family. I also feel a deep sense of personal fulfillment and contribute to the well-being of other people and my society.

At the same time I have tried to use the professional role of therapist, teacher, and guide to others as my ticket to being "a somebody". It's my way of attempting to answer, once and for all, the questions about myself which have tormented me since childhood. These questions only began to surface when I lost touch with my natural child consciousness/authentic self and spiritual consciousness and developed an adaptive child, and then soon began to progressively identify myself with my aggressive/defensive ego consciousness. The questions were: Am I good? Am I loveable? Am I worthwhile and valuable? Am I sufficient?

Repeatedly I would use my professional skills and

knowledge as my way of feeling safe, loved, and valued; of being good enough at last! As it turned out, outside of the professional respect, admiration, and acclaim I received, I truly did not know and, at a deeper level still could not *feel* that I was safe, loved, valued, or good enough.

What does a parched and dying soul do when there appears to be only one well of life-giving water? They drink from it. And... what if their thirst is only temporarily quenched, always requiring more arduous effort each time to quench that thirst? They do what they have to do to drink. I did what I had to do. So do you.

Eventually however, being singularly renewed and revived by the waters of my professional accomplishments became a recipe for disaster. The aggressive/defensive ego consciousness will attach itself to **any** face or identity as its way of obtaining the sense of being safe, loved, and valued. Each time it does, you will hear another chorus of judgements and condemnations.

Remember I explained the ego *never* rests? In taking on the project of writing this book, my ego consciousness has wrapped itself around a new identity and face: Author! True to form, this has been accompanied by a round of self-judgements and condemnations, so intense and protracted, that on many occasions it has thrown me for a loop.

The new identity that my aggressive/defensive ego would now like to cling to is my being the author of a book. Not just the author of "any old book", either. In order to meet my ego's standards for success my book has to be:

a) a timeless classic,
b) an international bestseller,
c) the greatest contribution to mankind's understanding of itself since Freud and Jung; and,
d) a source of unlimited income.

With these "tiny" expectations in the background, I'd like to give you an example of the tenacious and destructive ways in which my own aggressive/defensive ego has been judging me in the writing of this book.

I am not a writer by profession. I have never written a book before. Though I have put a few things to paper in my career as a psychotherapist, I have not written much in the past fifteen years, and nothing at all in the last seven. I have never been published. Not since graduate school, twenty-five years ago, have I written anything that demands the staying power and confidence of a major work, one that likely will require many months or even years to complete.

In putting my deeply held theories, ideas, and beliefs on paper, I've been bombarded by my own aggressive/defensive ego. Surrounding me at every turn, like noxious fumes, are judgements, condemnations, criticisms, and put-downs. These aren't only about writing this book, but also about who I am as a person and as a professional. I'm embarrassed to tell you how I have been filled with self-doubt, fear, worry, and self-loathing. In the beginning, every single time I sat down to write, I would feel sick to my stomach. My shoulders and neck would turn to stone. Frequently I would develop a mild headache or overwhelming fatigue. I'd sit paralyzed in front of my computer, convinced that I can't write, that I shouldn't write, that I've got nothing to say anyway.

As I will be speaking about later, in Healing The Ego, it often helps to put the voice of the attacking and punishing aggressive/defensive ego on "external speaker"; moving it from the hidden quarters of your mind into the public domain i.e., a journal, a tape, a close friend, or a therapist. If I would have exposed the judgmental, condemning voices of this consciousness to you, in regards to my writing this book, here's what you would have heard:

"Joel, forget it! Don't even try to write! You don't have what it takes. YOU'RE NO WRITER! YOU'RE NOT GOOD ENOUGH! You don't have the vocabulary, the knowledge of grammar, the understanding of sentence, paragraph, and chapter structure to succeed. YOU WILL FAIL! You don't have anything to say anyways and besides, you can't express what you do want to say in any coherent, articulate, creative or entertaining way. This is just a waste of time. No one will read it and it is taking valuable time away from other endeavours that you might be at least half good at—other things that you are able to make money at! DON'T BE A FOOL! DON'T EMBARRASS YOURSELF! DON'T GO AHEAD WITH WHAT WILL SURELY BE ONE OF THE MOST SIGNIFICANT AND HUMILIATING FAILURES OF YOUR LIFETIME!"

There is more—my own aggressive/defensive ego actually

gets much uglier. At still deeper levels, I could distinctly hear this chorus of attack and ridicule:

"YOU KNOW YOU'RE NOT THAT MUCH OF A THERAPIST! You're not as good, as talented or as unique as you think. People are not going to take you seriously. Especially other helping professionals. You exaggerate the contribution that you have made to others. You're a rather way-out, flaky, kook of a therapist anyway. Your ideas are way out there! They border on strange. They may even be dangerous and irresponsible.

"Deep down inside, you don't know what you're doing. Now you'll just expose your ineptitude and quackery to all and sundry. SAVE FACE, PRESERVE YOUR REPUTATION. QUIT WHILE YOU'RE AHEAD.

"WHO DO YOU THINK YOU ARE? You're no one! You've done some pretty bad things in your lifetime so you don't want to go too public with who you are. Shut off the computer and just forget the whole thing!"

Living with the unhealed aggressive/defensive ego is the equivalent of living under the regime of a malevolent and abusive dictator. This voice of judgement and condemnation, if left to its own devices, wreaks incalculable misery upon human beings. It severely limits and often entirely stops us from realizing our fullest expressions of creativity, love, and adventure. It prevents us from the fullest enjoyment of our lives, and from making the greatest contribution of which we are capable. Not only does it stop our light from shining, but the ranting judgements and condemnations of the aggressive/defensive ego consciousness can produce inestimable pain and anguish in our relationships, and crippling and deadly symptoms and diseases in our bodies.

So, at the same time as I am writing these chapters on the aggressive/defensive ego consciousness, I am putting even more time into healing my own.

Emotional Pain and Fear Underlie All Ego Judgements And Condemnations

Where do the mocking and derisive voices that we carry come from? Is there some kind of stored archive of judgements and condemnations within us which can somehow suddenly erupt, having such power that it can completely take us over and spill onto others? What are these attack thoughts really made up of? Where, inside us, do they come from?

Underneath the judgements and generalizations of the aggressive/defensive ego is a reservoir of unexamined, unhealed emotional pain and fear. The fusillade of biting, scathing self-judgements which were detailed in the previous section, arise out of unexamined and unhealed emotional pain and fear. They are the mental equivalent and intellectual crystallization of all of the fear that each of us accumulates over a lifetime. This is the fear I described earlier as the fear of which we are a part that passes all understanding.

To the same extent that you are filled with emotional pain and fear is the extent to which you will carry judgements, condemnations, and attack thoughts of yourself or others. Show me a frightened person and I'll show you a person whose mind is filled with judgements and condemnations. Show me a person whose mind is filled with judgements and condemnations and I'll show you someone who's scared (all the time).

To return to myself and the writing of this book as the current teaching example, underneath my aggressive/defensive ego's judgements and condemnations, what am I afraid of? I am afraid that I am a lousy writer. I am afraid that I am foolish or will look foolish to others. I am afraid that I am stupid. I am afraid that I don't have very much to offer. I am afraid of being incompetent. Worse still, I am afraid of being perceived by others as incompetent. I am afraid that you will not like me. I am afraid that you will disagree with my ideas, possibly finding them dangerous and irresponsible. I am afraid of putting a tremendous amount of time and energy into this project, only to have it be a complete waste of effort. I am afraid of other therapists and counsellors. I am afraid of being hurt and even devastated by the judgements and criticisms that I might receive. I am afraid of losing face. I am very, very afraid of failure. I am afraid to be known. I am afraid to be this intimate, this vulnerable, this open, and this honest.

I could go on and on. However let me address what I believe to be my deepest fears of all. Underneath my aggressive/defensive ego consciousness and its tenacious attachment to the face or identity of Joel the therapist; Joel, the teacher; Joel, the healer; and now Joel, the perfect writer of a perfect book is: *I am afraid that I am not good enough. I am afraid that without these faces of the ego and the esteem they bring me, I have no real worth; that I am not safe, loveable, or valuable. I am afraid that who I really am is no good.*

This, I believe, is the emotional pain and collection of fears which besieged me (and perhaps you?) when, somewhere in our childhoods, we lost our connection to our natural child consciousness/authentic self and our spiritual consciousness. It was the build-up of these fears and pains which forced the plug to become disconnected with its original socket—that created the necessity for the aggressive/defensive ego consciousness and the Universe Of Fear which it both creates and perpetuates. My own ego is no exception to the rule.

If you can relate in any way to this, here again we have another glimpse into how enormous the fear is in which we live. It is not that we have fear. It is more accurate to state that our fear has us. It swirls and twirls constantly in our minds. It fills our hearts. It kills our bodies. It destroys our relationships. Remember, as long as we are identified with our aggressive/defensive egos, we are identified with a fear-generating consciousness. Fear begets fear which begets fear—and, as we know all too well from human history, *fear begets savagery and human horror.*

A Brief Review

- The ego is made up of two aspects: the often crippling and destructive aggressive/defensive ego and the healthy ego-in-service (developed during the healing process);

- Its aggressive/defensive aspect originates *after* the natural child consciousness/authentic self and the spiritual consciousness are sufficiently neglected, hurt, mistreated, or harmed to create an adaptive child consciousness and the subsequent build-up of emotional pain and fear becomes overwhelming;

- Whereas the healthy ego-in-service contributes to your survival and well-being, the aggressive/defensive ego poses a major threat to them.

Originally brought into being to protect both your physical and emotional survival, (as a developing child or a maturing adult), this ego consciousness has turned on itself and lives by an attack-and-defence system which you, the adult, have become progressively more controlled by;

- As a result of the aggressive/defensive ego consciousness taking over an adaptive child consciousness that is overflowing with emotional pain and fear, it will perceive *any* additional pain or fear as a potential death threat. It will be determined to make sure that no additional emotional pain is experienced;

- One of the central features of the aggressive/defensive ego is that it is a massive judgement and generalization machine. This is a strategy or a tactic to maintain control and prevent the experience of more pain; and,

- The work of self-healing involves you identifying your aggressive/defensive ego consciousness, separating yourself from it, taking responsibility for it, helping it to heal, and restoring access to (and balance this with) your natural child consciousness/authentic self and your spiritual consciousness, This is done with the influence of a newly-forming independent/aware adult consciousness.

The Aggressive/Defensive Ego's Judgements and Generalizations Helped Us Survive

It is necessary to take a deeper look at the origins, purpose, and value of this aspect of the ego. Why is it a "judgement machine"? To begin, here is a metaphor:

A small and leaderless troop of soldiers is under attack by a formidable and relentless enemy. Significant casualties have been inflicted on the little troop. Faltering badly and outnumbered on every side, the troop is in real danger of being totally destroyed. No one in the group seems to know what to do. Death seems inevitable.

From out of nowhere, someone steps forward and declares that they are willing to become the leader. They will devise a plan and do whatever it takes to survive. The one thing this self-appointed leader insists on, from every soldier, is total, unquestioning obedience. Amongst the brilliant and imaginative schemes they must devise, the first and foremost is some way of discerning who the enemy is and where they are coming from. Then, what can be done immediately to protect themselves from complete annihilation. To get as clear a picture as possible, the leader begins by making rudimentary and sweeping judgements about the battle scene. They quickly assess who poses the most immediate threat amongst the enemy; how they operate; and what to do if or when they meet up with them face to face.

The accuracy and validity of the judgements that the leader forms could have life or death consequences for the little troop. Even if they are wrong about some of the judgements, or too broad and sweeping about others, if they are to instil any hope or confidence in the troops, they must operate *as if they are right about them all*. The leader *must* believe unequivocally in these judgements, abide by them themselves, and enforce them upon the members of the troop; otherwise, defenceless chaos will prevail. All will be lost and again, death will seem inevitable. If lives are to be saved, everyone must follow the exact and precise orders of this self-appointed leader.

It is thus with your aggressive/defensive ego. Born out of experiences of emotional pain and fear, this powerful aspect of your ego consciousness surveys your physical and psychological environment. It will detect any new or potentially new sources of pain and fear. The equivalent of a full-time radar system, it constantly scans your life and your environment, identifying any *possible* danger long before it can become a serious threat. "Enemy" forces will be recognized, their location pin-pointed, their power nullified. [And, the simplest way to achieve this is to classify *everyone* as potentially dangerous.] To become the alert, discerning, and sophisticated protector of the Inner Family, like the self-appointed leader with his troop, your aggressive/defensive ego has formulated all kinds of judgements and generalizations about life, love and other people.

These judgements and generalizations, and thought pro-cesses like them, are the cornerstone of its battle plan. It believes that emotional pain comes from all quarters with dizzying randomness and unpredictability—it and you are never consistently safe. This generates a Universe of Fear. It believes its judgements are critical to your survival (and sometimes they are!). According to your ego, the categorizing of *every*one and *every*thing as a potential or actual enemy allows you to live another day on the battlefield of life.

The aggressive/defensive ego is born out of more emotional pain and fear than the adaptive child consciousness, that's in a child, adolescent, or young adult can handle. The ego has to be incontestably *RIGHT* about its judgements, and has to enforce its judgements to physically and/or psychologically save the young person in its charge. Though its understanding and thinking have been and remain extremely limited, the ego always means well: *the ego is not the bad guy*. As a young and defenceless human being, no one stepped forward to offer you protection and assistance. Like the soldiers, you were outnumbered and helpless; and as a real child, with a pain-filled adaptive child consciousness, fighting for your every breath. Someone had to take over; someone had to take on the job. That job fell to the ego consciousness, and it got the job done by creating an aggressive/defensive ego. How do I know that? You're still here.

The Aggressive/Defensive Ego's Judgement Classification System

There are two principle categories of judgements in the aggressive/defensive ego consciousness' classification system. These are (i) Universal Judgements (four sub-types); and, (ii) Idiosyncratic Judgements.

Universal Ego Judgements refer to the judgements and generalizations that are common to all people. Your ego and the egos of everyone else, and I mean *everyone,* operate according to these universal judgements.

Idiosyncratic Ego Judgements refer to judgements and generalizations that are created and perpetuated by a particular person's ego in their lifetime. These are the personal deductions and conclusions a particular ego consciousness has drawn about the sources of emotional pain and fear it encountered, and personal (ego) strategies of how to make certain no experience of that kind ever happens again. In contrast to the Universal Ego Judgments (which we all share), no two people have exactly the same idiosyncratic judgements.

Four Universal Judgements Of The Aggressive/Defensive Ego

The First Universal Ego Judgement:
Externalizing the Cause of Pain—Hell is Caused by Other People

The aggressive/defensive ego consciousness perceives that all emotional pain and fear is caused by other people or outside circumstances. When we are controlled by this consciousness, we perceive and believe it is some external agent (of one kind or another) that *makes* us feel a certain way. Someone or something outside us is responsible for what we experience, particularly and emphatically when we do not like what we are experiencing. "My wife makes me angry." "My husband makes me unhappy." "My kid is driving me crazy." "My boss irritates me." "Rainy weather makes me depressed." "That other culture frightens me."

The aggressive/defensive ego constantly projects responsibility for *any* unwanted, unpleasant experiences onto others. To it, the people around us have a master control panel which determines our feelings and reactions. In their all powerful ways, by pushing various buttons on that control panel, it is they who determine how we react and what we feel. In other words: **The aggressive/defensive ego consciousness in us refuses to take responsibility for anything that we experience.** It does not even consider the possibility that we might be the source of our own experience, or that it is our own conditioning which generates the negative or painful experience. When we are operating from this consciousness, we are absolutely convinced that hell is caused by other people. Everyone has some degree of an aggressive/defensive ego consciousness that adheres to the incontestable conclusion that the emotional pain we experience is caused by something or somebody else.

Nowhere is this more apparent than in relationships. Though the details vary significantly from couple to couple, every marriage or relationship mired in acrimony and discord begins with some version of the following script: "My emotional pain and unhappiness is caused by you," claims the aggressive/defensive ego consciousness of one partner. "Wrong!" counters the other, "My emotional pain and unhappiness is caused by you!" Then they will itemize the misdemeanours: "Here's what *you've* done to *me...*" is usually what follows. "Well, you've done that to me and worse," is the counter-attack of the other.

Both members of the couple are (almost) completely controlled by their aggressive/defensive ego. As a therapist, I regularly see a long established, relentless cycle of hostility; an endless figure-eight loop of denied responsibility, judgement, blame, and "justified" attack. Husband blames wife and wife blames husband for the emotional pain, fear, and unhappiness that each is experiencing. The idea that it is their own aggressive/defensive ego consciousness is the larger cause of the emotional pain and fear than anything their partner (or child) has said or done is not something they have considered.

In life we have and will experience some emotional pain and fear associated with our fathers, mothers, brothers, sisters, husbands, wives, lovers, children, grandparents, uncles, aunts, cousins, in-laws, friends, neighbours, bosses, employees, co-workers and strangers. It will be our aggressive/defensive ego's perception and belief that these people have caused us to feel these ways. It will mobilize to defend and protect us against these purveyors of pain (and it will deny us access to the love and caring we seek to give and receive).

The universal ego-judgement that it is others who cause us to react and feel the way we do, perhaps more than any other single factor, is responsible for the deterioration and eventual demise of human relationships. By projecting the cause of our emotional pain and fear onto others, the aggressive/defensive ego feels indignant, justified, and always righteous, when it blames the "enemy". Then it retaliates by the most vicious means possible.

Our own ego consciousness is convinced we have absolutely nothing to do with being the cause of our own emotional pain and fear. *"I am innocent and you, it, or they are guilty,"* is its perfectly justified perception of everything in the universe.

The Second Universal Ego Judgement:
If I Experience Pain of Any Kind I Have Been Wronged!

The second universal ego judgement can be seen as a

variation or magnification of the first. It has to do with the way that the aggressive/defensive consciousness interprets the experience of pain; in its largest and most perplexing form—individual or universal human suffering.

Some of our greatest philosophers have wrestled with the question of why there is pain and suffering, often with little or no agreement amongst them. However one reality remains and that is: pain and suffering exist. They exist in every life. Raising the possibility that individual, collective, or global suffering, though unwanted and often unbearable, could have meaning and value, or even be necessary, is the equivalent of heresy in the judgement of the aggressive/defensive ego consciousness. Vehemently and vociferously, it will rebut this idea.

When we are controlled by this consciousness, we do not see our pain or suffering as something that just comes with the territory of being alive. We do not accept it as a mysterious, non-partisan component of being human; as something that all human beings (for reasons we can only speculate about) must experience. Our aggressive/defensive ego denies that pain could ever be an enigmatic teacher and healer guiding us in our spiritual evolution. Instead, whenever our aggressive/defensive ego consciousness experiences some form of emotional pain, fear, misery, or suffering it immediately makes the judgement that this is wrong and I (you) are being unjustly treated by someone or something.

When we are in this consciousness and experience suffering in any form, we do not deal with our human pain and misery as if it is something that just is and that is no one's fault. Rather, we feel perceive, and believe, that somebody out there is doing something to us, and that they are very mean or wrong for this. Our ego-mind then goes to war with whomever (or whatever i.e.: "God", Life, the Universe), that we are convinced is doing this "bad" thing. Once we have identified the "enemy" and have them in our sights, we have every conceivable reason to pull the trigger. We shoot bad guys, don't we? We have every justification for it, don't we? We pay them back with interest and why not... "We're innocent," says the ego.

If we are experiencing pain, what if *no one* is to blame? What if we have not been wronged? Yes, it hurts, it *really* hurts, but what if there is no injustice? If it is true, that there is no injustice, we may need to learn how to challenge our righteous, self-vindicating perceptions.

The Third Universal Ego Judgement:
Emotional Pain And Fear Are Bad;
They Should Never Be Experienced.

Remember that the aggressive/defensive ego consciousness, because it was both born out of, and carries overwhelming amounts of emotional pain and fear, has no tolerance for any new and fresh emotional pain. To it, emotional pain is death. It perceives emotional pain as an indignity, an affront, an enemy, a cancer. To allow *any* experience of pain serves no beneficial purpose and should be banished from our awareness.

Associated with the judgement that pain must be avoided (though I must say that my exposure is limited to Western culture), is that the *experience* of emotional pain and fear, of *any* kind and for *any* reason, is bad and wrong. "Don't worry, be happy!" may be a cute comforting cliché; however, to the aggressive/defensive ego consciousness, it becomes a tyrannical edict. Other derivatives of this dictate include these messages taken from the lyrics of American popular songs:

> *"When you're smiling, when you're smiling,*
> *the whole world smiles with you...*
> *But when you're crying, you bring on the rain."*
> *"When You're Smiling"*
> Shay, Fisher, and Goodwin

> *"Smile though your heart is aching,*
> *Smile though your heart is breaking,*
> *Although a tear may be ever so near..."*
> *"Smile"*, Charlie Chaplin

There is the song: "*Put On A Happy Face*." (Lee Adams, lyricist and C. Strouge, composer); and, of course there's the popular cliché: "Smile and the world smiles with you. Cry and you cry alone."

Individually, and as a culture, we seem determined to deny reality. We are taught in countless ways that emotional pain, or anything associated with fear and pain, is bad and should be avoided at all costs. Yet, emotional pain, loss, and hardship, are integral components of the human experience, no less than joy and love and happiness. They are all on the spectrum of the human condition.

The Fourth Universal Ego Judgement:
My Judgements Are Incontestably Right—They Are Laws of the Universe and the Way Things Are.

When we are identified with the aggressive/defensive ego, we are in a fear-based state of consciousness. Though this fear is so vast and limitless, which I have described as a Universe Of Fear (or the fear of which I am a part which passes all understanding), most of us seldom actually experience the physical symptoms of fear: shaking, trembling, perspiring, accelerated heart beat, etc. Fear is so omnipresent that we do not even notice it. It is not a part of our conscious experience. Instead, it is the *context for our experience, which is why we are unaware of being overwhelmed by it*. While ensconced in the aggressive/defensive ego consciousness (and in some ways this is one of its most useful features for our survival), we do not have emotional pain and fear. However what becomes a detriment to our survival is that in this consciousness our pain and fear have us.

Earlier I used the "fish in water" analogy". Here is where a clear understanding of this is crucial. Fish live "in" water and will usually live and die never having the experience of air or wind or people or land. They are completely oblivious to the existence of the universe outside of water and live their life ignorant of any experience beyond "water". This is context—the most powerful and controlling factor of their life, which they are blind to, is water. There is no facet of their existence that isn't influenced by water.

People, because of how we have orchestrated ourselves, and the way we perceive life and existence in this orchestration, live in an ocean of fear. We grow up, eat, play, create and procreate, earn a living, marry, live, and die, and are always ignorant of the universe of fear that we live in (context). Fish in the universe of water; people in the universe of fear.

Regarding content: The judgements, criticisms, attack thoughts, and self-righteous generalizations in the daily to-and-fro of our lives, and which occupy our thoughts each day, are "content".

Thoughts are seldom noticed as the overwhelming content of our consciousness. Only when you begin to notice the kind and quality of the thoughts you're having (which will require willing-ness, determination, and the development of your independent/aware adult consciousness), can you become aware of how harsh and cruel they are. In *some* situations they may be a dim reflection of truth, but for the most part they are harsh and unfounded.

Consider this: Start to notice how long you can go in a day without judging, criticizing, attacking, complaining, or generalizing. In my own case, I figure it's a good day if I can make it a couple of hours without them. Most of us are so furiously occupied forming judgements, opinions, conclusions, complaints, and beliefs, about someone or something—mind chatter that arises out of *our own* unknown emotional pain and fear (which reflects the universe of fear in which we live), that we don't even know we're doing it.

Instead of being consciously aware and realizing that we are looking at everyone and everything through a veil of fear and insecurity that is ours alone, we believe that we are just seeing the way things are. We see the world through a glass darkly. We believe that what we are perceiving is simply fact and truth.

The tell-tale sign of your aggressive/defensive ego consciousness in action is the strong, and often ferociously defensive attachment to its judgements, criticisms, opinions, conclusions, beliefs, and generalizations. To the extent that you are identified with this consciousness is the extent you will have to be **RIGHT** about them.

Self-righteousness is an unmistakable personality feature of an individual who is identified with their aggressive/defensive ego consciousness. Being mistaken or wrong about any judgement is equivalent to the death of their ego. Sadly and regrettably, most egos have to be forever right *at all costs*: divorces, abuse, violence, ruined careers, addictions, suicides, bombing foreign nations, obliterating foreign cultures—but they're right! Long after the original battle is over; long after the enemies of the past have retreated, changed, or died; long after survival in the world is firmly secure the ego glories in its righteousness.

For most of us, the fierce attachment of our aggressive/defensive ego's consciousness to being **RIGHT** can be compared to an incident that took place in 1974. A Japanese soldier was found all alone still fighting World War II in the jungles of the South Pacific, twenty-nine years after the war was over. It required a visit from officials representing the Emperor before he was prepared to drop his rifle and accept the fact that the war was truly over. Dropping the aggressive/defensive ego's judgements, criticisms, beliefs, and generalizations—releasing the stranglehold which the ego consciousness has over our life and love—is similar. That is, it needs the intervention of a higher "authority". This will be discussed later in <u>The Therapeutic Work of Healing The Ego</u>.

These are the four universal ego judgements that keep you in the universe of fear:

- Externalizing the Cause of Pain—Hell is Caused by Other People
- If I Experience Pain of Any Kind I Have Been Wronged!
- Emotional Pain And Fear Are Bad. They Should Never Be Experienced.
- My Judgements Are Incontestably Right—They Are Laws of the Universe and the Way Things Are.

To heal and experience authentic love you must be aware of them and be skilled in disarming them.

Idiosyncratic Ego Judgements

Each *individual* ego also has its own unique collection of judgements; a judgement classification system particular to itself. To each of us, this is our very own catalogue of judgements, opinions, conclusions, complaints, and beliefs that we have accumulated over a lifetime; about *every*thing we have experienced in our lives. The specific content of these judgements is unique to each and every ego. I call these types of judgements **Idiosyncratic Ego Judgements.**

As is the case with all of the workings of our aggressive/defensive ego consciousness, our idiosyncratic ego judgements helped us deal with experiences of emotional pain and fear in our formative years that were too much for us to handle. These arose in our particular environment and were unique to us. Idiosyncratic judgements helped us classify and compartmentalize things, giving us a way of anticipating and protecting ourselves from more grievous harm or pain. Here are some examples of idiosyncratic ego judgements:

- "Dad would never understand me if I opened up to him."

- "Mom cares more for her career than me."
- "My boss is only out for what they can get."
- "That person is and always will be nothing but a total jerk!"
- "Men cannot be trusted."
- "All women, sooner or later, will hurt me or leave me."
- "I'll leave them before they leave me."
- "Love isn't real or if it is, it doesn't last."
- " No one would like the real me."
- "If I want to be liked and admired I have to be rich or sexy or important or strong."
- "Good fences make good neighbours."
- "All… Arabs, or Republicans, or Americans, or homosexuals, or Jews, or Canadians, or Chinese, or __insert preferred group__ are __insert preferred prejudice__."

These are examples of judgements, criticisms, attack thoughts, opinions, conclusions, beliefs, and generalizations, that may exist in one person's ego consciousness but not another. Unlike the universal ego judgements, these are the content of a particular individual's aggressive/defensive ego; their personal way of packaging the world. Of course, others may share similar judgements, but they exist in subtly unique ways in each individual.

What are your idiosyncratic ego judgements? It would help develop your own awareness and insight if you were to take a few minutes now and reflect on your own ego's judgements. I invite you to make a list; even a short one, of your own judgements of others, of love, and of life by "forcing" yourself to write a few of them on paper.

If you are unsure how to begin, make a list of 30 recent topics in the news. i.e.: pro-choice/abortion rights, recycling, politics, the Olympics, violence in films, the internet, parenting, lawyers, seat belt laws, hospitals, capital punishment, food additives, naturopaths, gas prices, war, religion, cell phones, education, taxes… make a list. Beside each item note your personal views of each topic. Beside your views, write the name and views of someone who differs from you. These are representative of your and their idiosyncratic ego judgements. Owning your perceptions and prejudices is the first step in freeing yourself from them.

Regardless of whether they are Idiosyncratic or Universal

Ego Judgements, *when we are identified with our aggressive/defensive ego consciousness, we would rather be right than happy.* Needing to be right about our ego's judgements (righteousness), is in my opinion, by far our most popular addiction. And, arguably, the addiction to righteousness may be the most dangerous and destructive addiction there is. We would rather be right about our judgements, criticisms, beliefs, and generalizations, than live healthy and peaceful lives. We would rather be right about our opinions and conclusions than be in beautiful and loving relationships with the people in our lives. It appears to me the human race would rather be right than alive.

There is nowhere our idiosyncratic ego judgements influence us more often than with the people who are nearest and dearest to us. With those we love: we hurt them the most, and to them we are the most cruel. Spiritual leaders, insightful poets and authors, and therapists have known this for years. Now you can understand this is the machinations of your aggressive/defensive ego consciousness.

Built as a solid firewall against *all* the emotional pain and fear of the past, it associates some, and perhaps all of the pain with people with whom we were most vulnerable. These would be our family members, caregivers, and closest friends—those people we depended on and loved; those people who told us they loved us; and those with whom we were, and are, most vulnerable.

Years later, when we enter marriages and have families (that is, when we become similarly vulnerable and we try to allow people to get very close to us) these historical associations remain real and present to the aggressive/defensive ego. Our unhealed emotional pain and fear will get triggered all over again causing our aggressive/defensive egos to flare up and "protect" us.

I will examine the closest of all our relationships, the relationship of marriage or a primary love relationship to illustrate the horrible and destructive effects of idiosyncratic ego judgements. Remember: aggressive/defensive egos refuse to accept responsibility for their own emotional pain and fear and the hurtful and harmful things they are doing to the one they claim to love more than all others.

I will chronicle the devolution of love, caring, and goodwill by egos who would rather be right than happy. They will be RIGHT at any cost. I explain this in the hypothetical case of John and Mary.

Even though I use these names and discuss this dynamic in a heterosexual relationship, the dynamic applies equally to same-sex relationships. It also isn't necessary to be married or "living together". Any long-term, going-steady relationship will have a similar dynamic. It is a truly universal process.

Then I will tell the moving stories of three very different people who took responsibility for the workings of their aggressive/defensive egos. Not only did they return to the love they once had for their family member or partner, but they expanded it exponentially. To me, these are inspiring tales of individuals who decided to shift from people who would rather be right than happy to people who would rather be happy than right. These are Sam and Claudette and David.

The Aggressive/Defensive Ego Creeps into Even the Most Auspicious of Relationships

John and Mary meet and fall in love. Carried by oceanic waves of excitement, aliveness, novelty, romance, and passionate sex, they see only godliness and grandeur in their partner. It is as if they are absorbed and far removed from their ordinary day to day consciousness. It is a higher, more enlightened consciousness; an apparently egoless one free of fear, inhibition, and guile. There is no need whatsoever for the postures of attack or defence. It is a state of bliss, immune from all sources of hurt or harm; guided and cradled by the infallible power of heart and soul. They have not formulated any judgements, criticisms, attack thoughts, or generalizations about each other. All opinions, conclusions, and beliefs, which they hold about each other, are favourable and generous.

If they were interviewed at this early stage of their relationship, neither John nor Mary could probably even imagine formulating a negative judgement of the other person, not to mention conceive of a time (not that far down the road) when their ego-minds would be bulging with them. Each of them, to the other, exactly the way they are, is living, breathing perfection. All is wonderful; they are in love, and "love is all you need".

Yet sooner or later it happens: knowingly or unknowingly, intentionally or unintentionally, the karmic law that everyone hurts those they love comes into play. Mary is spending a little too much time at work and John feels that he is getting less and less of her attention at the end of the day, or John doesn't celebrate the big occasions like he used to. Without acknowledging it to themselves, for they are still very much in love, they feel slightly hurt and disregarded, or they feel ignored and saddened by this subtle shift in their perceptions of their partner.

These tiny beginnings of John and Mary's emotional pain and fear don't come out at that time. As a matter of fact, they don't come out as communicated feelings at all. Instead, one evening Mary, hardly meaning anything by it, delivers a comment on John's cooking skills that comes out surprisingly harsh. John, stunned by the first sign of a negative and critical trait appearing in his "perfect" partner, wonders how he could have missed this obvious character flaw in Mary when they were dating.

John doesn't feel like making love with Mary nearly as much as he used to. His disinterest in sex becomes apparent to her. She feels neglected, says nothing, and avoids the tension by putting more of herself into her work. Mary withdraws by being occupied with other things. John feels neglected. He sulks, becomes moodier and progressively more depressed, and avoids the tension by watching a lot of television.

What's going on here? Why does a love that was so promising, so generous, so full and powerful, start to sour? What's turning it into an experience of alienation and antagonism? What's controlling John and Mary and ruining their relationship in the process?

By the time John and Mary meet up with a therapist, each is usually carrying a truck load of judgements, criticisms, attack thoughts, and generalizations about the other. Both are convinced that they are absolutely **RIGHT** about the shortcomings of their partner. They believe they are right about their version of what has been happening in the relationship. They are right that it is the other person who is primarily responsible for the emotional pain and fear that they, themselves, are feeling. They are both right, *very* right, about the idiosyncratic ego judgements which each is carrying about the other person. They will also want the wise relationship therapist to agree and confirm that the other person (the bad one) has stopped caring, or never cared in the first place, or doesn't have the capacity to care, or is just like all men or women, etc.

The Aggressive/Defensive Ego Cycle
of Pain, Protection, and Retribution

The aggressive/defensive ego consciousness exerts itself in anticipation of, or a reaction to the experience of emotional pain and fear. In the relationship scenario described above, both John and Mary are experiencing emotional pain and fear of one kind or another. This is comprised of unexamined, uncommunicated, and, above all, *unresolved* feelings that each person is carrying in regards to each other. Within each of them, this pain is recycled and reinforced by being converted into idiosyncratic ego judgements in regards to their partner's ways of conducting themselves in the relationship. *Both John and Mary's aggressive/defensive ego consciousness has entered the relationship and, progressively and imperceptibly, begun to dominate it.*

How has this consciousness begun to control things? First and foremost it has moved John and Mary from their hearts (child and spiritual consciousnesses) to their aggressive ego minds. Rather than experiencing a heart-to-heart (spiritual) connection with each other, and appreciating the sameness and oneness of the human pain each carries, they now find this state of humble joining too difficult to endure. Convinced and astonished that their emotional pain and fear is being caused by the very person who had initially appeared to be the most accepting and safest they had ever met, their aggressive/defensive ego has successfully taken control. It has now become attached to a position of self-righteousness, and argued for separation by convincing each of them of the righteousness of their idiosyncratic judgements about the other.

If this process of relationship deterioration could be examined sequentially, it begins with one, or both, individuals descending into their aggressive/defensive ego consciousnesses' Universal Judgements. This allows them to explain, manage, justify, and defend against the real or potential experience of emotional pain and fear. Remember the four primary Universal Judgements we covered earlier?

1. Externalizing the Cause of Pain—Hell is Caused by Other People. In a primary relationship this translates to: *"My partner is doing this to me!"*

2. If I Experience Pain Of Any Kind I Have Been

Wronged. In a primary relationship this translates to: *"My partner is wrong or bad for doing this to me."*

3. Emotional Pain And Fear Are Bad. They Should Never Be Experienced. In a primary relationship this translates to: "I did not expect or bargain for these unpleasant experiences. *If I am experiencing any type of emotional pain my partner must change or I must be with the wrong person in the wrong relationship."*

4. My Judgements Are Incontestably Right. They Are the Laws of the Universe. In a primary relationship this translates to: "The way I see my partner is the way they are. *I am right to take whatever retaliatory or defensive actions I deem necessary.* I will attack and defend myself against my former perfect partner who has become an enemy."

These four Universal Judgements are what the aggressive/defensive ego consciousness creates and attaches itself to as the backdrop for surviving life and love. Then, it forms specific Idiosyncratic Judgements about the particular people that surround it.

In John's case, it judges the perpetrator to be Mary. In Mary's case, her ego judges it is John. There will be unique judgements, criticisms, attack thoughts, and generalizations which John's aggressive/defensive ego has formulated about Mary, and Mary's aggressive/defensive ego has formulated about John. With each new sting of emotional pain and fear, these judgements become more and more justified and entrenched. Both become more tenaciously attached to being right about these judgements, choosing the desolate and destructive path where they would rather be right than happy.

Let's return to the events which precipitated the gradual deterioration of John and Mary's promising relationship, and notice the increasing presence of their aggressive/defensive ego consciousness. At the same time, I will speculate on the content of the Idiosyncratic Ego Judgements which are amassing in the formerly open and loving space between them.

In relationship conflicts, what comes first the chicken or the egg? Who is responsible for the opening salvo? Who, in retrospect, was responsible for the first insult? In truth, in the bigger scheme of things, it hardly matters. However, I have to begin somewhere. I am going to arbitrarily say that in John and Mary's case it began with:

Event # 1: In John's opinion, Mary spends too much time at work and shares less and less of herself with him at the end of the day.

This subtle change generates a vague experience of emotional pain and fear within John. He may be completely unconscious or only marginally aware of this. Without awareness, he cannot know what he is thinking, feeling, or above all needing, from Mary. Without knowing what he needs, he cannot communicate in a direct and honest way with her. Instead, silently and privately, John's aggressive/defensive ego consciousness begins to dominate John's behaviour and attitudes and takes control. It might begin to formulate the following idiosyncratic judgements, criticisms, and opinions about Mary:

> Mary doesn't love me as much as she did.
> Mary doesn't love me as much as I love her.
> Mary's work means more to her than I do.
> Mary doesn't care how I feel about this.
> Maybe this is the real Mary and the one I fell in love with is a pretender.

Event # 2: John doesn't celebrate the big occasions with me like he used to.

This event generates a subtle experience of emotional pain and fear within Mary. She may be completely unconscious or only marginally aware of this. Without awareness, she cannot know what she is thinking, feeling, or above all, needing from John. Without knowing what she needs, she cannot communicate in a direct and honest way with him. Instead, silently and privately, Mary's aggressive/defensive ego consciousness begins to dominate Mary's behaviour and attitudes and takes control. It might begin to formulate the following idiosyncratic judgements, criticisms, opinions and conclusions about John:

> John doesn't care about me as much as he used to.
> John is quite self-absorbed and inconsiderate.
> John doesn't love me with all of his heart.

I am no longer special to him.
Well if he thinks I'm going to make him feel special,
he's got another thing coming!

Event # 3: Mary's delivers a rather harsh comment on John's cooking skills.

John's aggressive/defensive ego consciousness is now more present and sensitive in his relationship with Mary. It flairs up more easily; its hair-trigger is more easily and readily cocked. It requires less of a disturbance before it goes off. Listed below might be some of his Idiosyncratic Judgements that begin to circulate in his ego mind:

- Mary is giving everything to her work. I am, at best, only the second most impor-tant thing in her life. And yet, she has the nerve to criticize the way I cook! She can be pretty mean if she wants to be.
- Who I am and whatever I do around here isn't ever good enough!
- Mary reminds me a lot of the way my mother treated my father.
- I'm tired of doing most of the giving in this relationship. I'm going to pull back a little and wait for Mary to start delivering.

Event # 4: John's interest in making love with Mary declines.

As Mary's aggressive/defensive ego becomes increasingly engaged in her relationship with John, it creates more and deep-seated Idiosyncratic Judgements of its own:

- There couldn't be someone else, could there?
- If this is John's passive-aggressive way of getting my attention, well, screw him! (so to speak). It's not going to work!
- John doesn't find me attractive.
- Isn't it just like men? They offer you their best loving while they chase you. But as

soon as they have you, their loving is ra-
tioned out!
- John reminds me more and more of my
  father. And I swore that I would never be
  in a relationship like the one my mother
  had.

Event # 5: Mary puts even more of herself into her work and closes
off to John.

Now, ever more deeply in emotional pain and fear, John's
aggressive/defensive ego consciousness becomes considerably more
prominent in his relationship with Mary. Silently seething behind the
scenes, John takes off his kid gloves and puts on his boxing gloves.
His aggressive/defensive ego is now charged and charging; shooting
first and asking questions later.

- Screw her! I don't give a damn! She can
  bring a cot to work and stay there for all I
  care!
- Two can play this game. I'm going to be
  busy the night that she receives her award
  at the company banquet.
- Maybe I'll quit my job, take up golf, take
  up drinking or, better yet, have an affair!
- It just goes to show you a woman's love is
  like summer rain—you don't know when
  it's going to come or how long it's going to
  last!

Event # 6: John sulks, becomes increasingly moody and disappears
into the television.

Now more deeply in emotional pain and fear than before,
Mary's aggressive/defensive ego consciousness becomes more
prominent in her relationship with John. Silently seething behind the
scenes, Mary takes off her kid gloves and puts on her boxing gloves.
Her aggressive/defensive ego is now charged and charging: shooting
first and asking questions later:

- John is not the one I want to be with.
- He is not the right one for me; he is not my

soul mate.
- I made a mistake when I fell in love with him. Sometimes I make such stupid mistakes. I'm sure there's somebody much better suited for me around the next corner.
- Next time, I'm marrying someone who treats me right.

Similar incidents and escalation continues. Invariably, there will be progressively more dramatic displays of attack and defence between Mary and John. At this stage of the relationship's disintegration, the emotional pain and fear are so severe that the unhealed and brittle aggressive/defensive ego in each of them is in total control. Remember the emotional range of this ego consciousness vacillates between defensive/victim and vicious. Each ego-controlled combatant has assembled a dossier of judgements, criticisms, attack thoughts, and generalizations about the other which are cemented in place by impermeable self-righteousness.

John is **RIGHT** about his opinions, beliefs, and conclusions about Mary. Unquestioningly he knows them to be absolutely true. Mary is **RIGHT** about her opinions, beliefs, and conclusions about John. Hers are also unquestionably and absolutely true. In their cases against each other, the harshest judgements and the most hurtful words and behaviours appear justifiable and warranted by (a) the emotional pain and fear that each individual carries; and, (b) their perception of how unfeeling or mean the other person is. The process of separation and divorce, and the break up of two people who were so much in love, only amplifies this brutality. A love that was made in heaven ends with souls in hell.

Two Inspiring Stories

Fortunately, I have seen many wonderful, moving examples of the healing of relationships when people become aware of, and responsible for, their aggressive/defensive ego consciousness. This process, as I explain later, begins with modifying the aggressive/defensive ego; resolving some of the pain in the adaptive/child consciousness, and the development of an independent/aware adult consciousness. This consciousness lives with choice: word by word, thought by thought, feeling by feeling, and action by action.

A person who learns how to operate from their independent/aware adult consciousness, decides whether they operate from their aggressive/defensive ego and its universal and idiosyncratic judgements *or not*. In addition to having this freedom, such an individual has access to the wisdom and guidance of the other two Inner Family members—their **natural child consciousness/ authentic self** and their **spiritual consciousness.** Led by these other guides, love can return, relationships can heal, and then be recreated on a foundation that is more solid and real than ever before. Here are two real life examples:

Sam's Story

Sam's parents had been Holocaust survivors. When growing up, he had been exposed, first hand, to the terrible mental, emotional and spiritual damage that this horror had inflicted on them. Though not inclined to be religiously devout, Sam felt a deep, soulful connection to his Jewish identity. Sparked by his love for his parents and his extended family members lost in the Nazi death camps, he carried a fierce loyalty and passion for the preservation of Jewish culture and traditions.

The father of two, a boy twelve and a girl ten, Sam had been sitting down with them regularly to teach them Hebrew, read them books, and tell them stories about their Jewish heritage. Early on in these informal classroom sessions, Sam noticed that while his daughter was interested and keen to learn more about what Sam was teaching, his son was not. When given small assignments to do between lessons, his daughter would be attentive to the assignments and his son would not do them at all. In learning Hebrew, his daughter advanced easily and rapidly. His son (from whom Sam expected more) did not have his heart in it and lagged far behind.

Sam was aware of feeling extremely disappointed, upset, and angry with his son, which he tried to conceal during the lessons. Privately, he told his wife that he was feeling guilty and ashamed that his only son seemed to have such little initiative or desire to learn more about being Jewish, Sam confided to her that he felt, for him, this was somehow tantamount to betraying his parents and the deaths of six million of his people. Sam frequently, secretly vowed to himself he would be exceptionally patient and supportive of his son and his progress, but quickly descended into scolding and becoming sarcastic with him. He compared him unfavourably to his sister and eventually "blew-up" more or less every session.

Sam's outbursts of anger and attack with his son soon began to encompass other things, like the state of his room or his chores around the house. His son would protest by saying that Sam liked his sister better; that she could do no wrong while he could do no good. By the time Sam came to see me, his wife was now involved and unhappy with the escalating conflict within the family. His son was increasingly estranged and wanted to spend all of his time with his friends and avoided Sam's teaching sessions as much as possible.

Sam was a willing and open client. It didn't take long for him to realize that he was in extreme emotional pain and fear, firstly and most compellingly, about the alienation of his son. With a little prodding, he also started to realize he had been in considerable emotional pain and fear throughout the Jewish class sessions with his children (largely associated with his son's seeming disinterest in them). This was compounded by the sacred obligation he felt to his parents and the preservation of their heritage.

We began to identify how Sam's aggressive/defensive ego consciousness had influenced his behaviour to conceal his pain and fear. We pinpointed his judgements, criticisms, and generalizations *and* his opinions, beliefs, and conclusions that he had drawn about his son, himself, and what had happened. There was a litany of them. In regards to his son, amongst the most charged and darkest of these were: *"My son rejects being Jewish." "He is turning his back on his grandparents, his people, his faith, and his identity." "He will never return to his roots." "He is self-centered and disobedient." "He is a media-enslaved conformist more interested in being just like his friends than who he really is."*

Then there were those to do with himself: *"I am letting down and betraying my parents." "I am letting down and betraying my extended family members who were murdered by Nazi brutality." "I am diminishing the memory of six million brothers and sisters." "I am somehow diminishing their suffering and deaths by not instilling pride in my son for his heritage." "I am failing as a Jewish father." "The light of a noble and heroic people will go out and I will have contributed to its demise." "I am bad and wrong."*

Initially, Sam was steadfastly certain the judgements, opinions, beliefs, and conclusions that he had formulated to explain what was happening were just the way things are. He was convinced his set of interpretations were absolutely right and true. His view comprised the only way to see this whole unfortunate circumstance.

When I brought up the possibility that he would rather be right about his aggressive/defensive ego's judgements and conclusions than happy, Sam seemed intrigued but mystified by what I was saying. So I started explaining this in a way I thought he might understand. I asked him to imagine his son sitting across from him and to say aloud: "I would rather be right about everything I have been thinking about you than be in a beautiful and loving relationship with you." Sam tried it and I could sense something begin to soften and move within him. Then I went for the whole kit-and-caboodle; I asked Sam to say to his son: "I would rather turn you into a living memorial for the suffering of my parents and my people and the preservation of Jewish culture than be in a beautiful and loving relationship with you."

At first Sam resisted saying this. He said it wasn't because he wanted to be uncooperative. It was just because he didn't really get it. I asked him to try it anyway just to see what would happen; to say it slowly and deliberately three times in a row to his son. Sam began to tremble as he did this. Small tears began to well up in his eyes. His head fell forward. He repeated the sentence three times. By the third time he was openly weeping. Without noticing, he added the words: "Son, I'm sorry." And then: "Son, I'm so sorry!"

I knew that something very deep and hard inside him was softening. Using the ideas I have explained in this book, Sam was taking responsibility for his aggressive/defensive ego consciousness which had been controlling the relationship with his son. Sam was setting them both free from its ferocious attachment to the judgements, attack thoughts, and generalizations it had formed. In the moment of his admission and apology, an independent/aware adult consciousness came into being. Sam the adult, or more specifically Sam, the heart-and-spirit based adult and father, stepped powerfully forward releasing himself from the domination of his righteous aggressive/defensive ego consciousness.

I asked Sam to say one more thing to his son: "I would rather force you to be Jewish than let you choose to come back to your roots in your own time and way and be in a beautiful and loving relationship with you." Sam now willingly and effortlessly spoke these words. There were more tears. The therapy session ended with a rambling expression of Sam's mixed bag of feelings, which included surprise, regret, sorrow, relief, enlightenment, and determination. I asked Sam to consider in what way, if any, he would like to implement the realizations he had gleaned about his relationship with his son.

Sam was a totally different when I saw him next. He looked much, much younger. It would have been easy to assume by the way he looked that he had just returned from an relaxing vacation. On his own initiative Sam had apologized to his son. He told his son that he had been mean and too hard on him for not taking his home-schooled Jewish instruction as seriously as Sam would have liked. He told him this had to do with a deep hurt inside himself, inside Sam, that had to do with the way Jewish people had been treated in the past. He went on to say that he had no right to do this.

Additionally, since our previous session, Sam had remembered that he, himself, had felt forced to be Jewish by his parents and he never liked that. He recalled this had brought on a real acrimonious struggle between him and his father to which he eventually succumbed; but which left considerable negative feelings in their relationship. Sam told his son that he did not want to repeat this damaging situation with him. Lastly, Sam let his son know that he was truly free to no longer attend the home-school classes on Judaism. Sam said he believed that, sooner or later, his son would want to know more about his heritage, and if that happened, Sam said he would be glad to assist his son any way he could at that time.

I met with Sam once more about two months later. He told me that he was practicing the choice of being happy rather than right. He was applying this to his relationship with his son and to the other relationships in his life which had been controlled by his aggressive/defensive ego. He knew that there would be work ahead, especially as his children grew up and developed minds and wills of their own. If he was not careful, they could very easily again become the innocent victims of his own unhealed childhood pain. But for now, as he put it: "I can see clearly what I need to do and nothing is going to get in the way of my being the kind of father I want to be."

Claudette and David's Story

While Claudette was growing up, both of her parents, before they divorced, had been sexually unfaithful in their marriage. Her father compulsively so from as early on as she could remember, and her mother twice, the second time with the man for whom she eventually left Claudette's father. When David, her husband of six years, admitted to betraying her in a one night stand at a business convention, and with Claudette's family history, she felt completely torn apart. Though she loved him deeply, she could not imagine ever being able to trust him again. The torrents of emotional pain and fear that were unleashed within her were so severe that she wasn't at all sure that she would be able to live through this most grievous and personal wound.

David, though realizing that it might be too little too late, was also very clear (as he put it, "now more than ever") of his love for Claudette, He embarked upon a course of intensive therapy. With guidance, he willingly confronted the deeper origins of his need for a sexual fling. David did his inner work thoroughly and responsibly. He discovered deep-seated confusion and conflict he had carried about becoming intimate, committed, and monogamous with a woman. He admitted he "slid into" the *presumption* of a monogamous relationship, not because he freely chose to give this to her as a physical, emotional, and spiritual expression of his profound love for her, but because he wanted to be a "good boy". He wanted to be better than anything Claudette saw around her growing up.

David came to a point where he could admit that he had always viewed being monogamous as a sacrifice or a duty that he had to offer in order to please a woman, though not himself. It took several months of painful and sometimes embarrassing self-examination but David (and I) felt that for the first time in his adult life he was ready and able to enter an intimate, committed, monogamous relationship with a woman *by choice*. The woman to whom he was choosing to bring these new depths of love was Claudette. However the looming question was: Would Claudette be willing to reconcile?

During that time, I also saw Claudette in individual therapy. The emotional pain and fear she was experiencing at the start of her work was definitely deep and real. Now, several months later, I could see that she was not moving through it. Her emotional pain and fear were as severe and intense as they had been when she first discovered David's infidelity. Why was she still so stuck?

Her aggressive/defensive ego consciousness was somehow wreaking havoc with her feelings. How was it doing this? Somehow it was scoring points by maintaining absolute control of her fear and anguish *and* by being right (and righteous) about a collection of her Idiosyncratic Judgements.

Principally, she saw herself as being absolutely right in her moral judgement that she was the victim, and the *only* victim. She was entrenched in the belief that David was the perpetrator, and the *only* perpetrator of betrayal. Claudette "saw" that she was the naive, trusting, devoted mate, and he the two-timing, lecherous, dishonest degenerate. She had no doubt that men cheat on their wives—it's what they do and always will do.

Critical to this aggressive/defensive ego trap was Claudette's staunch and unquestioned conviction that she had always been monogamous in the relationship with David. In terms of her actual physical behaviour, she had. That is to say, she had never had any kind of overt/physical sexual contact with anyone outside of her marriage. But when I explained that *monogamy is taking responsibility for all of her sexual, romantic, and erotic thoughts and energy,* her indignant and righteous aggressive/defensive ego took the first of several significant blows. All of these blows we later found were required to open up her heart and spirit again.

She ashamedly admitted to having flirted with several men during her marriage, and had entertained (covertly encouraged) the flirtations of several more. Justifying this flirting/teasing as innocent and innocuous when it happened, in her healing she started to see it was not an expression of her commitment to monogamy with David. Furthermore, she admitted to holding on to sexual and romantic fantasies associated with a few of these men, and would occasionally use this fantasy material (unbeknownst to David) to enhance the likelihood of achieving orgasm during love making with him or during masturbation.

She remembered and admitted several sexually provocative dances with a man she met on a night out with her girlfriends; and she "conveniently forgot" to tell David she received a call from an old boyfriend who phoned her one day when David was at work. Claudette also "conveniently forgot" to tell her ex-boyfriend she was now married. For reasons that perplexed her, Claudette also admitted to feeling not nearly as close, less communicative, and less sexual with David for quite some time. None of this had ever been brought out for discussion with anyone, especially David.

The necessary and critical breakthrough for Claudette; the

one which took her out of her aggressive/defensive ego's tenacious attachment to its Idiosyncratic Judgements about her being the wronged and innocent victim of her husband's infidelity, was the startling realization that in thought, fantasy, and spirit she had not been monogamous and honest either. *That the inappropriate use of her sexual, romantic, and erotic energy, and more generally the breakdown in the state of authentic, open-hearted relationship with David, was her responsibility also and was not qualitatively different from how David had been with her.*

It was a question of degree not of kind. True, she was not the one who jumped into bed with someone else; and yes, physical betrayal was a terribly hurtful thing to do. In that way, she was a legitimate victim with many valid feelings of sorrow and heartbreak. However, she was not the only victim in this circumstance. She, too, was guilty of misbehaviours, some of omission and some of commission, not unlike those of her partner.

Aided by this and other illusion-shattering realizations over the course of her own self-examination, Claudette's aggressive/defensive ego consciousness came crashing down. She let go of her self-righteousness. In the humbled and open space within her that this brought forth, came her willingness to *take responsibility for a shared set of conditions in her relationship with David that were the breeding grounds for something like this to happen.* Her need to be right rather than happy was now out of the way. This, and the sharing of responsibility, allowed her to begin to love David once more.

Both David and Claudette had become acquainted with the workings of their own aggressive/defensive ego consciousnesses (consciousnesses of fear). They had watched as its cherished set of judgments, opinions, beliefs and conclusions lay in tatters on the floor. With the memory of the love they had once shared, they could begin the process of bringing their broken, yet considerably more authentic selves to each other to be known and healed. Each had been wrong and blind about a great many things. They were now choosing to give themselves over to their own heart- and spirit-based consciousness, producing a love qualitatively deeper and more enduring than any they had ever known.

Chapter IV

*"Your life is a journey into vulnerability, and you do not trust
that journey. The consequence of that mistrust is terrifying."*
Gary Zukav and Linda Francis
The Heart Of The Soul

Aggressive/Defensive Ego Strategies For Survival:
A look at the make-up of the ego-forged self

Another Perspective On the
Aggressive/Defensive Ego Consciousness

Though I have referred to the concept of the healthy ego-in-
service and the beneficial design functions it serves for the
individual, I have largely concentrated so far on what I call the
aggressive/defensive ego consciousness. This component of the ego
consciousness, one which in most of us tends to be significantly
more developed than the healthy ego-in-service, has been painted in
dark colors. This has been done for good reasons. Operating from
this unexamined and unhealed state of consciousness, humans beings
have produced savage and ugly expressions of our humanity.
Because it is fear-based and survival-oriented at any cost, and its
emotional range fluctuates narrowly from defensiveness on the one
hand to viciousness on the other, it must be viewed as a formidable
and dangerous power. To discount, sugar-coat, deny, or summarily
dismiss a consciousness that is responsible for man's inhumanity to
man only adds to our individual and collective potential for unabated
destruction and cruelty.

However, to see the ego consciousness as *only* a dark and
malignant force which should be excised from the consciousness of
humanity would represent another massive injustice and incalculable
loss for mankind. Our goal is to heal, not destroy. A healthy ego-in-
service, an ego consciousness which serves the Inner Family rather
than tyrannizes it, is capable of making an enormously positive
contribution to the world (and does so all around us on a daily basis).

If we are to heal the aggressive/defensive ego inside us, and help convert its potential for inflicting misery into a potential for good, it is not wise to make it a villain. Turning it into yet another enemy to be eradicated (this time an enemy within ourselves) would just be a slightly altered version of one of the aggressive/defensive ego's favourite ploys—externalizing the problem: denying any personal responsibility and finding enemies to blame. Using the tactics of the aggressive/defensive ego consciousness i.e. "blaming and fault finding" to heal it is folly.

We must bring understanding and compassion to this twisted and pained part of ourselves. We must open our hearts to see its humanity. Rather than seeing it as the villain, this model of self-healing asks you to see it as a member of your Inner Family. This family member is not unlike a lost, self-destructive brother or sister of yours—one who is in great need, yet at the same time one whose hurtful or harmful actions must be stopped.

To aid you in moving in the direction of claiming and healing this easy-to-judge and maligned consciousness, I'd like to propose another way to view it. Though capable of inflicting enormous pain and injury, at its core, your aggressive/defensive ego consciousness is *a twisted extension of your adaptive child consciousness and indirectly seeks safety, love, and value.* I'll explore the aggressive/defensive ego more, perceiving it through this softer, more heart-based point of view.

Returning Again to the Birth of the Ego Consciousness

It was a very traumatic experience when you first realized that you, living as your **natural child consciousness/authentic self** and **spiritual consciousness**) were not safe, loved, or valued. At the core of this reality-shattering experience, as a young "being-in-formation", completely dependent on the adults around you, you were catapulted into a fundamental crisis of identity. Wracked by an emotional pain and fear that was too much to bear, and threatened, like a survivor of a ship wreck, you floated alone, clinging to the debris of the life you once knew. With nothing to keep you away from the life-threatening trauma and rejection all around you, you were forced to confront a number of numbing, mind-boggling questions: Who am I? Who must I be in order to survive? How do I please the people I depend on? How must I be in order to feel good about myself? How must I act to receive even the most basic care? Do I have any intrinsic value as a person? Is my only value given to me by others? Can I, and must I, only depend on myself? How do I do that? Your answers to these questions were how you formulated a plan to preserve your life.

The aggressive/defensive ego consciousness comes into being in association with a chronic experience of not feeling sufficiently safe, loved, and valued. Its existence and enduring power is initially founded on the experience, then on the continuing belief, that rose from the experience, that true and lasting love for the person you really are is impossible. *"I am not, cannot, and will never be loved for who I actually am," is the core belief of every person controlled by their aggressive/defensive ego.* How do you live and get by if this is your fundamental belief?

To this earliest and most rudimentary form of our ego-minds, a potential life-saving solution comes: If I do not consistently experience being directly loved for the emotional and spiritual being that I am, then I will try being loved *indirectly,* even if it's very indirectly. Not feeling safe, loved, and valued in direct ways, you (a child) must now enter a "hall of mirrors" in order to experience being loved and valued. It is the outside world that becomes this hall of mirrors.

Put slightly differently, the external world becomes your mother and your father. You seek from it what you failingly received from your caregivers. You bestow upon the external world the status of a surrogate parent and try to turn it into a source of safety, love, and the experience of being good enough, which you did not receive from your caregivers or family. [The "external world" means power, beauty, money, status (good or bad), intellectual knowledge, etc.]

Obviously, what you derive from the external world cannot ever be your mother or father. As long as you identify yourself with your ego consciousness, and not by your natural child consciousness/authentic self, you cannot directly feel or let in the safety, love, or sense of being unconditionally valued that you need. Furthermore, the world can't offer you these. ***For as long as you present an ego-forged self to the world, you will only feel affirmed or approved as an ego-forged self.*** This is a hollow and transient source of emotional and spiritual fulfillment at best.

To the extent you have become an ego-identified (ego-controlled) consciousness is the extent that you have disqualified yourself from the actual experience of loving and being loved. You will never satisfy your longing for safety, love, and value. You will be looking for love in all the wrong places. You will look to the world to provide what it can never deliver and what you can never receive from it. Like a sunflower that long ago gave up on ever receiving direct sunlight for its growth, it has settled for the pale and diffuse rays of artificial light.

The ego consciousness and the ego-forged self which it generates, though unique, creative, and complex in how it goes about it, will never find that which it hungers for and desperately seeks. Its need for the experience of more love, safety, and value from external sources is insatiable. I will now explain the ways egos attempt to satisfy this craving; a craving that is not physical, but emotional and spiritual in nature.

Until now I have shown how the aggressive/defensive ego produces hurtful and destructive consequences to ourselves and others in its unremitting quest for survival. Now we can view it from a slightly different and considerably more benevolent angle—as an assembly of roles, strategies, and behaviours that are all indirect requests for safety, love, and value.

We Must Distinguish Ourselves in Some Way: The Endless Effort to Be More, Better or Different

"If you're not good enough the way you are,
it takes a lot of effort to get better."[1]

As soon as you become controlled by the aggressive/defensive ego consciousness; as soon as its games become your identity you immediately realize that you must somehow be or look better. The ego consciousness is a consciousness of scarcity. In it, and as it, you are never enough, and there is never enough. For example: you aren't good enough, successful enough, attractive enough, slim enough, or rich enough. There is never enough. Some of the commodities that there is never enough of are time, money, safety, security, or contentment. In this state of constant scarcity, you are driven to always be and do better; to be more than who you really are. You must dress up, assume airs, and *"prepare a face to meet the faces that we meet"*.[2]

The ego consciousness perpetually shops for a new and

better identity than the inadequate person you were "yesterday", and it has concluded exists underneath its displays. Ironic as it may sound, it goes shopping for a better or different wardrobe for the perfect emotional and spiritual being that you already are.

The endless search for something more, better, or different and the status that, it is hoped, these things will confer, is an obsession of the aggressive/defensive ego consciousness. Underneath the costumes, roles, and public faces it uses, and underneath the glittering, ever upgraded collection of baubles, bangles, and beads it uses to adorn itself, it is frantically trying to be exceptional and to distinguish itself in some way. *By being exceptional, the unhealed ego consciousness attempts to find the experience of safety, love, and being valued.* Demanding superlative perfection is its way out of the constant state of scarcity and the experience of not being good enough. In this manner, it attempts to escape the emotional pain and fear of the adaptive child consciousness and become a "somebody".

To become a "somebody" the ego consciousness has to attach itself to one or more of what I call *symbols of external power and status*. It uses them to forge an identity which it markets to the world in a manipulative self-advertising campaign. A symbol of external power and status can be almost anything: roles, possessions, personal attributes, skills, positions, belief systems, or group memberships. The ego consciousness will then identify with this symbol so completely that it will employ its entire arsenal of aggressive and defensive mechanisms to preserve and enhance itself in the world. Ego-identified human beings sometimes go to extreme lengths, even to willingly die on occasion, to prevent their identity (which is wrapped in external power and status) from ever being publicly questioned or tarnished.

All ego-forged identities, and this chapter will focus on a wide range of them, amount to some variation of:

1. establishing power and control over others; *and,*
2. a very indirect request for safety, love, and being valued.

These twin features of an ego-forged identity place the individual who is controlled by it on the horns of an excruciatingly frustrating and self-defeating dilemma. While on the one hand they can (by being exceptional) exert power and control over others in order to better ensure their survival, on the other hand this automatically prohibits them from receiving authentic love, safety, and being valued, which is what they wanted in the first place. This is always a lose-lose ego game. No one receives safety, love, and being valued, from the very people they are attempting to control.

Love, if it is to be real, is and always must be, a totally free offering to and from others. This means that any behaviour used to establish or maintain power and control over others will nullify any possibility of love freely offered. Consequently, anyone operating from an identity forged by an aggressive/defensive ego can never accomplish their goal of experiencing safety, love, and value with others. Furthermore, obscured by these complex ego power-games, any request for what they want is so indirect and obscure that it falls on deaf ears anyway.

The list of symbols of external power and status (which the ego consciousness strives to attach itself to)[3] is a long one indeed. Below are a few of the most common symbols for establishing external power and control.

- personality characteristics;
- personality roles and scripts;
- successes and/or failures;
- your work and career;
- education, knowledge, and credentials;
- possessions and socio-economic class;
- physical appearance and sexuality;
- special abilities and talents;
- special relationships;
- personal and family history;
- belief systems and values; and,
- political, nationalistic, racial, religious and other collective identifications.

In examining each of these in the next few pages I will show how, when these originate from your natural child consciousness/authentic self they will make a wonderfully positive contribution to others. Yet, when originating from your aggressive/defensive ego consciousness, they will separate you from others, contribute to the domination and subjugation of the people in your life, and guarantee you'll never really receive the safety, love, and value you seek.

Symbols Of External Power And Status
Used To Create An Ego-Forged Identity

Personality Characteristics

You can use your personality and any of its various features, traits, and characteristics, as the basis for an ego-forged identity. Absolutely any distinctive element of your personality can be turned from a lovely attribute—an endearing expression of your natural self—into a lavish spectacle that becomes a principle identity unto itself. For example: You can be funny, sweet, aloof, miserable, upbeat, outgoing, shy, silly, nice, loud, or self-effacing as a method of becoming more, better, or different than others, and attempt to use that as a means to gain power and control. Used for this purpose, any personality feature becomes your very own status symbol. It is honed, crafted, buffed, and polished by your ego consciousness for calculated affect. Like fine silverware, it is brought out at specific times to make a favourable impression on anyone you wish to impress (meaning control and manipulate).

Any personality characteristic, used in this way, is given center stage by the ego consciousness in order to cover up the unwanted natural child consciousness/authentic self within, which is only an attempt to indirectly secure the safety, love, and sense of being valued that is craved. By identifying yourself with a personality trait as a symbol of external power and status, like any of the others I will discuss, your relationship with your real emotional and spiritual self shrivels. You grow ever more distant from the buried emotional pain and fear you carry—the denial of which has forced you to act in these ways in the first place.

In contrast, when this or any other trait comes from your natural child consciousness/authentic self, this same aspect of your personality becomes a unique communication and expression of beauty rather than cover up of who you really are—a unique manifestation of your original self. It can represent a brilliant, entertaining, and creative form of being you and adds wonderful color and flavour to your interactions with others.

Personality Roles and Scripts

What I refer to as a personality role or script is broad and all-encompassing. This isn't a singular personality characteristic. It represents a large on-going role or a style of personality that a person is unknowingly living. The individual who becomes identified with a personality role is not all that different than an actor on a stage, except in this case the actor doesn't realize they are acting and the stage is their entire life. Behind these subtle, yet extremely powerful roles and scripts, invariably the ego consciousness is hard at work. Its attempting, by playing the star role in the play, to exercise power and control over others. The ego/actor will then manipulate safety, love, and the experience of being valued out of their audience.

Among the biggest payoffs gained by the endless repetition of these unconscious performances is that the aggressive/defensive ego consciousness gets to be right again and again about all the judgements, criticisms, opinions, and mass generalizations it has drawn about everything. Remember that one of the most gripping and addictive compulsions of the ego is its need to be right. Playing out a personality role or script allows it to be right about a good many things, while manipulating and ignoring the damage that righteousness causes.

Two Classic Personality Roles: Martyr and Victim

One that I have encountered on numerous occasions in my work is the Heroic Martyr. This is the person who plays the part of being passionately and magnanimously giving of themselves to a person, group, belief, or a cause, while feeling unfairly subjected to persecution or attack. Prone to an early self-sacrificial death, either at the hands of their opponents or by the very people for whom they are fighting (and to the martyr it is *fight*), the martyr perceives that the "genuine and pure love" they offer others is met with nothing but a lack of appreciation and/or disdain. An example of this might be a mother or father who "gives until it hurts" to their children and then feels ignored or unfairly treated by them in return. What judgements, opinions, or beliefs do you think the Heroic Martyr gets to be right about in an ego-script that expects or demands their "love" be returned with "love and cooperation" but instead is returned with defiance or ungratefulness?

The Victim is another extremely well used personality script that is quite closely related to the Heroic Martyr. The Victim, though, usually lacks an heroic or visionary cause for which they are prepared to sacrifice themselves. Instead, the victim script usually calls for them to see themselves as an ordinary, likeable, *innocent* bystander, who is singled out and picked on by fate, God, bad luck, or other people. The Victim's *constant* (mostly internal) lament is that life is unfair and unkind; they have been personally dealt a bad hand which they are powerless to change.

Critical to the role of the victim is their ability to convince themselves *and the audience* that they have done nothing to deserve the wounds inflicted upon them. [Note: All personality roles and scripts require an audience; the larger the better.] The universe has meted out a cruel and unusual punishment to them personally; a bitter and perverse punishment that they are in no way even remotely responsible for.

Though painful to the star of the show (meaning the victim) and to those cast in the role of "bad guys" (meaning the perpetrators of cruel injustice) in the play, we can easily and quickly see the twin features of the ego-forged identity that lies underneath it: (a) the attempt to wield external power and control over others; and (b), the very indirect request for safety, love, and being valued.

The need for power is so twisted and transparent, and the indirect request for love and safety is so manipulative and punishing to others, that the other "actors" (forced into the role of unsympathetic bystanders or villains in the play) invariably shut their love off and turn away. This, of course, only confirms to the victim's ego how unfairly others treat them. The whole destructive and manipulative cycle becomes entrenched and repeats itself all over again.

There are many other ego-forged personality roles and scripts. You may have acted out the "Reigning Monarch", the "Dance-away Lover", the "Free Spirit", the "Lost Child", the "Sensitive One", the "Spiritually Enlightened Teacher", the "Born Loser", or the "Rebel With (or Without) A Cause". A few from the foregoing list I have played out myself. I know first-hand how tenaciously the ego consciousness can cling to them, and how naked and vulnerable it feels without them. Yet, it is important to challenge them in yourself because the ego-fuelled drama which ensues from these scripts inevitably impairs the quality of your own and others' lives.

Delicate and compassionate challenging of your personality roles and scripts is essential. In the healing work clients do with me it is not uncommon for the very same ego consciousness that is directing the play to react with indignation and hostility when confronted with the possibility that, on some level, it is making the whole thing up. At first, it is painful to see how we are the ones producing and directing our sorrowful and unhappy dramas. Remember that underneath your need for these ego-forged roles is emotional pain and fear which you have not been allowed to have or bring out honestly and directly to others.

Here is one important caveat to the material on personality roles and scripts: *Do not make the mistake of concluding that every victim or martyr in our world is doing nothing other than acting out an ego-forged identity, aimed at manipulating power and control over others.* Such an assumption would be far from the truth.

There are legitimate victims and martyrs in life—victims of poverty, political injustice, sexism, racism, ageism; victims of suppressive and despotic regimes. There are real and brutal oppressors of the human spirit. Legitimate victims and martyrs are not fabricating and using their persecuted status as some extension of their aggressive/defensive egos.

Healthy, strong, outspoken, and courageous people (who operate from an ego-in-service) are required in great numbers to overturn the inhumane treatment of people everywhere. We must come to know and distinguish between the self-serving personality role of victim or martyr and the real and suffering victims and martyrs of our world. In this way we can serve our fellow human being and expand the possibilities of emotional and spiritual healing everywhere.

Successes and/or Failures

Believing we are not good enough the way we are requires that we have to go to great lengths to become better. "Not being good enough" means that one part of you (your aggressive/defensive ego) is condemning another part of you (whatever it is criticizing). If being your natural child consciousness/authentic self and spiritual consciousness isn't sufficient; if these are not enough to feel safe, loved, and valued in your world, then your ego may conclude that perhaps you can at least become good at something. Being good at "something" often includes a subtle demand to be perfect at it. One thing an aggressive/defensive ego excels at is internal self-rejection and criticism in order to become "perfect', which is of course impossible, so the ego always has something to complain about.

Here, again, the striving to become good at something (to improve, expand and excel at something) does not indicate, in and of itself, that an aggressive/defensive ego consciousness is operating behind the scenes. A person's endeavour to become good at something; to achieve goals, ambitions and dreams through the full extension of their mental, physical, emotional and spiritual powers is one of the finest and most noble aspects of your humanity.

A healthy ego-in-service is indispensable in the attainment of any goal. Adversities (and sometimes adversaries) will present themselves. Unexpected setbacks will occur and opposition in many forms can and often will challenge the realization of any goal or aspiration. Picking up the pieces, persevering, and finding the strength and courage to continue on are qualities and resources which derive in many ways from a strong and healthy ego-in-service.

Difficulty and darkness result when we become completely attached to something we are good at and use it as our complete identity. In such cases we exclusively define ourselves, and derive our entire sense of personal worth, from our singular success with work, skill, talent, or attributes. This becomes: "I have succeeded 'at this one thing' and therefore I am," or "I am only my successes," or "I am a walking resume of success and I present myself as this success to the world." The downside of this equation however, is I am only as safe, loveable, and valued as my success, and this belief severely limits your inner freedom.

Conversely and just as painfully, you can become completely identified with your most significant failures, mistakes, losses, or defeats. This too can become a place which the aggressive/defensive ego calls home and uses to create an ego-forged identity. In this dynamic, all that you are and all that you amount to is your shortcomings. It is just as easy to hold on to your failings as your mark of distinction as it is your successes. "No one loses like I do." "I am a born loser." "I can't win for losing," may be the plaintive cry here.

Successes or failures can be employed equally deftly to create an ego-forged identity. These represent an attempt to exert external power and control over others and an indirect way to try and experience being safe, loved, and valued.

As you read about aggressive/defensive egos, and the more common ego-forged identities, I must remind you that egos are very crafty. It is possible and common for a person to alternate between being identified with "successes" and then switch to "failure" in a matter of moments; or, to be identified with one "amazing" success in one area, and cling to that forever while being identified with failure in all other areas. Aggressive/defensive egos, in trying to experience being safe, loved, and valued, have the ability to switch and modify their identify in a matter or moments—please be mindful this is quite complex.

Your Work and Career

The work you do, and the skills you develop in your career, can become another basis for an ego-forged identity. Of course, in this matter, as is the case with all of the symbols of ego power and status, there can be an emphatically positive and healthy component to it. A genuine pride and sense of fulfillment can be derived from the competent execution of your professional and occupational responsibilities. Your work can be a way for you to make a wonderful contribution to society. It provides a reciprocal exchange of goods and services for yourself and others that satisfies needs which neither you nor they, acting alone, could meet.

Financial stability and security is a necessary and important by-product of the work you do. This is a way of caring for and protecting yourself and those you love by having food, shelter, clothing, education, and personal choice in how you or they live. Again, it can be a source of pleasure and pride in your abilities, as well as allowing you to have even more resources at your disposal to invest in the greater good of your world.

Your aggressive/defensive ego, however, can become so identified with your professional or occupational role that you cannot let it go and step out from behind it, even when that would serve everyone's best interests. It is then that your attachment to work-place roles and status becomes a straightjacket for you. You don't go to work, you *are* your work.

This does not only mean work for which you are paid money, it can also mean people who's "work" is being a full-time parent, or very affluent people who's "work" is organizing charities and benefits for poor or sick people. The ego under discussion here is one that is singularly forged around a narrow group of activities that, for convenience, I refer to as work.

If a doctor or some other professional must always be a knowledgeable, impermeable, and imposing authority figure (or a therapist must always be a 'guru'), even when they are with their own family, then something very natural and nourishing—their authentic emotional and spiritual self, is lost to themselves and everyone around them. The attachment to any professional role does not allow access to other sides, rich, rewarding, deep and undeveloped sides of their human make-up.

The minister who sees everyone in his private life as members of his congregation in need of spiritual direction is stuck in a restrictive, one-dimensional, life-diminishing role. The police officer who must always be hard nosed; the salesperson who sees everyone as a potential customer; the business leader who must always have the solution to every financial problem; the athlete who has to always win, are all examples of human beings embedded in the tyranny of ego-forged identities. There are thousands of examples of these.

To additionally complicate matters, almost all professional and occupational roles require the presentation of an ego-based *image* of capability. This is generally more about the cultivation and preservation of the image than the real person (underneath the image) who holds the position. No matter what the job, at the workplace it is presumed that you must always, always be competent and proficient (or at least appear to be competent and proficient). As an authority, you must look as if you always know what you are doing.

Another connotation of the word professional is: You must always be in complete command of every situation. To preserve an image of "occupational infallibility", never are you to be thrown for a loop. Never can you allow yourself to feel, worse yet reveal, feelings or mind-states such as being lost, confused, overwhelmed, or just plain not knowing what to do next.

This ego-forged image of expertise, professionalism, or detached objectivity may support you in *some* instances to more effectively carry out your professional or occupational responsibilities. Conversely, in *some* instances, it probably impedes this. However, if you are not extremely careful, eventually it will force you to lose contact with your natural emotional and spiritual self. The same ego-forged "professional identity" for which you may receive accolades and pay raises at work will fail miserably at home.

Your image may be fundamental to the earning of your daily bread and the attainment of external status, but it will be a killing field for your genuine connection to others.

Education, Knowledge, and Credentials

Closely aligned with the work you do is the status of *expert* that comes along with it. Implicit in the courses, credentials, and degrees you have attained and can show others (or show off to others), is the validation from society that you know something; something important and useful; something that very few others know.

It is not an over-statement to say the aggressive/defensive ego consciousness is the part of you that believes it knows everything. It is easy to see how an ego-forged identity can be created around special knowledge or education and endeavours that you are considered to be an expert at. Using your education and specialized training i.e., professional and occupational credentials, experience, degrees, honours, and awards, in place of your authentic self as a way of extracting safety, love, and value from your environment, amounts to: *"I know therefore I am"*. As is the case with all other symbols of external power and status (which are used to create an ego-forged self and thereby control others) this one bases the worth of its holder on external validation and not on our authentic inner natural child or spiritual consciousness.

Your knowledge and credentials, when used and guided by your other Inner Family members, become far more than a way for you to only survive life. They become true acts of contribution and service. Special knowledge or unique talent may be an expression of compassion or kindness emanating from the Universe of Love, and ways of helping and making life easier for your fellow human beings.

Possessions And Socio-economic Class

I have always been intrigued by the term "purchasing power" used by economists. It seems that being able to purchase (anything and at random and on impulse) gives you power. Accumulating material possessions and attaching your value, your self-worth, to them is an extremely popular way in which an ego literally attempts to provide emotional and spiritual sustenance. How large your home is; the kind of car you drive; the style and expense of the clothes you wear, are just a few of the economic and material mirrors which the ego can use to constantly gaze at itself to assess its self-worth. Inevitably, the ego's conclusion will be: "I am not worthy because I don't have...", or its derivative: "I am not worthy yet but I will be when...". This, in turn, brings forth the need for the acquisition of more "purchasing power"—products, goods, and services of fashion and enterprise, to be utilized as the "healing" tonic. But really, it's an avoiding tonic.

This is the aggressive/defensive ego's plight: Having given up on real and direct love, or believing this is impossible to attain, it goes in search of unreal and indirect surrogates. The ownership of things is a way of attempting to attain indirect love; it is about as indirect as "love" can get. Accumulating manufactured products adorned with corporate logos, and displaying public images lauded by the fashion and cosmetic industries, is about as effective in satisfying your need for authentic love and acceptance as drinking perfume for quenching your thirst. Yet, if you believe you are dying from thirst, it is probable you will drink anything.

Collectively, your possessions, personal wealth, and standard of living add up to yet another symbol of external power and status used by many people to create an ego-forged identity. Of course, it is one that is completely attached to your socio-economic class or income bracket. In yet another way, your ego consciousness will build its case for safety, love, and value on external criteria—its membership in an elite and exclusive economic group. The socio-economic class to which you belong can become a mark of distinction; a medal to pin on your chest, in your efforts to rise to the top of the heap in the hierarchy of other aggressive/defensive egos.

Of course, there is nothing inherently good or bad about wealth and the accumulation of things. Motivation and intent are crucial. It's just that they can *never* make you feel safe, loved, and valued for the emotional and spiritual self that you are. If you can truly offer to others safety, love, and value, and experience these things within yourself, then material possessions can be employed by your healthy ego-in-service to enjoy your life and surroundings and better the lot of others in need.

Physical Appearance and Sexuality

When your Inner Family members, the natural child consciousness/authentic self and your spiritual consciousness have become usurped by the aggressive/defensive ego consciousness, everything about you, including something as God-given as how you look, becomes another external factor on which you are evaluated and given rank and standing. When the world is ruled by ego, and that is certainly the case in our culture today, your physical appearance is too often used and exploited as a means of having external power and status.

The emotional and spiritual cost inherent in using your physical appearance, meaning your body and its aesthetic and sexual appeal and allure (in exchange for enhanced power and status), is that you must agree to becoming objectified. You must agree to reduce yourself to "a thing" absent of emotion. A thing deemed attractive, desired, and envied within the culture, but a thing nonetheless. And, once you have agreed to become a thing, once you present that-which-you-are as a commodity, you are forced to abide by the ever fluctuating market value of that thing. This is no different than the market value of an antique coffee table or a used car. This year "top dollar" goes to blondes and tri-athletes and next year it's brunettes and/or fast cars.

Women's beauty and sexuality is a perfect, striking example of this. As long as a woman is willing to be reduced to an inanimate object (like a coffee table) her physical beauty and sexuality can be insidiously and manipulatively used by the corporate culture, men, or by the woman herself, to achieve an ego-forged identity with various ego payoffs, but with devastating emotional and spiritual consequences. For business and profit, beauty and sexuality are used for the commercial marketing of anything from automobiles and chewing gum to hand soaps and beer. For the woman or man they can be used to enhance power, rank, or influence in the world of relationships—to be liked and wanted as a sought-after candidate (a "thing") for romance, sex, and material success.

In the world of an aggressive/defensive ego, our physical appearance and sexual appeal are just possessions—toys that I have and you want, or you have and I want, to be peddled to the highest bidder (cultural prostitution). The aspect of this that makes the players frantic, both men and women, is beauty and "sexual appeal" is almost entirely associated with youth (another ego gambit), and youth is startlingly temporary. Like a fake company on the stock exchange, youth is artificially injected with temporary value as a covert strategy for advantages taken elsewhere.

The ego's grip on sexual relationships alone is enormous. An entire book could be written on this subject. If we want to heal our sexual relationships and give ourselves a real chance at establishing a true heart and soul connection with people who attract us sexually, it is important and necessary that we understand and take responsibility for how the judgements, opinions, beliefs, and conclusions of our aggressive/defensive ego consciousness operate in our dealings with them.

At the beginning, owning these can be humbling, humiliating, and painful. It is not the stuff of self-flattery and not for the faint-of-heart. Our egos can be crude, callous, ugly and self-serving in how they view another's physical appearance and sexuality.

One of my male clients had the courage and clarity to put into words how his unhealed ego views women. In the cold and calculating, fear-based, survival-oriented mentality of his aggressive/defensive ego, he said: *"A chick in her twenties wins out over one in her thirties; one in her thirties wins out over someone older. If she's blond, she gets more points. If she's sexy and has a small, tight ass, she gets even more points. If she has big breasts, she scores even higher in value. If she's a twenty-something blond, with a small, tight ass and big breasts she wins the prize. What's the prize? The prize is she gets to be used by me."*

With a sense of embarrassed awkwardness, my own aggressive/defensive ego (with a few moderations) was resonating to every word he said. Though I have not had it as plainly articulated to me from a woman's aggressive/defensive ego, a therapist whom I've known for years, offered a startling example of this in a woman client of his. She determined the market value of men (and herself) — reducing them both to a physical and sexual thing. He offered this:

"A woman had been actively hunting her third husband. For over twenty years she had participated in excessive, harmful exercise routines (with a long history of related injuries). When asked about the consequences of this, she replied: 'How are you going to marry money if you're not slim and sexy?' She had paid for breast augmentation once; face-lifts twice; and liposuction twice.

"Her first husband, with a six-figure income, had to go on

permanent disability and their income was reduced about 50%. They had one son and had been married fifteen years. Even with the husband's disability, they could maintain a basic, no-frills lifestyle. When she was faced with this drastic loss of status (no tennis club, private personal trainer, or $300 hair cuts) she left her husband and forced custody of their son on him. Within two years she married one of her ex-husband's business associates (another six-figure income), who, according to her, had been 'hot for her' for years. Husband #2 became impotent and refused to indulge her spending. She divorced him after a few years.

"Within a year of her second divorce, now in her early 40s, she moved in with a man, ten or twelve years her junior. She made no bones about telling me, her therapist, she was 'trading up': he was more virile, had a bigger penis, and appreciated her beauty. Within a year he had left her, in her words, 'for some plain looking bitch his own age'.

"Now in her late 40s, she was angry, depressed, and suicidal. She had struggled desperately since her younger boyfriend had ended their relationship. Her ego had convinced her she had better catch husband #3 pretty fast. She vowed to her close women friends and to me, that her next husband would have a wallet 'thick enough to fall off'. She was planning more cosmetic surgery when she ended up in therapy which she entered to get help with grieving the death of her son; a suicide at 21.

"Thankfully she stayed in therapy long enough to make some sense of the self-destructive chaos in her life. Much of the work was around healing her Inner Family."[4]

This is another sad and tragic example of a person completely disconnected from their natural child/authentic self and their spiritual consciousness. As with the previous example, their aggressive/defensive egos are reducing themselves and others to commodities for sale.

Special Abilities and Talents

Sometimes an ego will become attached to the possession of a special talent, skill, or ability and forge an entire identity based around that. If you are an exceptional singer, gardener, athlete, artist, student, chef, or writer... an exceptional *anything*, it is extremely easy to become significantly or completely identified with your proficiency in that one area. This of course includes depending on and fostering the accolades that come with it.

What springs to mind are the stories of celebrities and how difficult (and frequently impossible) it is for many of them to find true and lasting love, and the unhappiness and ruin that befall these people after they are no longer adored by their fans. The cult of celebrity that permeates our culture, and what many people are willing to do for their 15 minutes of fame, is one of the more transparent and destructive ego-gambits to acquire external power and status. Most often, it reflects the insecurity of an individual who is desperately seeking the experience of safety, love, and being valued through notoriety, having power, or status by being adored.

Special talents and abilities of a person are a gift to us all. They are a joy to watch and behold when used by someone who is expressing and giving them away, needing little or nothing in return.

Special Relationships

"It's not what you know but who you know," goes a popular saying. Being seen with, associated with, with or loved by, a special or famous person can, in the world of egos, cast glitter over the not-so-famous, "less-talented" associate. The vicarious use of another person's ego-assets i.e., their looks, success, personality, position, wealth, notoriety, energy, etc., in order to feel better about yourself and improve your status amongst others, can become another full blown ego-forged identity.

The second-hand glory attained in this manner sometimes lies behind the mysterious process of people falling in love. Yet attraction of this type—the magnetism and worship of one ego for another—is also that which can cause a passionate and magical love to dramatically turn into a competitive and destructive one. Relying on the ego-status of another person to fill an emotional and spiritual hole in your own makeup will never work for very long. If your natural child consciousness/authentic self has been lost to you by being mired in unhealed emotional pain and fear (the adaptive child), the remedy of loving someone more worthy than you—a special somebody-else, will never be a permanent cure.

The magnificent spiritual work and source of instruction in A Course In Miracles[5], teaches us that any "Special Relationship" is doomed to failure. This is because a relationship orchestrated by the fear-based, survival-oriented aggressive/defensive ego consciousness cannot achieve or maintain anything close to real emotional and spiritual love. Many "special" love relationships are founded on the belief that each partner has found or will find in the other what they do not have within themselves. It is a long-known fact that *in matters of love, two halves do not make a whole.*

Relying on another person to compensate and/or act as a cover-up for your inadequacies, short-comings, insecurities, and self-doubts creates an alliance of excessive dependency. This only temporarily allows you to avoid responsibility for addressing or resolving your emotional pain and fear, by yourself and for yourself. In the "Special Relationship" both individuals are guaranteed to grow emotionally and spiritually weaker in the pact that they have struck with each other. Inevitably the initial expectations and early fantasies will turn to disappointment and then to aggression. The aggressive/defensive egos of the disgruntled partners will go for blood and all hell will break loose—every time.

As mentioned above, this is one of the signs of the "Special Relationship"—how quickly, and often cruelly good love goes bad; how people who initially couldn't get enough of each other turn into cruel and indignant enemies. I would slightly alter the Shakespearean quote from "Hell hath no fury like a woman scorned," to "Hell hath no fury like an aggressive/defensive ego scorned."

The two egos embroiled in a "Special Relationship", once their own unhealed emotional pain and fear resurfaces, may remain together lovelessly *or* they may leave immediately and self-righteously, blaming the other person for irreconcilable differences. Their egos march them off in different directions, only to soon thereafter fall in love again in another modified version of a "Special Relationship". Either way, regrettably, their ego-forged identities will triumph over love.

Family History and Family Roles

The historical family one belongs to, its triumphs and tragedies over time, its unique and colourful characters, and its status and place in society, form both a collective narrative and a bond that connects members of different generations in defining and meaningful ways. Knowing our ancestral roots helps us to better know ourselves and how and where we fit in the world. This can be with a sense of pride or shame, or both. The tribe we belong to is an integral part of our identity and within our tribal affiliation, there is no more powerful a source of personal identity than our immediate family of origin.

Both the tribe and the family to which we belong can become another symbol of external power or status from which your aggressive/defensive ego can forge an identity. In this way, simply because of their blood line, family members can consider themselves somehow more, better, or different than other egos. This can be as part of an elite clique of superior human beings, or (just as easily) a part of a group that's less than, different, or exotically dysfunctional.

This generates what appears, at first glance, to be seemingly opposite ego-based identities. However, as I have discussed earlier regarding the contradictory workings of the aggressive/defensive ego consciousness, any "opposite" presentations are exactly the same: they are ploys to establish power and control over others and are indirect requests for safety, love, and being valued.

Another dynamic of our family of origin which will dramatically shape the lives of the individuals in it, is the various roles that the family requires of its members. These roles are assigned and unconsciously assumed by necessity, convenience, personality, and most certainly by dysfunction. As with every other role into which we are cast in life (i.e., wife, mother, son, father, brother, daughter, sister, uncle, aunt, friend), family roles can act as a means by which we make a unique and valuable contribution to others. The roles we are assigned might also serve as pathways by which we experience emotional and spiritual growth.

Any team, no matter who comprises its members (including a family unit) in order to be strong and functioning, must find ways of blending different individuals with diverse attributes into a cohesive whole. Assigning roles is one way of doing that. For their survival and effective functioning, families require one or more of its members to play roles i.e.: Provider, Caretaker, Star, Problem Person, Adventurer, Sexual Person, Comedian, Rebel, Advisor, Confidant, Peacemaker, and Teacher, to name only a few.

Even though family roles are necessary, problems easily develop. Your ego can become so attached to the role you have been assigned in your family, that you cannot stop playing it long after it has served its purpose. An entire and permanent ego-forged identity can be fashioned around these family-originated roles.

In other words, your family needed you to be a certain way. If your ego creates an identity around that assigned role, you will soon be afraid to live without it; or cannot live without "being" whatever your family required of you. You will not know who you are if you aren't playing out your assigned role. Those times in your life when you are forced to shed those roles, and discover that they are no longer workable and probably detrimental, can be some of the most spiritually and emotionally challenging times to face.

When these family roles are abandoned, deep-seated questions that may have quietly haunted and distressed you for years can suddenly erupt. "If I'm not ___*the role*___ who am I?" "Do I even exist at all?" "Without my role, what value or meaning do I have?" "How am I important now?" "How will I get love and acceptance if I am not acting 'that' way?" "What is my purpose now?"

Feelings of being confused, disoriented, and depressed may accompany the loss of a long-lived role. Sometimes people become suicidal. The emotional and spiritual process of creating a new, authentic identity is rarely easy.

Belief Systems and Values

It is perhaps easiest of all to create an ego-forged identity based around your belief system and values. There may be no greater temptation than being completely attached to what you think, feel, know, or believe to be right, real, and true. This reflects the earlier discussion about the nature of the ego as a massive judgement and generalization machine. It is a depository of fear-based thoughts, opinions, criticisms, and conclusions, compiled over the course of a lifetime, regarding anyone or anything that has been deemed to be even remotely associated with experiences of emotional pain and fear. In its attempt to ensure survival, it has had to be RIGHT about the judgements and beliefs it has formed; often right regardless of any cost to yourself and others.

For many, our ego consciousness can become so attached or identified with what we believe that *our belief systems become who we are*. In these circumstances there is no separate and independent/aware adult consciousness present in the Inner Family. As such, there is no separation between the belief system and the believer or the judgements and the judge. That is to say that there is no conscious observer present who is aware they are rigidly holding certain judgements and beliefs. The person is so attached and identified with being RIGHT that, in extreme cases, they are prepared to reject, hate, or sometimes kill others in order to be right. This is the unquantifiable misery which is caused by an ego-forged identity based on personal belief systems.

This means of attempting to establish and maintain power and control over others is responsible for some of the most flagrant expressions of our inhumanity: dictatorships, religious wars, The Holocaust, racism, witch hunts, assassinations, The Inquisition, and terrorism. The brutality of self-righteous oppression of strong people and strong nations on weaker ones is horrific.

Maybe one day, I hope we will all have an awareness of how our aggressive/defensive ego consciousness views the world. Perhaps the future will provide as part of a standard medical check-up that each of us will be given an emotional and spiritual "x-ray" of how our own aggressive/defensive ego operates in regard to any conceivable subject matter or person. Imagine receiving a print-out on how your aggressive/defensive ego views "men", "women", "blacks", "Jews", "Arabs", "loggers", "environmentalists", or even the other sports team's "fans". Imagine finding out how it perceives "Mom", "Dad", "husband", "wife", "marriage", "god", "children", "love", "sex", "monogamy", or "trust". Though perhaps an extremely painful and humbling experience for us, I look forward to the day when each of us will have easy access to this kind of information about ourselves and how and where we need to concentrate our efforts on personal healing.

Political, National, Racial, Religious, and Other "Collective" Identifications

Once we understand how an ego-forged identity can so easily be constructed around a belief system, it is a short extension of this to develop one based on political, national, racial, religious, or some other collective identification. Your aggressive/defensive ego consciousness easily becomes so identified with the beliefs, philosophies, ideas, passions, or principles of a "group mind", it can prevent the establishment and development of your independent/aware adult in the Inner Family.

This group mind (like a collective ego) holds enormous sway over the participants involved. If "I am right" is a frightening force to be reckoned with in the case of an individual's ego, "*We* are right" can become, with the justification of God, majority vote, technology, religion, or country behind it, much more of a tyrannical, oppressive, and deadly bully. This is often the tyranny of the majority, righteously heaping persecution and condemnation in a tidal wave of violence upon those people who have different values and beliefs. The targets and victims of this brutality are, by simple definition, the "different" ones—people who by nature, choice, appearance, practice, or belief do not support the more powerful group's ideas.

The savagery committed by the human race on itself, animals, and the planet, in the name and for the cause of being "right" about political, national, racial, geographical, religious, economic, and any number of other collective identifications is without rival. By means of our attachment to the ego's symbols of external power and status, and our deep insecurities, we can become fanatical adherents that justify and rationalize the most gruesome atrocities, destruction, and misery upon each other and the world. This is why, for no other reason but saving the human race, each of us should sincerely confront our ego-forged identities and our own version of the abusive tyrant within.

One Final Ego-Forged Identity: Addictions

As I have already described, the aggressive/defensive ego consciousness is exclusively preoccupied with your survival as a physical and psychological entity. It does everything out of the belief that life, love, and other people are extremely dangerous and can precipitate potentially deadly experiences. Accordingly, then, you must follow its very strict rules to survive.

Ironically, and of course, sadly, as long as you are operating from your aggressive/defensive ego consciousness and its myriad of manifestations, your very survival becomes more and more precarious and, the opportunity to experience authentic love and acceptance is increasingly diminished. That is because the very same ego consciousness which rallies to preserve and protect you from any perceived external evil is one and the same as that which perpetuates and increases the fear that it defends against.

As an everyday example: What does placing a gun on your night table really give you? Your aggressive/defensive ego's answer would be a reliable and effective defence system. Another version of the truth, however, as viewed through non-ego eyes—the eyes of your natural child consciousness and your spiritual consciousness— would reveal that the amount of fear in your universe only increases through measures such as these.

Imagine *everyone* in your community carrying a gun; *everyone* having a gun on their night table: depressed people, angry people, poor people, afraid people, rich people, bank tellers, sales clerks, all motorists, furniture movers, everyone on the bus, all the people in the movie theatre, all the teachers in school, all the religious fanatics; *everyone carries a gun and has one in their home.* How would you feel at a sports event or in the grocery store knowing everyone carries a gun? What it would be like on a day to day, month to month, year to year basis, for anyone to live in that community?

Consider this from an "internal" perspective: What would it be like to live with an inner world in which *every* second of *every* minute was the experience of constantly escalating fear? By catering to your aggressive/ defensive ego, you escalate the level of fear until the real origin of the fear and emotional pain you carry is completely lost and forgotten.

What can be understood about any ego-forged identity is at its most innocent, it provides you with only a partial and incomplete identity; at its most damaging, a completely misleading and false one. You are not the image which your ego-forged identity insists you present to the world. The cleverly crafted appearances and impressions it generates are no more than a cover-up for your wounded and shamed adaptive child consciousness.

Defining yourself by completely identifying with any ego-forged identity is commensurate with taking up residence on the fifth floor of a building that has no foundation. No matter how much you renovate and upgrade the fifth floor; no matter how you design any room, or how you decorate the exterior of the premises, *the building you live in still has no foundation.*

What is it like to live your life without a foundation? What is it like to be displaying and living a partial or complete lie? What is it like to know, if only obliquely and fleetingly, that you are the one spinning the lies? When most hours of most days are spent fooling most of the people most of the time, what toll does it take on you?

These conditions, which are *un*supportive of the development and growth of an authentic, natural self, are the breeding grounds for addiction. In working with people who are addicted to substances of one kind or another; addicted to relationships or sex; to television; to righteousness (whatever the addiction), and in undertaking to heal my own addictions, the kind which are not only endorsed but frequently encouraged by this culture (i.e. the pursuit of money, recognition and external power), I believe addicts of every kind operate out of a false, ego-forged identity. No authentic, natural self is present at all. When an addicted individual glimpses what little truth holds up the image they convey to the world, a shudder goes through them. They know that underneath this "window dressing" there is no foundation at all.

The addict's natural child consciousness is hidden underneath an adaptive child consciousness, as the result of repeated early experiences they are unlovable, of little value, and most assuredly unsafe in a dangerous world. Invariably, in an addicted person, their aggressive/defensive ego consciousness dominates and controls everyone in their Inner Family. Access to a spiritual power which will help solve the problem is not possible.

I believe addictions are the inevitable result of too much time spent with the aggressive/defensive ego consciousness being the dominant consciousness. The Universe of Fear which it inhabits is barren and bereft of emotional and spiritual nutrients. There is no foundation for an authentic personality and a perpetual ego-need to be propped up with images and delusion. There is the increasing realization, which eventually leads to quiet and then frantic desperation, that *no* ego-bolstering agents or ego-attained rewards are going to be enough. Regardless of what they do, the addict's ego-forged identity will inevitably collapse.

A First Look at the Healing of the Aggressive/Defensive Ego Consciousness

The collapse of the aggressive/defensive ego consciousness and the ego-forged identities which it has created can be a very difficult process. It often feels to the person like they are dying. This near-death *emotional* experience will be the focus of future chapters.

For some people. sadly, the overwhelming defeat and breakdown of their ego-forged identities takes them down a path of despair which leads, one self-inflicted way or another, to their death.

Yet, the breakdown and fall of the aggressive/defensive ego also embodies the potential for the most profound emotional and spiritual growth of a lifetime. For though it may come dressed in the clothes of failure or humiliation, and feel like the death of all that we thought we were, it is only the loss of an adult consciousness which is completely identified with the aggressive/defensive ego. Now, this same person can identify with new and more fulfilling sources of identity and guidance: *the natural child consciousness/authentic self* and *the spiritual consciousness.*

When we discover there are other consciousnesses that can offer us an authentic identity, there is a significant experience of freedom, joy, and relief. Here is one of the cardinal assertions of this healing work: When we identify ourselves primarily with the *natural child consciousness/authentic self* and the *spiritual consciousness,* while at the same time helping the *aggressive/defensive ego consciousness* to heal (and inviting it into the Inner Family as a respected and healthy *ego-in-service*) we offer ourselves opportunities for a quality of life and inner peace that we could only dream about.

Chapter V

"Each man's life represents a road toward himself,
an attempt at such a road,
the intimation of a path.
No man has ever been entirely and completely himself.
Yet each one strives to become that –
One in an awkward, the other in an intelligent way,
each as best he can.
Each man carries the vestiges of his birth –
the slime and eggshells of his primeval past–
with him to the end of his days.
Some never become human,
remaining frog, lizard, ant.
Each represents a gamble on the part of nature
in creation of the human.
We all have the same origin, our mothers;
all of us come in at the same door.
But each of us–experiments of the depths–
strives toward his own destiny.
We can understand one another;
but each of us is able to interpret himself
to himself alone."   Herman Hesse

The Position Of The Ego In The Stages
Of The Adult's Emotional And Spiritual Journey

Irrespective of the culture, religion, or social status into which we are born, all of us are thrown into a life that is, if nothing else, a physical, emotional, and spiritual adventure. The ground rules of Life are the same for everyone. Some of the basic ones are: We are mortal and one day will die. No one knows where we have come from or where we are going to. Though we may deny it, each of us is a tiny and fragile creation in the incomprehensible immensity of the Universe. In the great sweep of time, we are granted very short life spans. We may be born wanted or unwanted by our parents; healthy or sick; rich or poor; or into democratic or demagogue societies. None of us has control over the circumstances into which we were born or has a final say on the events that befall us.

If life can be described as a game, it is a game which from beginning to end is surrounded by mystery and uncertainty. Its rules are more than a little vague and confusing. In significant ways the rules change from player to player. Winning and losing is hard (if not impossible) to define, and the definitions are ultimately left up to the individual. If life is a game it appears to be a random and chaotic one, often bordering on the absurd. To play it seems to require an incredibly high tolerance for insecurity, ambiguity, and lack of control. To put a positive spin on the absurdity of the game we could see it as being given maximum freedom by which to play. If our inclination is to see Life from the negative side, it would not be difficult to argue the game is nothing other than madness and no self-respecting player of any game would endure such a set of ambiguous and harebrained conditions.

Though none of us is given much choice over the ground rules and structure of life, it is clear that each of us is constantly making mental, emotional, and spiritual choices. Do these choices mean anything, or are they simply incidental superfluities that eventually signify nothing? I suggest that even with the apparently ridiculous rules, these choices are far from trivial. I believe *the mental, emotional, and spiritual <u>choices</u> we make, while playing the game of Life, is the real and only game going on.*

Every soul on earth is undertaking a physical, emotional, and spiritual journey. Through our choices, we determine how much time we devote to fear and survival (the aggressive/defensive ego consciousness), and how much we devote to expanding and living through our hearts and spiritual natures (our natural child consciousness/authentic self and spiritual consciousness).

It is also my belief that as much as our physical growth and maturity conform to certain predictable developmental stages, so too does our emotional and spiritual growth. The choices we make at each of these emotional or spiritual stages of our life will determine whether we do or do not grow and mature as souls.

What follows is a chart with an explanation of the emotional and spiritual stages in our journey through life. I explain the pivotal emotional and spiritual events that transpire at each stage; the impact these events have on our consciousness; and the conscious or unconscious choices we make. I will show that choices are key emotional and spiritual "forks in the road" which determine whether we do or do not become who we truly are in this lifetime—whether we go more deeply into the experience and expression of love and peace of the natural child consciousness/authentic self and the spiritual consciousness (thereby generating a Universe of Love), or more deeply into our emotional pain and fear and allow the aggressive/defensive ego consciousness to endlessly recycle the pain (thereby generating a Universe of Fear).

Stage 1
Birth as a natural child consciousness/authentic self connected to spiritual consciousness—the plug connected to socket. Then life circumstances lead us to either the…

The Universe of Love (or) **The Universe of Fear**	
natural development of the healthy ego consciousness (very rare)	*Stage 2 — onset of emotional pain and fear associated with the experience of danger, threat, neglect, abuse, and rejection of natural child consciousness/authentic self and spiritual consciousness*
	Stage 3 — development of the adaptive child consciousness/ inauthentic self (early, mild version of the aggressive/defensive ego consciousness)
	Stage 4 — adaptive child consciousness takes over and progressively develops a reliance on the aggressive/defensive ego consciousness
	Stage 5 — adult person becomes completely identified for purposes of survival with the aggressive/defensive ego consciousness
	Stage 6 — aggressive/defensive ego consciousness establishes complete control—toxicity and destructiveness begin
	Stage 7 — toxicity and destructiveness increase and reach a peak; calamity and damage to self and others apparent; conflict; illness; addictions; relationship dysfunction

Stage 8 — (a) adult identified with aggressive/defensive ego consciousness covers up; attempts to preserve old identity and ways with increasing unhappiness, conflict, pain, fear (will switch back and forth between stages 7 and 8); OR… a decision to heal is made.

*Stage 8 — (b) The person makes a **sincere decision to heal**; transformation and healing begin; adult identified with aggressive/defensive ego crashes or falls apart in crisis (move to Stage 9)*

Stage 9 — aggressive/defensive ego consciousness surrenders, heals and transforms

Stage 10 — independent/aware adult consciousness begins to appear

Stage 11 — natural child consciousness/authentic self and spiritual consciousness return

Stage 12 — independent/aware adult becomes leader of inner family; receives and honours input from all members; (healthy ego-in-service replaces aggressive/defensive ego)

A Description Of The Stages Of The Adult's Emotional And Spiritual Journey Through Life

Stage 1

There is a connection between your authentic self and a natural, internal emotional-and-spiritual process. This is always occurring within you. This natural process is tantamount to an individualized internal information system of extraordinary clarity, wisdom, and guidance. It is a personal compass of unmatched precision and dependability by which to navigate through life. Some people have lost this connection while still being carried in the uterus of their mothers. Other children may have only been able to sustain it for a few days or months after being born. A fortunate few may have been born into a family environment so emotionally and spiritually knowledgeable and supportive that they could sustain the connection for a few years. Rarer still are those children who have been able to maintain this connection through their formative years and adolescence into full adulthood.

When this inherent part of a child's humanness is celebrated, respected, and protected by their caregivers the child can bring this joyfully to the world. This may be the greatest gift that parents can give their children.

This is the situation in Stage 1 of our human emotional and spiritual journey as shown in the chart above. It is the truth of Life *before* emotional pain and fear; life before The Fall; life before there is a need for any kind of an aggressive/defensive ego consciousness. Put in terms of the Inner Family Model Of Self-Healing, in this stage we are identified completely with our natural child conscious-ness/authentic self and spiritual consciousness. There is nothing aggressive or defensive in our make-up. As described at the beginning of the book, the little plug is connected to its socket.

Stage 2

The world and the people in it, and especially those who were your primary caregivers, could be hard, very hard, but not necessarily because anyone wanted it that way. Though there are exceptions, few parents set out to be deliberate sources of physical, emotional, or spiritual damage to their children. Rather, it's in a largely unconscious clash of opposites, children—born without an aggressive/defensive ego—are placed under the unmitigated control of adults. Sadly, adults who have become almost completely identified with their own aggressive/defensive egos. One generation of humans (adults) who, for better or worse, know how to survive life by relying on complex patterns of attack and defense, are responsible for rearing a new generation of humans: their children, who, as children, live for things which have nothing to do with survival.

In this clash of two diametrically opposed consciousnesses, the child inevitably loses. In their encounter with these adult, ego-identified beings, the child is entirely dependent upon them for safety, love, and the sense of being valued that it needs. The child is clearly overpowered and begins to experience danger, threat, neglect, and rejection. Within the child, emotional pain and fear accumulate. The precious, irreplaceable connection between their authentic self and their natural internal emotional-and-spiritual process is severed. At and by Stage 2, the natural child consciousness/authentic self has been delivered such a series of devastating psychological and sometimes physical blows that the child, in order to survive, leaves behind the Universe of Love and plunges, perhaps forever, into a Universe of Fear.

These experiences of emotional pain and fear necessitate the creation of an adaptive child consciousness. This adaptive child is not the free and natural child who is connected to, and can bring forward, their spontaneous and natural emotional and spiritual process. It is a child shaped and molded by the aggressive/defensive egos that surround them. They learn to fit in, please, conform, and impress; or conversely to brood, withdraw, or rebel. They "adapt"; they do whatever the grown-ups want or don't want in order to receive some measure of the attention, affirmation, or affection they crave.

This adaptive child consciousness is the free or natural child shaped and molded to live for survival in a world of aggressive/defensive egos. The adaptive child is a socially fabricated entity that is the miniaturized version and precursor of the aggressive/defensive ego. The adaptive child learns how to use falsehood, manipulation, social roles, and control to get their basic needs met. It is schooled in *in*authenticity and quickly moves to Stage 3—the *practice* of inauthenticity. You might say that, subconsciously, realizing that since it can't "beat" the aggressive/defensive egos around them, the adaptive child joins them.

Stage 3

Stage 3 incorporates a fundamental shift in consciousness from the emotional and spiritual consciousness inherited at birth to an early version of the aggressive/defensive ego. Rather than being love-based and growth-oriented, the developing adaptive child consciousness is now fear-based and survival-oriented.

Like an artificial Christmas tree, the adaptive child consciousness can still fill an empty corner of the room—the adaptive child consciousness tries to fill an emptiness in the child's inner world. Though devoid of any real life or soul, the fake tree can be dressed up and adorned in any number of ways, and remind us of real Christmas trees and celebrations of long ago, that were more real, more pure, more true. Contrived and manufactured as it is, a fake tree can get us through an emotionally charged Christmas season. Sadly, this particular "season" of excessive emotional pain and dashed expectations that leads to the creation of an adaptive child consciousness can last the rest of the person's life. Hence, the need for an aggressive/defensive ego.

Stage 4

This is a complex and contradictory phase in our emotional and spiritual development. It generally parallels (chronologically) the adolescent and young adulthood years.

On the one hand this is a time when, ideally, the strong and healthy ego consciousness of a young adult is forming. That is an ego that experiences being capable, competent, and confident in succeeding at facing and meeting the challenges and expectations of the world. In the often confusing and overwhelming transition period between childhood and adulthood, a strong and healthy ego is a crucial and sustaining force for the young person to rely on. It helps them deal with emotional hurts, wounds, and disappointments that occur in interactions with others, without becoming paralyzed or incapacitated by them. It can show them how to incorporate delayed gratification, deal with life's adversities, cope with life's capricious unfairness, and persevere at goals and ambitions that require planning, time, and effort to achieve.

Adolescence, and the years of young adulthood, represent a unique and precious time in the human emotional and spiritual journey. A developing adult "should" be able to tap into the attributes and benefits of a strong and healthy ego consciousness, and the natural child consciousness/authentic self, *and* the spiritual consciousness. When a young adult's ego consciousness is operating in service to something larger than survival, something bigger than itself, they can feel the internal presence of friendly and guiding emotional and spiritual forces. They are a part of the universe not alienated from it. The balance of these three great forces produces young people who are passionate, adventurous, individualistic, and idealistic. Their life's energy and verve represent an unqualified vote of "Yes!" to the human condition. These young souls are breaths of fresh air, dream weavers, and superb detectors of falsehood and injustice. They are cradled in, and supported by, what could without exaggeration be called a magical state of inner unity and integration—precisely what the Inner Family Model of Healing encourages the fully-grown adult to develop.

Interacting with and relating to a large variety of people, the young adult is forming their predominate, lifelong character and personality. Hope, faith, creativity, and individuality, are at their height. Should they have had "optimum parenting" at this stage they are blessed, for perhaps the last time in their emotional and spiritual life cycle, by a natural child consciousness/authentic self, healthy ego-in-service, and spiritual consciousness (which are all balanced and mutually supportive of each other). They are a revitalizing and life-affirming contribution to the beleaguered and often jaded adult-world that surrounds them.

On the other hand, and simultaneously, in circumstances of frequent survival, what happens in this developmental stage is the fragile adult consciousness can become increasingly reliant on the aggressive/defensive ego consciousness as their primary identity and public face. In leaving the sheltered environment of youth, they are forced to enter the larger world beyond. That world is hard and unyielding. The world will demand they make it on their own; earn their own keep; watch their own back, and become very, very good at something that they can eventually rely on to survive. Competition is fierce. The bar on educational and career requirements is constantly raised higher and higher. The young adult must meet these demands.

Relying on their own resources, they will make it (or not) in the dispassionate world of the marketplace. In this indifferent environment, that is populated with sharks (other people's aggressive/defensive egos), they will be compelled to turn themselves into an attractive product or offer some valuable service which is in demand by others. In large part, it will be the intelligence, skills, and strengths of their ego for which they will get paid. It will be their ego which will (or won't) produce the observable and measurable results by which they will be evaluated and known.

The young adult is forced into another full-out battle for survival. By and large it will get progressively harder for them not to become completely identified with their job resume. Increasingly, in the battle for survival, their natural inner child/authentic self and their spiritual consciousness will become dwarfed by the aggressive/defensive ego. Hopefully, it will be a strong and healthy ego consciousness—an ego-in-service—that guides them through this. But as the battle for survival shows no signs of any quick and definitive conclusion, they will likely become more and more identified with their aggressive/defensive ego.

"Who am I really?" asks the twenty- or thirty-something person in a rare, quiet moment of introspection. "What have I accomplished lately? Oh, I know. It says right here on my business card, I'm a _____." These emotional and spiritual events usually occur towards the end of Stage 4. The aggressive/defensive ego consciousness is ascending; it's reaching its greatest stage of power and influence. The young adult is forced to put away their natural child consciousness/authentic self, their spiritual consciousness, and their healthy, ego-in-service. They are now quaint anomalies, no longer fitting or useful on the fast track and fast times that both entice and enslave them.

Stage 5

By this time the adult is now almost completely identified with their aggressive/defensive ego consciousness. It is their only identity. There is no separate witness or observer; no independent/aware adult consciousness is present. As I have discussed earlier, the aggressive/defensive ego consciousness can employ a multitude of contradictory and often opposing faces and personae for its purposes. For instance, by Stage 5, the ego-identified adult may present themselves as a rising star. Perhaps they have become a productive, successful, well-connected, renowned "conqueror" at their profession and can publicly display a range of culturally endorsed images of "winner". Conversely, by this point, they may have already badly stumbled or failed (be it in love, education or career) and in the process, have become identified with one or more of the range of culturally maligned images of being a "loser".

At this point in our emotional and spiritual journey the aggressive/defensive ego consciousness, generally speaking, has all the bases covered. It can shrewdly play both ends against the middle. Because it is so deft at the manufacturing and wearing of masks, it has us tied up in knots. By Stage 5 it is by far and away the dominant consciousness—the ruler of the Inner Family. The natural child/authentic self and the spiritual consciousness have become trivialized. If they are remembered it is with a nostalgic sentimentality and perceived as ineffective in the real, dog-eat-dog world. The absorption into a fear-based, survival-oriented world of the aggressive/defensive ego consciousness is now complete.

By Stage 5 no other members in the Inner Family have *any* influence. The aggressive/defensive ego is in absolute control. Its perceptions have become our perceptions; its values and priorities, our values and priorities; its ways of operating, our ways of operating. By this stage *the aggressive/ defensive ego consciousness offers us the only version of experience we have available to us; the only perception of reality that we trust.* Any other version of experience such as those that could be offered by our natural child consciousness/authentic self, our spiritual consciousness, or by an independent/aware adult consciousness, that might influence us to make wiser choices are given no credibility or importance. This is because, according to the aggressive/defensive ego's assessment, these other consciousnesses do not advance the cause of survival. Therefore, they are at best irrelevant and at worst they threaten survival.

Stage 6

At Stage 6 the aggressive/defensive ego is at the zenith of its powers. It is at the top of the heap. In terms of its ability to establish and maintain power and control, the ego consciousness will not gain more influence than it has attained by Stage 6. Its power and control is not, however, used in the service of a higher good, like the authentic well-being and empowerment of other people. Instead, its power is used to:

(a) perpetuate the survival of the ego-identified adult;
(b) wield its power over other egos to keep them at bay;
(c) prop up an ego-forged identity;
(d) justify blaming and externalizing responsibility; and,
(e) avoid and suppress an inner self embedded in emotional pain and fear.

By now, the aggressive/defensive ego-identified adult is often a parent. No longer a member of the subjugated and oppressed class to which they belonged as children, these people (and their egos) are now in the position of being rulers rather than ruled. Now they have the power and authority to *tell* their children how to be, what to say, how to think, and what to feel. In the marketplace, the aggressive/defensive ego-identified adult is likely established in a career, and often at the height of their ability to command external power and control. Here, too, they will try to tell others how to be, what to say, how to think, and what to feel.

And what of people who fall under the dominion of an aggressive/defensive ego-identified adult? What do they do? If they cannot leave they will obey. They will mold themselves to fit in. For the most part, they will tow the line and do as they are told; but they will do so out of fear not love, always feeling subordinated and stifled. Whether they find themselves in a marriage, a family system, a business, an organization, or a country, the oppressed subjects of an aggressive/defensive ego consciousness will invariably, and often subconsciously, resist its rule. The stage will be set for the power struggles, relationship discord, toxicity, and high drama of Stage 7.

Stage 7

In Stage 7, alone and disconnected from any natural emotional and spiritual process occurring within, the aggressive/defensive ego-identified adult is now, for all intents and purposes, out of control. Completely embedded in the Universe of Fear, they attack anyone whom they see as the cause of the emotional pain and fear they experience. There is a war in their inner and outer world. The aggressive/defensive ego consciousness dominates the Inner Family and has essentially excluded and suppressed the natural child consciousness/authentic self, the spiritual consciousness, *and* the adaptive child consciousness.

Any relationship between people—parents/children, siblings, dating, business associates, friendships, and *especially* marriages, with one (or more) out of control aggressive/defensive egos, will be marked by power struggles. There will be, overtly or covertly, a massive build-up of resentments, frequent eruptions of hostility, invisible walls of separation, and withdrawal.

For many relationships, the *overt* war that now exists will produce high drama and abuse i.e.: shouting, fights, altercations, slammed doors, affairs, law suits, corporate in-fighting, substance use, vicious put downs, sometimes violence, and divorces with all manner of accusations and blaming. For many other relationships there will be the *covert* conflict and "low drama" of snide remarks, sarcasm, petty insults, invisible lines of emotional and spiritual alienation, repressed anger, unbreakable silences, and untouchable bodies. This is a "love life" spent going through the motions without substance or meaning. Mired in the toxicity of psychological and emotional battles there is usually little possibility for change until one of the antagonists is prepared to, or actually does, leave.

The damage done to children controlled by an aggressive/defensive ego is significant. Defenseless and completely controlled by ego-identified adults, these children will be forcefully expelled from the Universe Of Love in which they were born and forced to survive in the Universe Of Fear. This repeats the entire, hurtful chain of events (Stages 2 to Stage 7) that happened to their parents before them.

When children are raised in an environment where they have to "survive" their caregivers, connection with their natural child consciousness/authentic self and spiritual consciousness cannot be maintained. The aggressive/defensive ego of the parents begets the aggressive/defensive ego of the child as the child is indoctrinated into the parent's Universe of Fear. [When the child becomes an adult they will, in turn, perpetuate that cycle with their own children.]

Usually by Stage 7, the public faces and images which the ego-identified adult has carefully employed and polished (to effectively hide unpleasant private truths and realities) start to sway and will sometimes collapse. The person can't seem to "fake it" any longer even if they want to. The underbelly of an ego-based life is now exposed to themselves and others. It becomes harder and harder to hide or control the damage they do to themselves or others (very similar to the escalating damage in addictions). The often used justifications, rationalizations, and explanations for their behavior begin to become meaningless excuses. Personal declarations of willingness and intention carry no credibility. The pain-inducing, pain-inflicting behavior patterns continue.

Hurtful behavior and any related addictions are now out of control. Marriages are in serious jeopardy or ruin; family relationships are full of conflict; personal and professional worlds are in chaos; and the inner world of emotions is unbearable. Like a paratrooper falling from an airplane, in Stage 7 the aggressive/defensive ego-identified adult desperately tries to open their parachute in time to avoid a crash landing. The parachute won't open. They now face the real possibility of self-destruction and the obliteration of happiness and perhaps life itself.

Stage 8

The crash occurs in Stage 8. This is the proverbial point of "hitting bottom", and perhaps the most consequential of all of the stages in an adult's emotional and spiritual journey. The fear-based, survival-oriented, ego-identified adult has collapsed. The many ego-forged identities that were used in their attempts to feel safe, loved, and valued have failed. The actor they turned themselves into (since childhood or adolescence) has forgotten their lines; or they continue to recite the old familiar lines over and over again and nothing works. The "audience" has markedly changed and is no longer mesmerized and admiring of the roles the ego-actor has so finely developed. Even the play itself, once thought to be timeless in its appeal, is now looking dated and flawed. The critical reviews and the boos that can be heard from the balcony generate substantial emotional pain and fear in the formerly confident performer.

The play of life that the aggressive/defensive ego has been directing has become a calamity of painful reality. A tremendous sense of personal failure and rejection are part of this experience. A person in the throes of this process feels disturbed, disoriented and unhinged by what is happening; there is a real sense of a loss of meaning. No matter what is tried, they cannot seem to recover any equilibrium. The dramatic illusion of the play has suddenly vanished and they are left facing reality.

A critical choice presents itself to the faltering and flattened ego-identified adult at Stage 8. *As frightening and difficult as this choice may be, it may well be the first real choice the person has had to make since childhood—choosing to define and declare who they really are.* With the pieces of a fractured ego-forged identity lying in tatters all around them they can realize, even fleetingly, that their real identity is not comprised of their ego alone. They have the opportunity of discovering they are more than everything they thought they were. They are more than all of the identities provided by an aggressive/defensive ego consciousness.

Though perhaps shaken and barely standing, some consciousness other than ego remains intensely alive and present, even if it's just to inspect the devastation of their life as it was. This is the beginning of an authentic independent/aware adult consciousness.

Remember: The ego consciousness, and all of its identities and ways, have been the only reality until now. What, and more importantly *who*, remains after the aggressive/defensive ego has fractured and fallen; a fall from which it cannot seem to recover? Is whoever remains real? Do they have any place in life?, any power?, any value and worth? Is there anything about them which is embraceable?

The adult, at this stage, is no longer exclusively identified with their aggressive/defensive ego consciousness and its ego-forged identities. They are more real and more themselves at this moment than they have been since they descended into the Universe of Fear. Yet, even if they are more real, more natural, and more authentic than they have been for years, can they survive? This is a terrifying state to be in. Will life and other people simply mutilate and destroy them like they did before? Being emotionally and spiritually killed once was hard enough. In this new awareness that borders on real, will they be re-born only to painfully perish again?

To the aggressive/defensive ego consciousness, a monumental and humiliating catastrophe has occurred out of which nothing good can come. We (and the ego) have fallen short of everything that it has insisted we must be. From its creation and arrival into our consciousness it has insisted that "we" be (or at least appear to look) fearless, strong, together, beautiful, smart, capable, successful, and pleasing.

It has perpetuated and enforced the beliefs that we are our own creator; we are the center of everything; we know everything, and perhaps most critically, that we can control everything. In Stage 8 we can demonstrate none of these. In this period of extreme personal disorganization and disintegration, we cannot demonstrate any of these beliefs or traits.

At Stage 8 a significant choice with great emotional and spiritual consequence presents itself to the adult consciousness that witnesses the ego's loss of dominance. Broken and often disgraced by some form of seemingly ignominious failure, rejection, defeat, or loss, the tightly-wound and complex structure of blame, anger, and fear inside the adult is torn wide open. The aggressive/defensive ego will scream: "Damage control! Damage control!"

If the now fragile, independent aware/adult consciousness can endure this rupture, it may feel relief but not know *exactly* what it is relieved of. And, it may simultaneously feel an experience of unshackled freedom from the life-denying oppression of the aggressive/defensive ego.

The now aware and temporarily unbound adult consciousness is at an unmistakable fork in the road of life. Here is the monumental choice: Do I pick myself up and do everything in my power to return to my old personality: the successful ego-driven actor in an ego-controlled life, *or* do I quit that and leave the stage, and sincerely attempt to live life as just me, the person I actually am; my authentic, natural self? Which path do I take from here?

The arrows at Stage 8 (see chart p. 127) represent the choice that must be made. Having more clarity on the agenda of the aggressive/defensive ego (meaning a life lived in the Universe Of Fear), the arrow pointing from the right to the left column) represents a possible return to the Universe Of Love.

Being at Stage 8 [going from 8(b) to 9 on the chart] presents the opportunity to discover and facilitate the re-emergence of the other Inner Family members—the natural child consciousness/authentic self and the spiritual consciousness, which were concealed and forgotten long ago. It also creates the possibility for the development of the new independent/aware adult consciousness that is *not* the same as the formerly governing and belligerent aggressive/defensive ego consciousness.

Persevering through Stage 8 to Stage 9 creates an opportunity for profound change. It allows for a fundamental choice that the events of life will periodically offer to us. It is the opportunity for personal transformation; that radical shift in consciousness necessary for permanent and lasting change in the quality of our lives. It is the opportunity to shift from a fear-based, survival oriented, hostile consciousness to a loved-based, growth-oriented one. It allows for the transformation from an Inner Family dominated by the aggressive/defensive ego to one led by an independent/aware adult who, in turn, is led by the natural child consciousness/authentic self and the spiritual consciousness.

The arrows on the chart also indicate that many individuals at Stage 8(a) revert to Stage 7—back to the aggressive/defensive ego consciousness as the source of their primary identity. Once the crisis has abated; once the acute and piercing emotional pain and fear can again be reduced to a dull, chronic, throbbing familiar ache; once some reasonable form of personal equilibrium can be reestablished, these travelers return to their old, familiar "comfortable" ways. They conclude that whatever the exceptional and temporary "fall from grace" was which they have recently experienced, the old ways have carried them this far in life and, no doubt, will take them a long way further.

Thus, these individuals see the ego's fall from grace as a small blip on the screen of their lives. Relying as soon as they possibly can on their recovering aggressive/defensive ego consciousness, these individuals elect to keep their dark personal odyssey away from others. They return to their quest for external power and control as their way of feeling secure. In short order, the aggressive/defensive ego restores itself to the dominant position in the inner family. Sooner rather than later, it's pretty well "business as usual".

Some individuals, however, realize that they cannot go back to the old ways; or, even if they could, they don't want to. The dark night of the soul through which they have passed has allowed them a glimpse of a new way of being. They feel or sense a new potential for freedom, peace, sanity, love, harmony, richness, and depth of life which they want more than anything. Many realize that they have always wanted these things, and perhaps wanted *only* these things; they just could never figure out how to experience them. In Stage 8 they have come to realize their ego consciousness, operating by itself, will *never* be able to acquire them. These are the intrepid travelers who go on to Stages 9 through 12.

As I sometimes say to clients displaying this emotional and spiritual courage and sense of adventure: "I guess you're at a point in your life where you'd rather die crossing the Atlantic looking for a New World than be already dead in old Madrid!" However by this point in their journey, many of these survivors have placed their feet on the soil of the New World, and nothing I say or do is going to keep them from staying there.

At this point it is common for people on their healing journey to vacillate between the old ways prescribed by their aggressive/defensive ego consciousness and the new ways suggested by the other emerging and reawakening Inner Family members. Frustration, disappointment, loss, failure, emotional pain, and fear may be required down the healing road for these individuals to see the grievous limitations of identifying themselves with their ego consciousness. This will eventually bring them back to the pivotal choice in their emotional and spiritual journey which Stage 8 represents. Again and yet again, they will return to this consequential fork in the road.

For most people, even though we may delay leaving behind the ways of our aggressive/defensive ego consciousness for a long, long time, we cannot postpone it forever. If not in our living, then in our dying and the physical, emotional and spiritual process which surrounds it, many of us will be forced to abandon our old ways. Personal healing, a process which begins with the life-altering choice made in Stage 8, and its implementation into our lives in Stage 9, asks us to leave the ways of the aggressive/defensive ego behind while we are living.

Stage 9

To paraphrase Paul Tillich in his timeless masterpiece *The Courage To Be*, God is the God that shows up when our version of God dies. Stage 9 marks the earliest beginnings of a unique, organic personal spirituality. The individual who has passed through the shattering dissolution of their aggressive/defensive ego at Stage 8 (which I refer to as an ego-death), knows in every cell of their being they are one of a fortunate few survivors of some disaster. Their life has been spared.

Not only have they been miraculously granted life, but have

been given the opportunity to heal and transform it. The version of God they experience will be unique to them. The meanings and symbolism they ascribe to "God" will be based on the experiences they have been through. For the second time in their life, and the first time since childhood, access to a spiritual consciousness can come through their heart and not their head; through (and by means of) their own unique emotional and spiritual process, and not the imposed precepts, suppositions, doctrines, and laws of a collection of egos (caregivers and culture).

Stage 10

Whether we are forced to shed our attachment and identification with the aggressive/defensive ego consciousness through a personal breakdown of one sort or another, or we do so voluntarily, space opens up for a God which this ego does not know. The eternal link between the inner child consciousness and the spiritual consciousness, which surrounds and protects that child, can be re-established. The growth and development of a separate independent/aware adult consciousness (emerging as the head of the Inner Family) is the developmental work in Stage 10.

This is a "new adult" that is learning to lead the Inner Family with compassion and step away from complete identification with the aggressive/defensive ego consciousness. Rather than presenting false identities and manipulating tactics for external power and control, forged and supported by their ego, this new consciousness embarks upon the exhilarating (albeit trepidatious) work of creating a new identity. This new consciousness is aware and responsible.

A person at this point in their transformation is aware of their ego's aggressive/defensive ways. They take responsibility for their ego and its healthy, unhealthy, hurtful, and destructive behaviors; are willing to learn how to be an effective adult in the world; and know how to get their feelings respected and needs met, *without* having their fear-based, survival-oriented ego harm anyone.

This practice may feel painstakingly slow. Old ways die hard because, after all, they are associated in the adult's mind with survival. A person may feel awkward, shaky, and occasionally foolish with these new levels of vulnerability. The old aggressive/defensive ego consciousness will sometimes return, seemingly out of nowhere. Once again its negative judgments, opinions, and criticisms will shout things like: "You look like a wimp in this situation!" "You're too vulnerable!" "Doing this could cost you dearly!" "Who'll love you now?".

The familiar blaming refrain of the aggressive/defensive ego consciousness, based on its need to externalize the problem, will reappear: "They deserved it!" "This is *their* fault." "They are *much* more of the problem in our relationship than I am!" "They can go to hell!" "Screw this—we're out' a here!" Whoever chooses to give birth to their own independent/aware adult, and be led by their *natural child consciousness/authentic self* and their *spiritual consciousness* (rather than the aggressive/defensive ego) will be tested and tested repeatedly.

You may be wondering: Can this "new" adult—*me*—be more vulnerable, transparent, and humble in the real world and *still* be taken seriously? If I don't attempt to control others, will I still get my needs met? Will I be important to others? If I don't adapt, conform, or please, will I still feel safe, loved, and valued? And most critically: Will I survive as this "new" adult?

What must be remembered is not all of the ego's old ways of operating were damaging or hurtful or even problematic. It accomplished and provided many things. The aggressive/defensive ego on rare occasions, has been a wonderful asset. It has been a valuable and necessary Inner Family member, required for your continued safety and survival. It will be up to the newly formed and developing adult consciousness to separate out the aggressive/defensive ego from an emerging ego-in-service, and create a new way of carrying out its old role.

Can the aggressive/defensive ego, the former head of the Inner Family (and one that could often turn into a bully and a tyrant), learn how to be a team player? How does the fledgling independent/aware adult consciousness assume leadership of the Inner Family? Can the Inner Family move from a hierarchal system with the ego at the top, to an egalitarian one? How does the newly developed, independent/aware adult prevent the aggressive/defensive ego from automatically feeling threatened at every change? More importantly, how does a person prevent the ego from returning with a vengeance to reek havoc on the Inner Family all over again? Stage 10 is the time for delicate and patient negotiations and transitions to promote a fundamental shift.

Stage 11

Stage 11 is the opportunity for significant and unparalleled personal healing. Now able to have a will and voice of their own, separate from that of the aggressive/defensive ego, a person can formulate a healing program aimed at further loosening the grip this consciousness has had over them. They may take on certain repetitive, self-defeating behavior patterns (or addictions) which have been used in the past to "protect and aid" in survival.

For example, a person may confront what has really been going on *underneath* their excessive busyness or underneath "falling in love" with inappropriate people. They may want to face their use of food, alcohol, money, or sex to heal the deeper wounds which have precipitated the use of these ego-bolstering agents. All of these ego-bolstering agents are the little plug finding *dis*connection.

At a deeper level still, their healing journey will take them into an examination of their adaptive child consciousness—the one who survived childhood in an unnatural state by having to adapt to the conditions dictated by the egos around them. A person may elect to do the work of healing that adaptive inner child (Chapter IX) by learning how to show this child, perhaps for the first time, the committed love and caring of a sensitive adult who is determined to protect, mentor, and cherish their inner experience. This will go a long way to reducing the size and power of the aggressive/defensive ego consciousness.

At this point the ego's need for external power and control is no longer usurping the role of a higher power. The independent/aware adult consciousness is now in a position, if they so choose, to deepen their connection to their authentic self and authentic spirituality. In healing they may be willing to develop a personal relationship with an Intelligence or Presence which may have been briefly experienced when their ego was falling apart. This willingness to live more authentically may take them to a formal religion; to no particular formal religious expression; into community or away from community; more deeply into a primary intimate relationship or out of it; more heartily into their career or away from it.

Regardless of what form this takes, there is a clear and visible freedom from the tyranny of the aggressive/defensive ego consciousness and its Universe of Fear. By incorporating the input and guidance of their *natural child consciousness/authentic self* and their *spiritual consciousness*, the now aware person can choose to be true to themselves.

Stage 11 brings with it the opportunity for the independent/aware adult to gain an understanding and appreciation of their previously conflicted Inner Family members. *They can come to experience, within themselves, the look and feel of a truly connected and supportive family*, thus ending the internal civil war that ravaged any possibility of experiencing an integrated and whole consciousness. This stage marks the transformational shift from the fear-based and survival-oriented consciousness (developed to survive life) to the heart-and-spirit led consciousness which was theirs at birth.

Stage 12

Stage 12 solidifies and integrates the inner transformation that has occurred. The new independent/aware adult consciousness, now separated from and responsible for the aggressive/defensive ego consciousness, can continue to grow into a leadership position within the Inner Family. This new leader will not be under the assumption that they know everything and impose their will upon others. This new adult will be aware they can *never* know everything and refuse to impose their will upon others.

This "new" person has the utmost respect and faith for the wisdom of the members of their Inner Family. A leader, who is akin to the chairman of a sage and powerful committee of discerning experts, listens deeply and reverently to what each of them is saying and advising. A leader who knows that each committee member has wonderful skills and a certain mastery of insight regarding their perspective of any problem or circumstance (including relationships). Each Inner Family member is extremely knowledgeable about different things.

Possibly the most important role of this independent/aware adult leader is to facilitate, absorb, and weigh the free flow of information between the members of this brilliant team of diverse experts. Then, after all is considered, to make the final decision for the direction to be taken. I believe, in this negotiation within the Inner Family there is always an everybody-wins solution.

There may be matters before the Inner Family that end with the adult's decision to follow the suggestion of the ego-in-service. Its vast experience in matters of protection and survival (remember, the ego-in-service is the transformed aggressive/defensive ego), should count most heavily. There may be other times when the simple, pure feelings and perceptions of the natural child consciousness/authentic self will be given the greatest weight; or times when the gentle and loving suggestions of the spiritual consciousness, which has no concerns about survival at all, will be followed. Every decision (and every circumstance) is different. The independent/aware adult consciousness doesn't resort to standard formulas for solving complex problems.

In "real life", every member of a family or team should be consulted and contribute to the solutions of the problems that affect them. With patience and collaboration there is always a win-win solution. It is no different as regards the Inner Family: At various times different Inner Family members get to have their solution be most valued; all however, continue to operate in the service of each other.

The new independent/aware adult consciousness presides over your integrated and supportive Inner Family with compassion and integrity. It knows it belongs forever and always to something greater than itself. As this adult consciousness you are the leader and the led; the healer and the healed. The inner wars and conflicts have been largely stopped. When conflict erupts it is easy to negotiate a new, peaceful harmony. No longer attached to ego-forged identities, you are comfortable living in authentic humility, service, and peace. The greatest gift of all, that is only available as the result of this healing, is the experience of being loveable and loved for nothing more and nothing less than being who you really are.

Chapter VI

*"When we get out of the glass bottles of our ego
and when we escape like squirrels
turning in the cages of our personality
and get in the forests again,
we shall shiver with cold and fright
but things will happen to us so that we don't
know ourselves. Cool, undying life will rush
in, and passion will make our bodies taut
with power, we shall stamp our feet with
new power and old things will fall down,
we shall laugh, and institutions
will curl up like burnt paper."*

D.H. Lawrence

Healing The Aggressive/Defensive Ego Consciousness

At first, to take on the work of healing the aggressive/ defensive ego consciousness might feel much like being a solitary, protesting citizen standing up to a totalitarian government. The lonely, objecting citizen will tell the dictator that their ways of governing are cruel and harmful to everyone and that they should change their ways immediately or resign. We could reasonably expect the response of the autocratic authority to be some version of: "Thank you for sharing, citizen. Now, I will kill you."

Much like that of a dictator, the regime of the aggressive/defensive ego has this kind of strangle-hold over our consciousness. It dominates us so completely that we operate unknowingly out of its fear-based, survival-oriented state of consciousness, in many cases, practically from cradle to grave.

We do not know ourselves separately from it. We remain hopelessly enmeshed with it instead of becoming independent/aware adults who have both the determination and skill to discern when we are operating as this unhealthy and (usually) destructive Inner Family member. Rather than learn to disengage from it, we consider it an obligation or an inalienable right to indulge it, regardless of the consequences to ourselves and others.

This consciousness is our governing ruler; our supreme commander and the highest authority, controlling all the affairs of our lives. Though we may perceive ourselves as free-thinking, self-governing citizens (of a free society), in practice we are harshly, and many times brutally enslaved by the dictates of our aggressive/defensive ego. If it is true that world peace begins with inner peace, one glance at the front page of any newspaper will tell us how much "inner peace" most of us are experiencing.

Here are some questions to consider if you want to move from theory to practice—from reading about the aggressive/defensive ego to healing it:

- What will you do to negotiate change with the controlling, oppressive dictator living inside of you?
- What steps will be necessary for you to establish sovereignty and peace in your inner life, such that it is your *usual* way of life?
- In the matter of your personal healing, what is it actually going to take to heal your aggressive/defensive ego so that you can *reliably* live in an authentic, love-based, growth-oriented consciousness?
- Is it possible to leave the self-contained, self-perpetuating Universe Of Fear which you (as an ego-identified adult) have created and lived in?
- Is it possible to routinely reside in the Universe Of Love, which once surrounded and protected you as much as the Universe of Fear does now?

This chapter will focus upon the answers to those questions and the steps required for this radical healing to occur. Each of these steps, in the healing of the aggressive/defensive ego consciousness, is a difficult and challenging one. Each one forces you to confront and take personal responsibility for your conditioning, your belief systems, and your habitual behavior patterns.

Your aggressive/defensive ego will remind you that this conditioning got you this far in life; it has been indispensable to your survival. It will pressure you with logic and fear to abandon your healing path. Vital and beneficial aspects of these elements of your ego consciousness—which will now appear through a healthy ego-in-service—have allowed you to feed, shelter, and clothe yourself and your loved ones. For whatever your contribution to the world has been, your ego has facilitated that. Yet, if you are still reading this book, hopefully you will have realized that your ego consciousness, even though it aided and abetted your own and other's survival, is now the single greatest threat to it.

Before I detail the inner work involved in healing the aggressive/defensive ego consciousness, I will offer you some simple and practical (though not necessarily easy) ways to live differently on a daily basis. These will create spaces or gaps in the iron-clad grip it likely exerts over you. There are three: (a) *Slow Down*; (b) *Endure Boredom and Aloneness*; and (c), *Put More Attention on Yourself.*

A. Slow Down

> "*Even if you win the rat race, you're still a rat.*"
> A Client

Most of us, because of how we created out lives, simply do not have the time in the course of a typical day to pay any attention to ourselves. We don't have time to observe our state of consciousness and what we bring to the people around us. Our lives are very busy. Often harried and buffeted from task to task and person to person, we tend to live fast, often at breakneck speed. The refrain sung by many in this day and age is:

> "*I'm late, I'm late, for a very important date.*
> *I have no time to sit and wait. I'm late!*"
> Lewis Carroll (Charles L. Dodgson)
> *Alice's Adventures in Wonderland*

To establish even a meager toe-hold for the work of healing the aggressive/defensive ego, **you have to slow down.** Having seen it in my own life and in the lives of my clients, I know that the ego is addicted to, and thrives on, life in the fast lane, not life in the bus lane. In a constant search for stimulation and excitement, your aggressive/defensive ego operates on only one speed: fast. It lives in a "frantic time zone", loving the adrenaline rush that comes with action, movement, chaos, and speed. By its very nature, the aggressive/defensive ego needs to get pumped up to face the world.

Never allowing a leisurely pace, and always insisting upon slightly too much for you to do in a day, it imprisons you in a dazed, disoriented, and agitated state. *Living in this perpetual condition, you* are *not* going to be connected to and informed by your subjective *emotional and spiritual experience*.

When living hard and fast, developing the independent/aware adult consciousness of your Inner Family, that is detached enough to notice when you are operating from your aggressive/defensive ego, will be next to impossible. All you are likely going to notice is the external frustrations and impediments to getting where you're going and doing what your ego tells you you have to get done.

How does this happen? (a) The aggressive/defensive ego detests and avoids self-examination; (b) it needs frustration and anger *apparently* rooted in external sources as a deflection from itself; and (c), it will therefore create tasks, goals, plans, and itineraries, that are impossible to complete. Your ego keeps you frantic and focused on your inability to get everything done. It constantly creates too much to be done. *You are forever externally focused and always frustrated, without time to self-examine*. Which brings you back to point (a) — your ego avoids self-examination.

To take on the work of personal healing and extricating yourself from the grip of the aggressive/defensive ego consciousness, you must **learn to move slower**. You must learn how to become comfortable in a "laid back time zone" where there is no edge and little seems to happen. If you are asked what time it is, you might answer: "I don't own a watch, but I think it's October."

Taking on the work of healing your aggressive/defensive ego means you will alter the speed at which you react to life. You will have to adjust and reduce the number of things you commit yourself to doing. Are you willing to reduce and and/or eliminate any unnecessary commitments? Are you willing to closely *examine* what commitments are not necessary, even though you have "convinced" yourself they are? Are you willing to stop impressing yourself and everyone else with how much you try to accomplish? Are you ready to stop being reactive and force yourself to do less — a *lot* less? Are you willing to live in such a way that you force yourself to have time and space to quietly reflect on how you have been living? [That does not mean while stuck in traffic between appointments.]

The aggressive/defensive ego consciousness (which has controlled you) will always be too busy and move too fast for you to examine and take responsibility for it. It is not going to stop on its own. It doesn't want to. If you are to grow beyond the limited things it can offer you, you are the only one who can stop it. This leads us to the second thing you can do to create a healing space for yourself.

B. Endure Boredom and Aloneness:
Change Your Ego's Propensity for Drama.

Should you decide and commit yourself to this (temporarily) arduous work you will discover what lies behind the perpetual-motion machine. You will learn why it (*you*) has to be constantly moving, darting hither and yon, and to and fro. If you do this work, and it is work, you will be rewarded with an understanding of why you cannot be quiet and still, internally or externally, very long.

A large part of this is because of the ego's insatiable need for drama. To the extent that you are identified with the ego consciousness (as your primary identity), is generally the same extent to which you will need to present yourself as a larger-than-life action figure, living a highly dramatic and sensationalized life. No Inner Family member needs to experience events in such bold strokes and high energy as the ego. Out of generated drama, your ego gets high and manic in the good times and depressed in the bad times. Everything is fabulous in the beginning and devastating in the end. That's your ego in action.

It is the ego that will place the wreath of hero on you one minute and the badge of failure on you the next; see you as superior to everyone one day, inferior to them the next. At first it will see your new love interest as the person with whom you are certain to live a charmed, conflict-free and magical life. Later it (*you*) will be *devastated* to detect a grievous flaw or several glaring character defects in that once-perfect partner. Your ego will withdraw love with the same lightening-like speed it once offered it.

To begin the process of becoming aware of, and separating yourself from, the aggressive/defensive ego consciousness, **you will have to live a life without manufactured drama**; a life devoid of over-stimulation, histrionics, and self-generated spectacle. (This is harder than most people realize.) In doing this you will have to experience boredom as you no longer inject artificial sources of stimulation and excitement into your day. Additionally, you will experience some solitude as you move yourself away from the performances and pageants your ego once created; a solitude that is a healthy opposite to the drama which kept you away from reflection and self-examination.

Few states are as distasteful and uncomfortable to the aggressive/defensive ego as boredom and aloneness. These represent an affront to the images the ego attempts to cultivate. Boredom and aloneness represent forms of emotional pain and fear, and to the ego *emotional pain and fear is death.* If you eliminate the drama in your life, and allow yourself the experience of boredom and aloneness, you may feel like you are dying (to all that you have been). If you eliminate all the drama you have used to manufacture an image of yourself; if you can experience and endure these sometimes difficult and frightening states you, can wean yourself off of the grip of the false images you have been presenting to the world. Your aggressive/defensive ego has employed self-generated drama to masquerade as your real identity.

C. Put More Attention On Yourself

In one way, it would be accurate to say as long as you are identified as the ego consciousness you put almost all of your attention on yourself. Surviving life and the world of other people is neither easy not simple. Your deepest resources were expended in an endless and futile search for protection from known and unknown enemies. You need to continuously assess and reassess your position in regard to the universe.

This forces you into an aggressive and/or defensive emotional mindset in which you are perpetually looking for danger or constantly trying to find things to be afraid of. Seldom can you get out from under the effort of preserving your self-image, and seldom can you escape from the exhausting task of creating a list of people or things to be afraid of. This is selfishness, and according to the ego's belief system, is a trait by which the fittest survive. Noticing, empathizing, and attending to the needs of others is a luxury; trusting anyone is dangerous; compassion is a game for fools.

Being "selfish" in this manner is the state you (we) usually live in. Why then would I suggest you put more attention on yourself if you want to undertake the practice of healing your ego?

The attention you need to develop is a "second order of attention". Rather than struggling to dominate people and ram your survival-agenda down the world's throat, the second order of attention is watching your aggressive/defensive ego as it tries to do just that. It is the cultivation of neutral observation—what I call a non-involved witness or observer; or in terms of the Inner Family Model, developing an independent/aware adult consciousness.

This is (or will be) a new adult consciousness; one that is not completely identified with the aggressive/defensive ego and can see the ego in action rather than be it in action. In some Buddhist meditation practices this is referred to as developing your third eye— being able to quietly, mentally, step back and watch yourself going through the motions of your life; "observing without being a part of"; watch yourself being yourself.

In this way it (your mind) can begin to step out of the domination of the aggressive/defensive ego by becoming aware, watchful, and responsible. I discuss this in detail later.

Steps in Healing the Aggressive/Defensive Ego

In addition to the three things I already discussed—slow down, endure boredom and aloneness, and put more attention on yourself, there are seven related tasks in healing your aggressive/defensive ego. They aren't easy, but they work.

Step 1: Discernment

You need to be able to discern when you are in the aggressive/defensive ego consciousness. The first order of business is to learn all that you can about the actual experience of being in your aggressive/defensive ego consciousness so you can accurately recognize it and know when you are operating from it. How can you work on healing a consciousness which can severely hurt yourself and others; how can you remove yourself from its fear-based, survival-oriented obsession and choose to see things differently if you do not know when you are in it?

1 (a): Body Cues

The first set of tangible clues that can inform you about this come from your body. When you feel afraid, anxious, or nervous (or angry, irritated, frustrated, or annoyed, which are emotions we create to camouflage our fear) how does your forehead look and feel? Is it soft and smooth or is it tight, hard, furrowed, and tense? How do your eyes look? Do they seem gentle, open, peaceful, and accepting, or are they narrowed, piercing, wary, or strained? Are your shoulders hunched, lowered, or raised? Do your shoulders (do *you*) feel braced and brittle or supple and relaxed? Is your heartbeat fast? Are you perspiring more? How does your voice sound when you are afraid—how does the tone change from your regular speaking voice? Perhaps you sound louder or more demanding; maybe you have a faint or thick voice in your attempts to hide or compensate for fear. Does it contain a subtle tremble or waver in it?

In my own case, more than any other physiological cue, the quality and timbre of my speaking voice gives my aggressive/defensive ego away. When I am feeling afraid or insecure, I immediately try to cover up any sign of fear in my voice by thickening and hardening it. When I speak with this voice I notice that I sound cold, rigid, and authoritarian. In those moments when I am actually experiencing a great deal of vulnerability and uncertainty (fear), to hear the assuredness of my voice and the certainty of its tone, you would think that I am a world-renowned authority on whatever the subject is. Using my voice to present the confident image my aggressive/defensive ego is attempting to convey—a person who is absolutely right about what he is saying, is a cover-up for my fear.

Routinely accompanying this "know it all" voice is another trademark clue that I am operating out of my aggressive/defensive ego—inflexible, categorical, black and white thinking. Something is either good or bad, right or wrong, either/or and acceptable or unacceptable, and of course my ego's way is *always* right. When I am thinking in ego mode (and I usually only realize this after the fact), the idea of gently opening and sharing my tentative perceptions and thoughts on the matter at hand, and seeking input or collaboration and help from others, does not even cross my mind. I (my ego) knows *every*thing! I know what is best for *every*body! If I am patiently self-observant, all of this can be gleaned from becoming aware of the quality and timbre of my speaking voice which indicates I have fallen into black-and-white thinking; there are no shades of grey.

I have noticed several other "body clues" that tell me my aggressive/defensive ego consciousness has taken over. An ache or heaviness shows up in my left temple (as if it is pinched too tightly in a metal brace or a helmet). This physical ache informs me that my aggressive/defensive ego is near. When my forehead gets furrowed and tense and my vision blurs slightly I know that I am identified with this consciousness and about to launch into some critical judgments (spoken or unspoken). This is usually the time when I need restraint, and then at a later time, attention and care. My most frequent targets are immediate family members like my wife or children. On these occasions I have learned I would be wise to "button it up" or leave the room. Silence or withdrawal would be a much higher act of love than anything I could say in that moment.

What body clues might suggest to *you* that you are spending a lot of time in the aggressive/defensive ego consciousness? How does your whole body (or any part of it) feel to you these days? Healthy or unhealthy? Light or heavy? Tense? Relaxed? Phantom pain? You may spontaneously answer: "Just fine, thank you!" Do you feel youthful or aged—not so much in weight or age, but in spirit? Be advised that these body tensions are subtle and you may be so inured to them, your ego has you convinced everything is fine.

What psychological and emotional states seem common for you? Would you describe your private inner experience as feeling empowered and optimistic or more depressed and defeated? What can you sense from your overall levels of energy and fatigue? How are you sleeping? Can you fall asleep easily? Does your mind become quiet and still quite quickly or do persisting and jangled thoughts take you over? What is the quality and content of your dreams? When you wake up, what do you notice about your attitude and emotions? With quiet reflection, the answers to these questions will yield considerable and valuable information about your relationship with your aggressive/defensive ego consciousness.

1 (b): Your Reactions to People and the World Around You

Your reactions to the people in your life can provide valu-able clues about the state of consciousness you are in. Are you feeling patient, accepting, and loving towards your spouse and children or annoyed, hostile, and distant? Do you experience the people around you as more of a blessing or a burden? What type of thoughts are you having about them?

Remember that the aggressive/defensive ego consciousness, because it both originates from and perpetuates a Universe of Fear, is a judgment machine, constantly spewing forth negative opinions, beliefs, and conclusions. These are about people and things it perceives as external causes of pain. Observe the thoughts you are having these days about significant partners, lovers, family members, people at work, the driver in front of you, and perhaps most critically about yourself. How critical and judgmental are those thoughts? Are you manufacturing ugly scenarios in your mind about the motives and behaviors of others?

Notice how other people are reacting to you. Do they appear trusting and relaxed around you or cautious and defensive? Are they willing to open up to you or just patronize you with what you want to hear? If the people in your life were interviewed privately by a third party and asked to be unreservedly honest about you, what would they say about what it *really* feels like to be around you?

Your physical environment and events that occur in it will be another mirror that is being held up for you to see. You will have an opportunity to understand and take responsibility for your state of consciousness. As simple a thing as cutting your finger, breaking a dish, getting into a minor car accident, or a heated and unsatisfying argument, will usually mean more than an unfortunate, freak occurrence. But to see the deeper meaning requires thoughtful, quiet introspection. Though it may seem foolish to turn this into an indisputable law, these kind of events—the apparently trivial, self-defeating or mundane annoyances and setbacks—are indicative of the presence of a hurtful or harmful energy and might indicate the aggressive/defensive ego is in control and in need of urgent attention. Again, it may seem foolish to push it to this extent, but in my experience, and in the experience of an associate of mine (who specializes in addictions and energy psychology), *minor misadventures and mishaps always indicate something amiss internally in your state of consciousness.*

Ideally of course, it would be a blessing to yourself and others if you could stop the destructive thoughts, feelings, and especially behaviors, of the aggressive/defensive ego consciousness before they even happen. This, though a very lofty aim, is the longer term objective of this healing work. This is a huge undertaking, so begin slowly. Here it is thus far:

- Slow down; volunteer for less; commit yourself to less; do less and slow down;
- Be even a little willing to face boredom and aloneness. This may be terrifying, but it (and

slowing down) give you time for more inner reflection; and,

- Put more attention on yourself—develop your "second order of attention" by watching how you try and dominate or manipulate your world and the people in it. Spend more time analyzing your character and motives, and *very little* or no time analyzing others.

The first specific step in reorganizing your ego is to examine your body's reactions to the world around you (which includes your attitudes and emotions). In the beginning you will probably only notice the destructive behavior in hind-sight, but that is where we all start from. As small as this awareness may seem, it is a wonderful beginning for taking responsibility for your state of consciousness.

Step 2: The Soft Touch — Treat Yourself with Compassion and Understanding When You Realize You Are Operating from your Aggressive/Defensive Ego Consciousness

The aggressive/defensive ego consciousness is never far from the surface. Like a flash of lightening, it can erupt suddenly in clear and peaceful skies. There does not come a point, even with diligent practice over many years, where we permanently transcend our aggressive/defensive ego; where we fully and forevermore leave it behind. Only a few of the world's most gifted and elevated spiritual masters may achieve this. Thinking or believing we have done so is typically an egotistical position of its own, bound to lead to more subtle and slick forms of self-deception, and the production of yet another ego-forged identity. And, if it is denied, it will hatch even shrewder plots to maintain its grip over consciousness.

This must be emphasized again: The goal of the Inner Family Model of Self-Healing, and working with the aggressive/defensive ego in particular, is not to eliminate, abolish, or destroy it, but rather to foster its healing. We, and certainly I, will be in an ego state of consciousness most hours of most days for a long time to come. In my case, even though I have been doing my own diligent inner work on the healing of my aggressive/defensive ego for the last decade of my life, I get gripped by it on a daily basis. I still occasionally spend days engulfed in the Universe of Fear. This is gradually less; however, even in those minutes, hours or rare, complete days when I am centered in my natural child consciousness/authentic self and my spiritual consciousness, I can be overtaken by the aggressive/defensive ego faster than the time it takes to switch off a light.

Do not take on the work of healing yourself and your ego to get to a promised land of uninterrupted and permanent bliss, love, and inner peace. If you do, when permanent bliss does not materialize (and any bliss is never permanent), your ego will use that "failure" to justify its righteousness. A more reasonable and promising alternative would be to be able to visit a peaceful state more often, and have the ability to return there *by choice*. Each time you could deepen your awareness of what it took to return and how you might remain there just a little bit longer. Inevitably and inescapably however, on this side of enlightenment, the aggressive/defensive ego consciousness will reassert itself. Once more, you will banish yourself to the cold and desolate Universe of Fear and struggle for survival.

Success is shifting out of the fear-based, survival-oriented ego consciousness one more time than we fall into it. Even if it is true that we will spend a good portion of our lives in suffering and fear; and though we may repeatedly return to becoming identified with (and run by) the aggressive/defensive ego consciousness, we must accept and forgive ourselves each time we allow this to happen.

It is only by feeling compassion for ourselves that we can incrementally advance. Being stuck in the aggressive/defensive ego equates to being terrified. Being afraid is nothing to be ashamed of; it is part of our humanity. Choosing compassion and love rather than fear is a critical step on the road to healing. Judging, criticizing, and attacking ourselves for being afraid will never work. Like having a gun on your night-table, *judgment never dispels fear, it compounds it, for judgment is just another form of fear.*

The aggressive/defensive ego consciousness will never be healed by increasing fear, self-attack, or self-criticism. Only the practice of self-acceptance and forgiveness can divert us from this march towards ever-deepening darkness. We must learn to treat ourselves gently, with compassion and understanding, when we discover we are operating out of our fear consciousness.

Paradoxically, and at the same time, we must also learn to be firm with ourselves. We must be vigilant so our fear does not transform itself into a host of cruel and destructive behaviors. This takes us to the next step in the healing of the ego.

Step 3: Personal Responsibility

Doing the work of personal healing can be compared to riding a bicycle down a narrow, ditch-lined country road. If we are to ride safely we must steer down the middle and avoid the ditches that are on either side. In the work of healing the aggressive/defensive ego, one ditch is being too rigid and demanding of yourself, and the other is being too self-forgiving and taking no responsibility. These ditches are at opposite ends of the same spectrum: condemning through perfectionism to ignoring through irresponsibility. The extremes are harmful.

The novice at personal transformation, thinking they have successfully avoided self-condemnation (one ditch), and believing they are progressing nicely down the road, may be stuck in being too self-forgiving (the other ditch). Similarly, at another moment, the opposite will be true—thinking they are not being too lenient with themselves but are trapped in destructive self-condemnation. It's tricky.

Addicts, in their twelve-step recovery from addictions, have described addictions as "cunning, baffling, and powerful", and so it is with the aggressive/defensive ego. I will discuss how this mind-set of aggression or defensiveness is never more than a thought or a feeling away. But, so too, is the spiritual consciousness—always only a thought or a feeling away.

Being gentle and forgiving with yourself when you realize that you have been operating out of your aggressive/defensive ego is an important and necessary step in your self-healing. It helps you avoid the ditch of being too hard on yourself. See if you can let go of any punishing and judgmental reactions (fearful responses) in the attempt to heal a consciousness that is already overloaded with blaming and fear. An ounce of self-love and acceptance is more helpful than anything else.

On the other hand there is a ditch to be aware of on the other side of the transformation road. To avoid it, you must be personally one hundred per cent accountable for your aggressive/defensive ego consciousness and all of its toxic and destructive ways. It is possible to be too easy on yourself in this regard. If you deny or deflect responsibility for its hurtful and harmful effects, you are acting shamelessly and unconscionably. Your refusal to be personally responsible, you might say accepting and forgiving yourself *too* much, enables its damaging reign of power and abuse to continue. No healing can occur until personal responsibility is taken for all actions that have resulted from your unhealed state.

You need to treat yourself compassionately when you know yourself to be operating from the aggressive/defensive ego, *and* you need to be firm in your willingness to be entirely accountable for it and anything harmful generated by it. No one, other than yourself, is responsible for the thoughts you generate. Neither is anyone or anything ultimately responsible for your feelings and reactions to the circumstances and people you encounter. And certainly, no one can decide for you if and when you are ready to take on this inner healing work. Steadfastly moving away from the aggressive/defensive ego into a more heart-and-spirit based consciousness stands on the principle that you are completely responsible for the state of your consciousness and the quality of your life.

To take on the healing of the ego we need to be willing to uncover aspects of our make up that are unflattering, humbling, painful, and difficult to accept. In this we must also hold ourselves one hundred per cent accountable for the darkness and negativity of this consciousness and all the consequences that come out from it. Whenever we are experiencing negativity of any kind, we must have the courage to gaze at ourselves in the mirror, wince if we must, but still ask: "What part am *I* playing in all of this? How is *my* aggressive/defensive ego involved in this?"

Step 4: Developing the Beginnings of an Independent/Aware Adult Consciousness by Cultivating A Neutral Inner Observer

This transformation is founded on the cultivation of the ability to actually have a choice over our state of consciousness and therefore our ways of being in the world. Cultivating this choice is the rudimentary beginnings of liberation from the tentacles of our habitual fear-based, survival-oriented mind-sets. It offers a quantum leap in the stages of our emotional and spiritual journey. Rather than being so completely identified by (and absorbed in) the aggressive/defensive ego consciousness—which was our *only* way of seeing and being—we can become autonomous. By creating a wise inner observer, we can use our aggressive/defensive ego when we deem it necessary and detach from it when it is not serving our purpose.

This model of self-healing, like a few other disciplines for psycho-spiritual growth, emphasizes the development of an internal witness or observer. This inner observer watches and evaluates our participation in the world and it especially watches our fear-based responses to life's circumstances. In the Inner Family Model of Self-Healing, this neutral observer equates to the creating of a new consciousness—the **independent/aware adult consciousness.** This is separate and distinct from the aggressive/defensive ego. The creation and development of this consciousness, that will exist independent of the fear-based, survival-oriented perspectives and actions of the aggressive/defensive ego will represent (within you) nothing less than a paradigm shift in how you view the world. This adult consciousness will be an aspect of your mind that holds back some of its attention from the externals of life so it can be put into the stance of being "in the world but not of it".

This is similar to other psycho/spiritual healing practices that cultivate this type of inner "third eye of self-awareness" regarding the real world. However, it is an eye of awareness about yourself and no one else. [It is a crucial step that goes beyond some meditative disciplines that only practice this level of awareness during disciplined meditation.] By creating this level of *self*-awareness and *self*-observation, through your independent/aware adult consciousness, you dramatically increase your level of responsibility *and* the possibility of success in your personal healing.

Why is creating this neutral self-observer such a crucial and necessary event? Because, for the first time in our psychological and spiritual evolution as conscious beings, there can be separation between the aggressive/defensive ego consciousness and who we are. Slowly, deliberately, we can become identified with something other than the set of learned responses which we employed to survive as a young person in a world that was adverse to our basic emotional and spiritual nature. A non-attached, clear, responsible, independent and aware adult consciousness can govern the conditioned reflexes of fear and survival. This new person can forge within their consciousness what I call a *sacred gap*—the equivalent of an inner space that lasts a precious few seconds of real time with which to observe their aggressive/defensive ego in action and to make another choice. The development of a neutral and responsible witness is indispensable to having these moments of choice.

Rather than unconsciously and automatically living as an aggressive/defensive ego, this new Inner Family member—the independent/aware adult consciousness—can *observe* the aggressive/defensive ego. It can develop into the ego's governor *and* as the genuine leader of the Inner Family. As this independent/aware adult consciousness gains in influence, in a manner that is both gentle and firm, it can give the aggressive/defensive ego a new role, that of an Inner Family *member* not an Inner Family *ruler*; a committee member not a unilateral decision-maker; a significant and valued inner voice not the voice that by virtue of aggression intimidates and controls all of the others.

This new independent/aware adult consciousness of the Inner Family is in charge of remembering that there are other options to those ways formerly dictated by the aggressive/defensive ego. This consciousness is charged with finding, evaluating, and using other options. This fledgling adult consciousness is the one who can develop the links to the natural child consciousness/authentic self and the spiritual consciousness.

With the demonstration of vulnerability, honesty, and humility (previously avoided and unwanted) we, as independent/aware adults, can become responsible for the hurtful and harmful things that we have perpetrated on ourselves, the people in our lives, and the world. As we grow into this new adult, we often feel impelled to apologize for (and clean up) the messes that we have left in our wake. This is the next step in healing the ego and transforming your life.

Step 5: Admission, Responsibility, and Apology

It is easy to see why so few of us want to be conscious, maturing adults, responsible for the past, present, and future workings of our aggressive/defensive egos. As we free ourselves from total identification with this consciousness, and take personal responsibility for what it has done to ourselves and others, the picture that we gaze at in the mirror will look quite different from the public faces and presentations we have shown the world. Initially we may look so *un*appealing that we can easily understand our reasons for having hidden "ourselves" in the first place.

We have done whatever we needed to do to survive. Countless times we have denied the fear that we have been experiencing and displaced it, in one hurtful or harmful way or another, onto ourselves or others. We have judged everyone, privately and arrogantly forming and hardening beliefs, opinions, and generalizations about them. We have used these to make ourselves right and them wrong; to make ourselves good and them bad; to see ourselves as innocent and them as guilty. We have manufactured ego-forged identities and selfishly used power and control to subjugate others to the tyranny of our aggressive/defensive egos. In our twisted search for safety, love, and being valued, we have been cunning and manipulative, deceptive and antagonistic, exploitive and avaricious. Our ways of conducting ourselves have made others, especially those who are nearest and dearest to us, more afraid.

In what may be our most aggressive act of all, we have become perpetrators of the formation and entrenchment of aggressive/defensive egos of the next generation. We have added to the fear and aggression that is already swallowing up and destroying humankind. We have manipulated others to further our own ends; to try and get "them" to fill the gaping holes in the foundation of our emotional and spiritual self-worth. Our ego-forged selves, in their ravenous hunger for indirect sources of security and protection, have consumed environmental resources, material goods, other people (in relationships), and attacked adversaries like wild animals devouring their prey. And yet, even after having gnawed the last meat off their bones, we have found no appeasement for our insatiable appetites and no relief from our fear.

If we are to heal our aggressive/defensive ego we must bring the hurtful and harmful thoughts, feelings, words, and actions it has generated to some kind of moral and public reckoning. This clean-up operation begins with the step of admission.

It takes tremendous courage and strength of character to face the people whom we have hurt and used and admit how we have made things hard or worse for them. As we recover a connection with lost Inner Family members, specifically our natural child consciousness/authentic self and our spiritual consciousness, we will be guided as to how and with whom we are to conduct these personal acts of atonement. For instance, it may become clear that we must approach one particular person face to face offering some form of reparation. Or, we may be guided to simply envision the faces of our victims, admit and take responsibility for our hurtful or harmful ways, and ask for forgiveness. It is possible we will be led to make amends to specific people, or to a large group of people i.e. a particular race, religion, or nationality, or men or women, by taking concrete actions to serve and benefit that group.

Sometimes we may think it is too embarrassing to admit our wrongdoing to the people we have mentally, emotionally, physically, or spiritually harmed. In these circumstances we must examine our reluctance. This may be a gambit of the aggressive/defensive ego trying to hide and avoid responsibility. We must *closely* self-examine to determine if we are avoiding this hard, humbling, and self-deprecating step out of an unwillingness to be responsible for our past behavior. It is also possible, in my view, that this lack of willingness to approach those we have harmed comes out of a love and compassion for ourselves. This expresses itself in our decision to release ourselves from the obligation to approach the other person. [This is not the view presented in twelve-step addictions recovery programs. Here, I am presenting my own experience and beliefs.]

Sometimes, resurrecting the old pain and hurt we caused others may not be in the best interests of the injured party. In some rare circumstances the most responsible course may be to refrain from bringing up past wrong-doing. This is delicate and requires a very deep commitment to personal honesty.

Even with all this, a significant step in our healing and trans-formation is taken when we share our "crimes against humanity" in some public forum. "Going public" may be an acknowledgment of our misdeeds to a neutral and compassionate third party—a minister, a therapist, a sponsor, a spiritual mentor. Other forms may be letters carefully crafted, whether sent or not; entries in a private diary or journal; or a petition or prayer of admission and the request for forgiveness in our private relationship with our God. This issue of making amends is very complex. For a very detailed examination of amends for harms done, Richard Clark's book *Addictions & Spiritual Transformation* (Trafford Publishers) is a good guide.

Critical to the clean-up operation of the aggressive/defensive ego are the steps of admission, taking personal responsibility, and the repairing of harms done, along with the earnest determination to learn from our mistakes and misdeeds. How we go about doing this is not as important as making sure that it is done, and is done particular to each person that was harmed. Our Inner Family, led by the spiritual consciousness, will guide us to the right action.

An Example of My Own Damaging Aggressive/Defensive Ego

This healing work is forever humbling. Here is an example from my own life; of becoming identified with my aggressive/defensive ego consciousness and the significant pain and hardship I caused others.

First, a bit of family history: My father lost his mother when he was six years old. She was suffering from an infected tooth (in the early 1920s) and she went to see the person most approximating a dentist in the tiny Russian community in which she lived. She died there right on the spot from complications associated with the anesthesia. My mother's father, again unexpectedly, died in her arms from a massive heart attack when she was a young teenager. Both of my parents' were no doubt deeply affected by these deaths. Subsequent to these deaths, their physical and emotional survival depended on a strong extended family and step-parents.

For myself, in some measure as a child but more insistently as a teenager, I experienced being forced by my parents to attend every social function of my extended family. I had to be on my best behavior when I went, and was pushed into feeling "close" to all my uncles, aunts, cousins, and grandparents. I had no understanding of it at the time. Along with intense emotional reactions, my aggressive/defensive ego vehemently resisted both the compulsory involvement *and* demonstrating forced affection for my extended family.

Because of this dynamic, throughout my twenties and well into my thirties, I went into exile from my family. I moved away, developed a life of my own with my wife, and would not attend any functions that involved my extended family. This included staying away from significant events in the lives of childhood friends, especially if those occasions took me back to my home town. I never explained my abrupt and prolonged withdrawal to any of the people involved. If asked why I hadn't attended I would routinely use my work demands as an excuse or some other ambiguous (invented) half-truth, or I'd out-right lie. On those *rare* occasions when my absence was discussed I could sense the confusion my behavior was causing. Throughout those years I was conspicuous by my absence. I knew that my family and friends were, at the very least, perplexed by my anti-social behavior and that some felt quite disappointed, hurt and upset.

It was during a course of intense inner work in my late thirties that I came to realize the deeply buried emotional pain I was carrying from my childhood and adolescence. I saw how these unexamined, unhealed feelings had carved up and damaged almost all of my relationships, especially those with people whom I had (at one time) felt most vulnerable or needy. I created a list of people I had harmed. This list was a lengthy one and it was difficult and painful to see all the names on it. These included all the relatives and friends whom I had deserted and severed my connection with years before.

I still wince as I recall the discovery of these realizations and my personal responsibility for the toxic and destructive ways in which I (my aggressive/defensive ego) had acted towards the people closest to me. I came to admit to myself that these human beings were being punished for nothing more than being related to me. I saw that I had turned my un-owned emotional pain and fear into a punishing avoidance against them. My love and acceptance of the newer people in my life was more generous and vastly more enduring than for those people who knew me from my childhood and adolescence.

In hearing from my natural child consciousness/authentic self and my spiritual consciousness, I was gently guided to start attending extended-family functions, no matter where they were held or what the expense. I was entirely willing, if it felt right at the time, to sit down with any family member, explain what the real truths were behind my self-imposed exile, and take complete responsibility for my behavior. I accepted these firm but loving directives from my emotional and spiritual Inner Family members and was fully prepared to carry them out. However, this was never necessary.

Upon returning to my extended family, accompanied by my wife and little boys, I was greeted by such an immediate and unconditional embrace and celebration that it was as if I had never left. My return was enough for them. In deciding that in this situation I needed to say nothing, I carefully examined myself to see if I was just avoiding awkward and potentially embarrassing conversations about my hurtful absence. However, my child consciousness consistently informed me that nothing more needed to be said.

These realizations and experiences were very enlightening. Having accumulated and hardened my judgments, opinions, criticisms, and conclusions of my parents and extended family for over two decades (while perceiving myself to be a kind and loving person), I (my aggressive/defensive ego) had become tenaciously attached to being right! What a humbling and liberating realization it was to discover that those that I had judged and rejected had been loving me all along; that the quality and durability of their love for me was considerably higher than mine for them.

At every new occasion that my extended family gathers I make a sincere effort to attend. We share our love and affection for each other. I still wonder, usually *enroute*, if I need to say anything to anybody to do my own clean-up work. I also wonder if I need to seek forgiveness. What happens, though, is that upon showing up, I just get too busy having a good time. Some wise person once said that 80% of friendship is just consistently showing up. My experience of my extended family is that consistently showing up has been 100% of what was needed for me to feel safe, loved and valued by them, and for them to feel respected and loved by me.

A Client's Clean-Up Operation

Samantha came to see me towards the end of yet another love-relationship which was concluding in disappointment and heartache. Now in her mid-forties, she had been involved in five or six primary relationships over the past twenty years, all of which lasted between one and three years. Though clear at the beginning of therapy that she was attracting people who could not ever commit to her, Samantha came to her first surprising realization during her healing work: she, herself, could not and had not committed to any of her partners, either. As our work together went deeper, Samantha came to see herself as a romance and relationship addict.

What is a romance and relationship addiction? Like all addictions, romance and/or relationship addiction are attempts by the aggressive/defensive ego consciousness to find something external that will make it feel safe, loved, and valued. In the case of this particular addiction it is the excitement and the passion which accompany "falling in love" which acts as a mood and reality altering drug for the fragile ego. New romantic relationships are a mood-altering experience.

Because the aggressive/defensive ego consciousness knows nothing about what authentic love is, a person like Samantha, suffering from a love addiction, doesn't really experience any love for the unique self of the other person. In reality, this is more a way of escaping her unremitting emotional pain and fear. Samantha's "beloved partner" is actually more a supplier (or a supply) of mood altering experiences than a unique self in their own right. This makes Samantha's partners interchangeable and dispensable. In relationship, romance, or sex addiction people become disposable.

What is crucial and mandatory is the need to find the narcotic that "love" delivers. This was the fix Samantha's aggressive/defensive ego was dependent on for its survival: the adrenalin that comes from new "love and romance". One of the most common distinguishing traits of ego-based love is that the beloved tends to be idealized and adored as long as the high lasts, but once it wanes the partner becomes the permanently fallen disposable angel.

Upon acknowledging the ways that her aggressive/defensive ego consciousness had operated in her primary relationships, Samantha could at last truly understand what had been happening in her love life. She realized why all her relationships did not, and could not, last: they arrived with all of the splendor of a comet and departed just as quickly.

Here, however, it is the nature, depth, and quality of Samantha's ego clean-up operation that I want to emphasize: She began by methodically seeking out *every one* of her former partners and asking them if she could pay them a visit. To be very thorough she included a person for whom she had experienced a romantic infatuation, who was not even of her sexual orientation, and the minister of her church whom she had idealized and romantically fantasized about. In discussing the extraordinary lengths she had gone to in twisting these people to fit her ego's romantic needs, Samantha laughingly said: "Where there was a will, there was a way!"

Having received their permission to meet with her, she told all of her former partners that she had never been committed to them and had not loved them for who they actually were. She admitted that she was entirely and completely accountable for this. She informed them that she did not know how to love without using addiction and manipulation to do so. Samantha admitted that real intimacy—the ability to deeply connect to another without turning them into a drug-like fix—was too frightening for her and considerably beyond her grasp during the time of her relationship with these people. She apologized fully to each of her former partners and asked for their forgiveness. Lastly, she let them know that her ways of operating in relationships had everything to do with her unhealed emotional pain and fear from her early life in her family of origin and declared she would do whatever it took to get to the bottom of this.

Samantha did get to the bottom of her unhealed emotional pain and fear and the aggressive/defensive ego consciousness which had been erected on top of it. For the past nine years she has been in a healthy intimate, committed, and monogamous relationship.

Step 6: Coming to Know the Story of Your Aggressive /Defensive Ego

Acknowledging the suffering caused by your aggressive/defensive ego consciousness *and cleaning it up,* even if it is done after the pain and hardship have been inflicted on others, is effective healing work at any time. But there is more you can do to heal your aggressive/defensive ego consciousness than take responsibility for how you have acted in the past. There is more you can do than just clean up the physical, mental, emotional, or spiritual havoc or damage you have caused. And, there are preventative measures to lessen the likelihood you are going to act in these hurtful ways again.

I have defined a shift as having occurred when you can't go back to the old ways of operating even if you want to. In essence that is what the remainder of this book will address—the inner work to heal your aggressive/defensive ego in such a fundamental way that a permanent and lasting shift in your state of consciousness will occur.

This path will lead you deeper into the make up and workings of this consciousness than you have gone to this point. To do this, you will be asked to explore the story of your ego consciousness and the original emotional pain and fear which gave birth to it. With the participation and aid of another Inner Family member—the adaptive child consciousness, this buried emotional pain and fear can be shown to you. It is these early experiences of emotional pain and fear that constitute the original fire. You will then be able to do more than put out the brush fires continually ignited and inflamed by your aggressive/defensive ego.

This step, of coming to know the real and actual events associated with the birth of your aggressive/defensive ego consciousness, is so important that I have devoted the entire next chapter to it. In it you will learn how to know and understand this Inner Family member as well (and maybe better than) anyone you have ever met.

Step 7: Reliance On Other Inner Family Members

Fortunately, who you are is much more than your aggressive/defensive ego. Who you are is also (a) a natural child consciousness/authentic self and (b) a spiritual consciousness. These two other consciousnesses also live within, patiently waiting for the day when you awaken from your long and tormented slumber in the Universe of Fear and become motivated enough to begin the process of self-healing.

Upon disentangling yourself from the clutches of your aggressive/defensive ego you will have sustainable access to these other two consciousnesses. Access to them opens up the possibility of a whole new world.

How and why is this so? Instead of being survival-oriented and fear-based (living out of your aggressive/defensive ego consciousness) you can live out of your two love-based consciousnesses—*the natural child consciousness/authentic self and the spiritual consciousness*. These are life-oriented, not survival-oriented, Inner Family members and can become your guides to the perception and experience of a different reality. If you can learn to identify yourself with them you can transform your life.

Being able to live out of these life-oriented, love-based consciousnesses at will is the equivalent of being able to switch channels on your inner television. Reflect for a moment that you may have lived your entire life (or at least most of it) being completely unaware there are other channels available with which to perceive and experience life. Imagine being skilled at switching from the Survival and Fear Channel to the Authentic Love Channel. Imagine also that you can not merely see, but experience first-hand that the love channels provide far greater safety, clarity, sanity, and peace than you have ever known!

Perhaps for a time your deeply entrenched ego-based thinking will try to convince you that these "new channels" cannot be
lasting; that you cannot remain tuned into the Authentic Love
Channel permanently and indefinitely.

Perhaps in the initial stages of your journey into self-healing
that is true; but so what? Wouldn't living with just a little less fear, a
little less destructiveness, a little more love be a good start? Might
not these loved-based consciousnesses be a nice place to visit, and
visit more and more often? Might they not give any poor adult,
hopelessly identified and ensnared by the aggressive/defensive ego
consciousness a much needed vacation from their anger and
defensiveness? We take vacations from the pressures of our jobs
each year—why not take a vacation from our aggression and fear a
few minutes each day?

Your access to the natural child consciousness/authentic self
and spiritual consciousness (and being both willing and able to be led
by these Inner Family members) is the last and most powerful
requirement for healing. In many ways, all of the other steps lead up
to this one.

Chapter VII

"As we try to practice mindfulness, we see that the Ego does not cease to exist - it simply ceases to tyrannize us or to offer the only version of experience available."
Ram Dass, from *Still Here*

The Actual Work Of Healing
The Aggressive/Defensive Ego

Getting To Know Your Ego

Until now I have described the characteristics, features, and traits of the aggressive/defensive ego consciousness in extremely general terms; painting it with the largest possible brush strokes. I wanted you to (a) get a sense of what I mean by an ego consciousness; and (b), to see if you could notice any semblance of it within yourself. If you have read this far, I can safely assume that you are interested in the longer term and deeper work of healing this consciousness. It is now time to move from an understanding of the ego consciousness in general to an understanding of the make up and workings of your aggressive/defensive ego in particular; to understand as much as possible about your ego's unique "personality".

True, this is not a straightforward venture. This particular Inner Family member is known for its complexity and contradictoriness. It has been described by four adjectives: cunning, baffling, powerful, and patient. It can present itself in compulsive opposites: a compulsive drive to be the best or a compulsive need to fail, and it can switch in a matter of moments. As an ego-controlled adult you may present yourself to some people as loud, bold, or attention seeking; yet twenty minutes later you may present yourself to others as timid, solicitous, or self-effacing. Getting to know your aggressive/defensive ego will require the skill and deftness of seeing yourself *without distortion* in a hall of warped mirrors. Regardless of this, I believe it is well worth the effort.

How do you get to know this consciousness? The same way

you came to know any significant person in your life. You probably asked a lot of questions about the life of the other person and listened to the answers. You discussed things and got a sense of their history and background; their ways of thinking, feeling, and expressing themselves; their priorities and core values, and their deepest fears and highest hopes. You spent a lot of time with them and watched them in action with a wide assortment of different people in varying situations and circumstances. You noticed how they conducted themselves. In these ways, over time, and by devoting time to the relationship with them, you established what you believed to be a reliable profile of the other person. In exactly these same ways you will come to know your aggressive/defensive ego consciousness.

The more time and effort you put into this relationship the better you will know yourself. This is why I recommend (earlier in the book) to slow down.

An Exercise in Becoming your Aggressive/Defensive Ego and Letting it Tell Its Story

How do you begin the process of getting to know the particular nature and identity of your aggressive/defensive ego consciousness? This Inner Family member, one that has also been described as your fear consciousness, is usually not far away from the surface of your life. Any of the so called "negative" feelings i.e.: anxiety, stress, worry, agitation, jealousy, envy, blaming, impatience, anger, or hurt, have a fear consciousness at their base. Anytime you notice that you are judging or finding fault with someone or something, whether you declare this openly or not (whether you realize it or not) you are operating from a fear-based consciousness. Some of us spend so much of our lives in an aggressive or fear-based emotional state that a better question might be: "When am I *not* operating from my aggressive/defensive ego?" In any event, for most people, this Inner Family member tends to be the easiest one to find within themselves.

What follows is an exercise which asks you to hand yourself over and become your aggressive/defensive ego consciousness, and thereby let it *start* to tell its story. More value tends to be derived from the exercise if you can do this in the presence of a therapist or confidante (someone with whom you feel safe and will not be judged). This other person will simply listen to your disclosure. You can also effectively give yourself over to this Inner Family member on your own, become it, and let it take you spontaneously and deeply into its private and often tortured realms.

Here is one of the simplest and most powerful ways: In a quiet, private room, place two chairs close together and facing each other. If you are doing this exercise with another person watching, place their chair, a third one, in a corner of the room out of your field of vision.

Sit in one of the two chairs that face each other. During this exercise, this particular seat will be reserved for you as the independent/aware adult consciousness. As long as you are seated in this particular seat you are **not** your aggressive/defensive ego consciousness, but rather a witness or observer to it. Using all the knowledge and information you have gained about it from this book, and including your own intuitive understanding and emotional and spiritual insight, imagine what your aggressive/defensive ego consciousness might look like if you were to give it a physical and symbolic form. In other words, using your own creative visualization, allow an image, a picture, or a symbolic representation to come to you that would be a snap shot of your present day aggressive/defensive ego consciousness. What does it look like?

Don't force anything to happen. Just take what you get. Feel what you feel. Let yourself go and just see what image or images flash before you. What or whom do you see in the chair before you? Trust your first, most immediate impression. If no image or symbol embodying your aggressive/defensive ego comes to you, simply let that be and proceed with the exercise anyway.

I do not wish to unduly influence your own personal creative visualization. If you feel it might be helpful, and would like a little prompting, in the next paragraph I will give you examples of what other people have perceived when they invited their aggressive/defensive egos to appear before them. On many occasions I have known people who have initially encountered a void and picked up no concrete image or picture of their aggressive/defensive ego consciousness, only to have one come to them later which proved both rich and relevant. To that end, if you don't want to know other peoples' portrayals of their aggressive/defensive egos, just skip the list that follows. On the other hand, for those of you who would like to take a bit of a lead from others, you're welcome to consult the depictions below to see if any of these portrayals might resonate with you.

Some of the representations of their aggressive/defensive egos that clients and seminar participants have envisioned include:

- a battle-weary knight or guard compulsively patrolling a castle wall;
- a school-marm, her hands on her hips, scolding one or all of her students;
- a bloody and crazed warrior in the middle of a battlefield;
- a delicate, attractive but poisonous flower;
- a brilliant, flamboyant university professor, pontificating about life;
- a resistant, terrified sheep being led to slaughter;
- a stand up, cardboard figure of a gorgeous and seductive siren;
- a Moses-like figure coming down from Mount Sinai with the Ten Commandments;
- an immaculately dressed president of a company;
- a volcano;
- a mouse with fangs;
- a general who plots military strategy on the eve of battle;
- a depleted and resentful Mother Nature;
- the Mad Hatter from *Alice In Wonderland* (Lewis Carroll);
- Darth Vader from the movie *Star Wars* (Lucas Films);
- a lonesome cowboy riding out into the sunset (and a host of other archetypal figures from movies, fables and popular literature); and,
- various known celebrities and political figures.

Back to the exercise: Now regardless of whether you have an image or not, give yourself over to this depiction of your aggressive/defensive ego consciousness. Get up from your adult-consciousness' seat and take the chair opposite or intuitively take another location in the room—one which you sense would be a position which this ego would find familiar and in keeping with its stature or status. For example, as an aggressive ego, you may insist on standing while the adult consciousness sits so as to present yourself as more powerful; or, you may wish to take centre stage by choosing a central position in the room; or, you may elect to stand near the door so that a speedy or stealthy exit can be made.

You may want to adjust the furniture or employ any objects in the room to serve as props for the aggressive (fearful) character you are about to portray. For instance, you may want to use a ruler as an imaginary wooden pointer in your hand; a cushion as a throne; a pen as a sword. The room becomes an appropriate backdrop for your aggressive/defensive ego's imminent performance. Regardless of how silly or ridiculous you may initially feel, let yourself be "channeled" into a role, and create a scene which gives your ego the kind of commanding or dominating (or subservient) presence it might enjoy.

Once you've done this give your physical body over to this Inner Family member. Let your aggressive/defensive ego shape, sculpt, or hold your body in such a way that your body becomes an actual expression of this consciousness. Another way of saying this is physically notice the changes in your body as you surrender to your ego consciousness. To illustrate: clients regularly report that their body will tighten and stiffen, a scowl will often come over their face, their eyes will narrow, their jaw will harden, their teeth will feel like they are gnashing. I have often witnessed a client's face take on the hollow features of a mask. People doing this exercise may initially experience the sudden emergence of bodily discomfort, aches, physical pain, or nausea. If you feel overwhelmed that your body is taking on more than it can handle, *stop* and return to this exercise sometime later. If you can persist through these challenges (from my experience, they rarely last more than a few minutes), keep letting your body become the body of your aggressive/defensive ego.

Once you are as physically and psychologically identified as you can be with this ego presence, then allow yourself to begin speaking in the voice of your aggressive/defensive ego. Two very useful opening sets of statements, which rarely fail to jump start the process, are:

> "My name is Ego. I am <u>insert your own name's</u> aggres-
> sive/defensive ego. I have learned how to survive life and love. This
> is what I'd like you to know about me today..."
> "My name is Ego. I am the aggressive/defensive ego con-

sciousness of this Inner Family. And this is what I'd like to say today..."

Again, just keep letting go (spontaneously surrender to whatever comes up) and see what happens. Perhaps nothing will happen; perhaps you will hear from another splintered-off ego-based voice which will say something like: "This is nuts!" or, "If I'm not careful, this could be really embarrassing!" or, "How do I know if I'm not just making the whole thing up?" Notice these voices but see if you can just bracket them off and stay as much in the character of your ego as you possibly can.

If you are doing this work with some trusted companion, have the other person prompt you from time to time with open-ended questions. These will keep you, as your aggressive/defensive ego, "on track". Here is a sampling of a few questions to keep you in the process:

- Aggressive/defensive ego, what's it really like to be you?
- What's it been like to be you all these years?"
- Aggressive/defensive ego, what's one thing that you'd rather not tell us about yourself?
- If you had only three words to describe the three feelings or states that you experience most often as *name's* aggressive/defensive ego, or the ego of this Inner Family, which three would they be? Tell me about them, please.
- Aggressive/defensive ego, what are you most afraid of or concerned about these days?
- Aggressive/defensive ego, what is your principle role or job description in *name's* Inner Family?

If your aggressive/defensive ego consciousness does start opening up, you might want to try slightly more probing questions that delve into its history. You may give these questions to your support person, ask them aloud yourself, or respond on paper, writing as this Inner Family member. Here are a few that may fit nicely:

- "Aggressive/defensive ego, when were you born in _name's_ life?"

- "Why were you born?"
- "How have you helped _name_ or this Inner Family survive life?"
- "How have you helped _name_ or this Inner Family survive love?"
- "Ego, talk to me about your pain or hurts or disappointments."
- "How do you feel about the inner child, the adult consciousness, or the spiritual consciousness of this Inner Family?"
- "What do you most need from your Inner Family?

When you are ready to stop the exercise, conclude by returning to your original chair, sit there for a few minutes (as the adult consciousness), and absorb the experience. Debrief with your support person; or write down at this point or sometime soon, all of the impressions and experiences you had as your aggressive/defensive ego.

The purpose of this exercise, and all the work on healing your aggressive/defensive ego, is to make it safe for this consciousness to start to tell its story to you. As its story unfolds, you will begin to get a sense of the deeply buried emotional pain and fear which have been instrumental in the formation of this part of you. Accessing these feelings and experiences, difficult and painful as that may be, is to make great progress. Instead of unconsciously acting them out, you now, as a fledgling independent/aware adult, become uncontrolled by your aggressive/defensive ego. Furthermore, you can start forming a non-adversarial relationship with it, one in which mutual understanding and support can develop.

Remember, from earlier chapters, the aggressive/defensive ego is typically denied, shunned, and perceived as the darkest and ugliest member of the Inner Family, because it is capable of such hurtful, destructive, and vicious thoughts and acts. Yet, if you truly want to heal yourself, it is important you perceive it as a part of you. This Inner Family member, like all the others, is in aching need of the experience of safety, love, and being valued. In the final analysis, you will be the one to help your aggressive/defensive ego feel like an included, respected, and esteemed member of your Inner Family.

The Written Work

Several of the techniques for healing your relationship with yourself will require a little bit of writing on your part. Before I explain these exercises, I recommend that you buy yourself a particular kind of pen. This is a four-colored pen with blue, black, red and green ink cartridges. Or, if you prefer, buy four different colored pens. Allow each of the four primary Inner Family members: (a) the aggressive/defensive ego consciousness; (b) the child consciousness (both natural and adaptive); (c) the fledgling independent/aware adult consciousness; and, (d) the spiritual consciousness to choose the color they prefer which will always be "their color" in any writing assignments.

For illustrative purposes, let's say that after a quick process of consultation your aggressive/defensive ego consciousness has chosen red ink; you, the fledgling, independent/aware adult consciousness, black ink; the child consciousness (be it natural or adaptive child), green; and, the spiritual consciousness, blue.

For writing assignments, writing as the child consciousness (be it natural or adaptive) is always done with your *non-dominant* hand. Writing as any other Inner Family member is done with your dominant hand.

A. Interviewing Your Aggressive /Defensive Ego

Another productive way of getting to know the nature and identity of your own aggressive/defensive ego consciousness is by giving yourself over to it in writing. Dialoguing with your ego consciousness on paper, or otherwise conducting an interview with this Inner Family member in which you ask some key, specific questions, can yield a great deal of understanding and enlightenment about it.

Before you begin this, get as clear a sense as possible of your interview subject. In having read this book to this point, and done a bit of the suggested inner work, you have probably already formed some sense of your own aggressive/defensive ego. You may already have had thoughts, feelings, physical sensations, and memories which you have identified as originating from it. You may also have been visited by a spontaneous image, picture, or visualization of what this consciousness might look like.

Take a minute now to reflect on what have you come to

know about your own particular aggressive/defensive ego thus far. Your ego may be tempted to reflect on the dynamics of someone else's aggressive/defensive ego (which it is quite good at!). At times it is quite gifted at recognizing what's "wrong" with others. Resist this and reflect on yourself. Consider what else you would like to know about it. What topics or specific incidents would you like to discuss with it? What matters would you like to address? What questions do you have for this Inner Family member so that you can come to know it better?

The first interview I suggest be between your aggressive/defensive ego consciousness and "you"—the fledgling, independent/aware adult consciousness. What follows is a list of some key questions to ask your ego. To put this into practice, if you are using the same ink-color associations as above, write down the first question from the list below: "Aggressive/defensive ego consciousness, who or what are you?" in black ink. Then change your ink color to red and write your response to this question from the perspective of your aggressive/defensive ego. *Write as spontaneously and freely as you can.*

Don't censor anything, especially material that you may not immediately understand or like, consider irrelevant, or even be startled by. Please let your ego consciousness write *anything* down on paper that it wants to in response to any question you ask it. Accept whatever answer you receive. Then do the same thing, using as many of the following questions as you sense might be useful and informative:

1. "Aggressive/defensive ego consciousness, who or what are you?"
2. "When were you born in my life?"
3. "Why were you born?"
4. "What past hurts or trauma brought you into being?
5. "What were your earliest beginnings?"
6. "What people, events, or circumstances played a role in making you what you are today?"
7. "How did your entire world become fear-based and survival-oriented?"
8. "What have you done to help me survive?"
9. "What are your deepest beliefs?"
10. "What are your biggest fears and worries?"

11. "What are you most sensitive about?"
12. "What are your unique features, traits and characteristics?" (i.e. has your ego specialized in aggressiveness or defensiveness? winning or losing? trying to be larger than life or hardly visible?)
13. "What are some of the masks you have used?"
14. "What public faces and roles have you identified me with?"
15. "How have you shielded the natural child consciousness/authentic self from hurt or harm from others?"
16. "How and when have you used external power and control over others as a method of indirectly seeking safety, love, and a sense of being valued?"
17. "What personal successes and failures have you identified me with so that we use these to define who we are?"

In this question and answer interview, you (the fledgling independent/aware adult) may recall other incidents and circumstances that you now realize were orchestrated by your aggressive/defensive ego. It is also okay to ask your ego a question about those or anything else that comes to mind. [Remember: accept whatever answers you receive and to switch ink colors as you switch roles.]

And the most important questions of all:
• *"What can I (the newly independent/aware adult consciousness) do to help you heal your pain?"*
• *"How can I support you in ways that no one ever has?"*
• *"How can we become committed partners to each other and to this Inner Family?"*

B. Writing Spontaneous Letters from your Aggressive/Defensive Ego

Another often surprisingly easy and effective way of getting to know the particular nature of your ego consciousness (and its personal story) is to become this Inner Family member and write spontaneous, free-flowing open letters using the first person pronoun "I". For example: "I am your aggressive/defensive ego consciousness and this is my story...".

I feel honored to present a few sample letters from clients

and seminar participants. These letters can offer you an inside glimpse into the immensely bewildering and sabotaging behavior this consciousness can wreak and the dedication to inner work that's required to heal it.

Most of the letters I have chosen are on the theme of relationships, particularly the primary love relationship. I have found no other area of inquiry which shows us the workings of the aggressive/defensive ego consciousness as starkly and powerfully as love relationships. Also, for many of us, there is no area of life more baffling, frustrating, and deeply painful as intimate relationships.

Though we may have considerable intelligence and good will, and even consciously intend to deliberately *not* recreate past mistakes, this often fails to be enough to prevent disaster. Yet coming to know the nature and dynamics of our aggressive/defensive ego consciousness, and uncovering the emotional pain and fear underneath it, can produce a transformational shift in your ability to give and receive love in new ways that are healthy and exciting.

Here are several examples of where the healing work began—in love lives that were run and sometimes ruined by a dominating and controlling aggressive/defensive ego. These letters show that **nothing on earth frightens this consciousness more than love**.

*

Amanda, aged 47, "received" this letter from her aggressive/defensive ego on the theme of "Loving, Trusting, and Committing to a Man". This is an ego, which, as she put it to me, "wasn't born yesterday, baby!"

"I am the aggressive/defensive ego consciousness in this Inner Family and here's what I have to say about loving, trusting, and committing to a man - NO FUCKING WAY!! Trust is something someone made up to get you where they want you. Love is a fairy tale—no happy ending though. The only person you can depend on completely is yourself. Everyone is in it for themselves and if they tell you otherwise, they are lying!

"Men enjoy you for their own pleasures. Sex, comfort, food—other than that, they can get what they need from their buddies. It is too risky to invest your time and energy on something that will not last and end up feeling lousy. Starts off with excitement,

novelty, feelings of euphoria and quickly becomes standard and routine, requiring minimal participation. Love, trust, commitment— BULLSHIT! Give me what I want and I'll tell you that I love you if you want me to. You won't be valued for WHO you are but WHAT you do. Look pretty, smell pretty, deliver the sex on command and do not talk back. Don't challenge any ideas. [Men see...] women as typically foolish creatures, flighty at best. No brain capacity.

"It is ridiculous to think you can actually find someone who is genuinely loving, trusting and committed to you. Only in the movies, baby! You have to give to get and eventually you'll be doing all the giving and getting nothing in return. Don't dare complain about it either or you'll be punished for that."

*

An extremely competent, successful, and well-liked businesswoman, Judy's track record in love was, according to her, "not resume material". Her first deep insights into why her love relationships had turned out the way they had came from this letter:

"I am the aggressive/defensive ego of this Inner Family and I have learned how to survive life and love by distancing myself from others. I would get hurt physically and emotionally if I got too close.

"I've learned to be fun, funny, smart, and accomplished. I can do anything I set out to do—and I've done a lot. I am good at a lot of things to a certain level, and then I move on for a new experience. I like to say I'm "experiential". I'm afraid to go too deeply into one thing or one person because that may bring failure at some point. I have a lot of friends but don't let them get too close. They may find out that I'm not so likeable when they get to know the real me—the girl who was always in trouble and hated by her family. Because if a person's family hates them, then they must really be a bad person.

"I am also reactive. I am controlling. I can be business-like and I can be seductive and manipulative.

"On the other hand, it's been a lot of fun to be me and a ton of hard work. I have lots of successes in work and sports, yet have not had a successful long-term committed, intimate, monogamous relationship with a member of the opposite sex. Ever. And I've even been married!

"I've been perpetually exhausted on this treadmill."

*

Now in her late 30s, Bonnie had only known one repeating pattern in her love relationships: all of them were short-term, intense, sexually passionate, dramatic, and invariably explosive relationships with unavailable men. Here is a short excerpt from the earliest of her aggressive/defensive ego's letters:

"I came into existence about the time little Bonnie (her inner child) *started to argue back with her father, about the time when she was four or five. She was no longer his cute little girl. Instead she yelled back at him. Then he would hit her and make her feel so, so ashamed.*

"I learned to survive love and life by trying to be invisible and say nothing like my mother or be angry, yelling and hysterical like my father. I am the combination of their two egos."

*

Joy experienced very little pleasure and happiness in her history with men. One uncanny, incredibly painful pattern she kept repeating was that all of the men with whom she became involved, including her husband, were, in due course, unfaithful in their relationship with her. Though initially overcome by profound helplessness and frustration, the letter from her ego (below) gave her a sense, for the first time ever, of her part in her selection of partners. It showed her that her experiences with men had a lot to do with her relationship with herself.

"I am Joy's aggressive/defensive ego, and I have learned how to survive life and love by stopping her fruitless search for lasting love. I appeared early in her life, just after her third birthday. It was about that time when her parents decided that she was nowhere near as good a child as her brother. I taught her to be cunning and avoid their wrath as best she could. I continued to protect her from getting too close to anyone throughout her life. Occasionally she ignored me, but she usually paid for that in the end.

"By the time she was twenty-five I was finally getting through to her that she was not loveable and she could give up

looking for it. Sadly I let my guard down for an instant that summer and John somehow snuck in and got her thinking she was loveable. Well she was so convinced that he was sincere that she married him, but eventually she found out I was right all along.

"Imagine the triumph I felt when he admitted a couple years later that his feelings had changed! 'You were just a holiday romance!', I crowed. 'What a fool you were to get married and have children with him!'. She listened to me for a year, but sadly, somehow, after living apart for awhile, she let him come home. She really paid for that one. He had an affair. Now he is preparing to leave her again. I have made certain that she knows better than to try again. I will be on duty ensuring that she doesn't try this love game again."

*

In any primary relationship, whenever there is an absence of love and happiness, there are always two unacknowledged, combative aggressive/defensive egos fighting it out for supremacy. To gain an appreciation of the deeper, hidden ego dynamics which play themselves out in many intimate relationships, imagine one of the aggressive/defensive egos portrayed above, falling in love with one of the aggressive/defensive egos depicted below.

At the start of his healing Ted was a 43 old salesman, married and divorced, with no children, and was living alone. Though perplexed by the turn of events in his love life, he had already identified a few self-imposed obstacles in the way of the kind of love relationship he yearned for. One of those he called his procrastination. A letter from his aggressive/defensive ego consciousness showed us more about its history, beliefs, and approaches to women and love, and gave us considerably more understanding on his need to procrastinate. This is the first correspondence of several that were to come on this subject:

"I am Ted's aggressive/defensive ego and I have learned how to survive life and love. If I don't get close then I can't get hurt, so I run. When I sense that someone is getting too close, I create distance. That distance could be moving to a different province or moving to a different city. It could mean withdrawing emotionally. It could mean focusing all my energy on my job. It also could mean

withdrawing from all meaningful conversation with family and friends. More relevant to the matter at hand, it has meant enjoying women romantically and sexually but turning into a wall of stone when they wanted my real self.

*"It is easier to live on my own. All I have to do is think about me and, as I am on my own, I don't have to exert myself surviving life and love. Life is simple. I can take a break from outside demands, but there is no break—I am always on alert; ready to be called into action. I am tired. I am tired of the game. I am tired of the old patterns. I am tired of my endless list of wants. It seems that "everything" still isn't enough. I procrastinate because I am scared. I am scared that if I don't procrastinate then I will get what I need, and if I get what I need then I will be happy and content. If I am happy and content, then I, [Ted's aggressive/defensive ego] **will not survive**. So in order to survive, I run and procrastinate."*

*

Instigated by Margaret, she and her partner Bill came to see me for relationship work. She described their relationship as dull, dry and meaningless; lacking spontaneous fun, feelings, or sex. Though both people in a love relationship are responsible for its state and are creating it, albeit in very different ways, here is one side of that equation. It won't take you long to see how fun, spontaneity, or sexuality were at a premium here. This is a letter from Bill's aggressive/defensive ego, far and away the most dominant member of his Inner Family:

"I am the aggressive/defensive ego of your Inner Family. I have learned how to survive life and love. I do not let anyone get close to me. I carefully select the people I befriend and cull, on an on-going basis, those who no longer bring value and/or who interfere with my ability to carry out my priorities. I organize my life to be as effective as possible in carrying out my priorities, trying to maintain an orderly, regular schedule, while leaving sufficient flexibility to deal with unforeseen issues.

"I am ordering and systematizing the activities in my life to allow me to be more productive and effective, and to take on more meaningful challenges. I am regularizing my food intake, my social activities and exercise regime so as to maximize my health and minimize my risk of injury or illness.

"*I am undertaking on-going study and involve myself in business organizations and conferences so as to maximize my business efficiency and extend my network of human contacts. I arrange my activities so as to allow enough time to perform all my work and business commitments and adjust my other activities accordingly. I take two or three vacation breaks a year, and try to take most of them in a far away location. I try to limit the amount of time I spend socially with other people. I generally eschew spontaneous fun.*"

*

Here are more letters from the aggressive/defensive ego con-sciousnesses of male clients:

"*I am the aggressive/defensive ego of the Inner Family and I have learned to survive life and love by isolating myself from all people to some degree. No one is ever in a position to make it hurt such that I can't make it stop. I never commit to anything, except to never commit to anything. I expect as little as possible of what can be freely given from others. I demand what I want and take what I need.*

"*I always strive for control. If I lose control I constrict my living environment until it appears I have control again. I can even feign disinterest in survival. Nonetheless if I experience an unwanted risk, I can instantly scramble into damage control no matter how exhausted—with whatever effort, vigor and ingenuity is required.*

"*I consistently search for a better understanding of the art and practice of war. I add to my armory by reflex. I assimilate everything I possibly can. I accumulate territory as a buffer. I hone my judgments. I can be ruthless in perpetually amputating anything that might bleed too much.*

"*I never accept responsibility if I can avoid it, unless it suits my purposes and enhances my security and power.*

"*I measure everything.*

"*I deny the immeasurable. I hide my vulnerabilities and fears. I create whatever it seems to take to keep them away from the eyes of others. Yet, at the same time, I am constantly in touch with fear such that my guard never drops and I justify my existence and value. I am therefore indispensable and will always be.*"

*

"*I am Calvin's ego. I am the person he created at age five to get other kids to like him and to keep the bullies at bay. I am the one who had to act tough and brave when Calvin was afraid. I am the one who had to laugh and have fun when Calvin was miserable. I am the one who had to ask out girls, because Calvin was too afraid. I am the one who had to act like he didn't care when other kids teased him, while the words tore Calvin apart.*

"*Thirty-three years after Calvin created me I am still the one who will fight and fight and fight until the day I die, even as Calvin pleads with me to stop. He tells me the enemy has long since disappeared but I can still see the enemy everywhere. I am on constant guard. I never rest. I am relentless.*"

*

"*I am the aggressive/defensive ego in this Inner Family and I have survived life and love by:*

- *keeping people at a distance;*
- *telling people as little as possible about what is going on in my life, and by never being known;*
- *being quietly critical of everything and everyone;*
- *avoiding surprises by spending a lot of time planning for the future and worrying about the future;*
- *investing a lot of energy in being right; and ensuring that my suspicions and criticisms are justified, no matter what it costs me or my relationships;*
- *not getting attached to anything or anyone;*
- *never taking risks;*
- *blaming my parents for the things I don't like about me;*
- *creating, maintaining, and perfecting an agreeable "public relations" image;*
- *hiding all of the things I'm afraid of, ashamed of, or feel guilty about;*
- *being on guard against each man's ego and fearful of every woman's inner child; and,*
- *when all this doesn't work, I know I can always count on my addictions to help me survive the moment.*

"*After almost 45 years of life like this, I am growing tired of being responsible for everything in the universe. I deserve to have some fun in this lifetime. I am human too, after all."*

*

What bears repeating one last time is, to the aggressive/defensive ego consciousness, survival is (physically) the preservation of life and the accumulation of material security; and (psychologically), the preservation of a sense of safety, love, and value in the world of other people. No matter how natural, safe, or at ease we may feel one moment, the aggressive/defensive ego consciousness is never more than a fear-based thought away. Sometimes it seems as if the very experience of inner peace *itself* triggers a disapproving reaction from this Inner Family member. In my own case, I have noticed that on occasion that I can become judgmental and mean-spirited towards people around me only moments after I have completed a meditation!

One last letter from a seminar participant illustrates how quick the ego can change. Cam had just spent the past forty-eight hours in my intensive Inner Child Seminar. In it, he had allowed himself to be acutely vulnerable and shared himself honestly and openly with others. He had used the seminar to powerfully reconnect with his child consciousness and, as the seminar was coming to an end, he spoke about feeling relaxed, relieved, and cleansed.

As a way of showing participants some of the possible work that lay ahead, and to maintain the breakthroughs they were experiencing, I ask them to spend a few minutes hearing what their aggressive/defensive egos had to say about the healing work they had done in the seminar. This is the letter Cam received from his ego:

"Ego calling Cam! Ego calling Cam!

"Wake up call! Party's over! Tomorrow is Monday and you're on deck. Enough of the mushy shit. You know what brings home the bacon. You know where you get your strokes from. And it isn't blubbering in front of strangers. I've learned hard lessons and I'm not about to forget them. Here are some of them I want to reinforce:

1) Better to be nouveau-riche than never to have been riche at all. Yeah, yeah, money can't buy happiness. But neither can poverty. Go to work!

2) Men are valued by women for their money and power.

Once your head is in the noose, you're just another piece of furniture and a meal ticket. Better to be alone on your own than lonely inside the trap of a relationship.

3) Wallowing in this mushy shit never gets you anywhere. Helloooo! Wake up! Once you blow your nose, it's back to reality. Anywhere you've got in life, it's because I've showed you the way.

4) The only thing you know for sure is one day you'll wake up dead. In the meantime, make your stash, have a blast and for Christ sake, if you have to get laid, don't get tangled up in love again.

5) This weird thing you've got about Daddy not being there for the little boy... Give it a rest! You go picking a scab and all you get is pus. It won't scar over until you stop picking it! For Christ sake, stick a band-aid over it and leave it alone. You're embarrassing me.

"Now, get out' a here."

*

Letters from your aggressive/defensive ego should be as uncensored as possible and the product of a free-association process. Over time your writings can and will become the equivalent of an ego autobiography. Keep in mind throughout your writings that your objective is simply to get to know as much as possible about this consciousness. Do your best not to judge or criticize this Inner Family member.

Judging and criticizing it will only add fear to a consciousness already overrunning with fear.

C. "Aggressive/defensive ego, what are you afraid of?"

A final simple, yet powerful exercise which can assist you to understand the nature and identity of the aggressive/defensive ego consciousness is to keep posing the question: *"Ego, what are you afraid of?"* and immediately write down whatever comes to you. Here are some typical responses from people who have tried this:

"Ego, what are you afraid of?"

- men
- people

- women
- feelings
- rejection
- being vulnerable
- losing
- power
- death
- poverty

- failure
- whether other people
  like me or not
- looking foolish or weak
- feeling lost
- the unknown
- love
- being conned

These. and other ego responses like them, can be psychological and emotional gold mines—openings for the intrepid inner-adventurer to explore.

A Concluding Note On Working With the Aggressive/Defensive Ego

In all of the suggested exercises described above, when coming to know your aggressive/defensive ego, remember that *this consciousness ultimately does not trust anyone but itself*. To encourage it to begin to open up to you will likely require a slow and gentle pace and a non-judgmental, non-coercive approach.

See if you can bring respect, tolerance, and patience to all of your requests of the aggressive/defensive ego consciousness. Treat it like someone in your life you are just beginning to know, who is sharing deeply personal and sensitive information with you. Remember you are dealing with a terrified consciousness that has experienced deep wounds, mostly in conjunction with other people, and often from those who were closest to you. It has been aggressive or defensive in its dealings with others for good reason.

As you attempt to make a heartfelt connection with this side of you, you will be returning to scenes and memories that are full of emotional pain and fear. The process of bringing out this consciousness will only succeed if you, the now independent/aware adult, show it consistent understanding and acceptance. Go gently. Tread lightly. Show kindness.

Statements like: "Ego, I am here to get to know you. I will not judge you. Please tell me more." "Ego, I'd like to know more about you. What else do you feel comfortable telling me?" "Ego, I will wait for you to reveal yourself in your own time and at your own pace," can, if sincere, work wonderfully well in gradually eliciting more involvement and information from this Inner Family member.

Your motives for getting to know the ego consciousness will be questioned and tested by it. Do you want to know it in order to judge and condemn it for past transgressions? Do you want to cast it into exile or worse yet, kill it? None of these agendas will be helpful in its healing. Your goal is to befriend this Inner Family member, not to slay it.

There will be other kinds of tests. How capable are you, as a new independent/aware adult to take over the leadership of the Inner Family? To entrust you with this, your aggressive/defensive ego will have to be gradually convinced (actually shown) that your emerging leadership role will not cost the Inner Family's survival; that its survival will be absolutely guaranteed (though in new and previously unimagined ways). The aggressive/defensive ego will need to be reassured that its own healing is not the equivalent of some terribly costly and disgraceful indulgence with grave or even fatal consequences.

Remember, the ego considers itself to have been the best, moreover the *only* friend that this Inner Family has ever had. Upstart "friends" with no proven track record, like the newly independent/aware adult, the natural child consciousness/authentic self, or the spiritual consciousness, will have to prove their effectiveness. If they show any sign of failing to carry out the sacred duty of protecting the Inner Family, from what the aggressive/defensive ego perceives to be a hostile world, it will immediately struggle to reassert dominance and control. Be mindful: The aggressive/defensive ego will do whatever it has to do to test the shift in consciousness which is now starting to occur within you.

The First Step In Personal Transformation: The Emergence of the New Adult

With this inner work, a major step has now begun in the transformation of your consciousness. In coming to know, be responsible for, and begin to heal your aggressive/defensive ego, bit by bit you are developing a new independent/aware adult consciousness. You are no longer totally controlled by (and immersed in) the fear-based, survival-oriented set of conditioned responses that you relied on to get you through life. A real opportunity arises in which you can identify yourself with a more heart and spirit led consciousness.

No longer unconsciously and automatically run by what Herman Hesse called *"the slime and eggshells of* [your] *primeval past"*(cited at the beginning of Chapter V), this development in you has the potential to create a new consciousness. This can give birth to an identity which is love-based and growth-oriented, and with that, allows a new array of life-enhancing choices. Having choice over which universe you inhabit and what you bring to others (either the Universe of Fear of your aggressive/defensive ego consciousness, or the Universe of Love of your natural child consciousness/authentic self and your spiritual consciousness), will open up a whole new world. "You"—the new independent/aware adult who emerges from this healing work, is capable of leading and simultaneously being led in this process of inner transformation.

Chapter VIII

*"As a child I had known that the excitement, fears and wor-
ries the grown-ups went in for, had no real foundation. I
knew it in flashes, but the others would always manage to
convince me that I was wrong and once again I would feel
guilty or fearful or both."*

J. Van De Wetering,
Journal of Transpersonal
Psychology No.2, 1977

The Therapeutic Journey Of Healing The Adaptive Child

A Very Brief Look At My Healing Journey

In my own case, I was (and eighteen years later I still am),
shocked at how much pain and crisis I had to create in order to
disengage enough from my aggressive/defensive ego to set my self
free to do the work of healing. By the time I was twenty-five I was
dominated by my aggressive/defensive ego. I was completely blind
to the amount of emotional pain and fear I was hiding inside.
Although I didn't know it clearly: Life terrified me.

In my mid-thirties I was very cavalier about the pain and fear
I was causing my family and had completely justified my behavior;
but this wasn't enough to wake me up. Clients that had formerly
recommended my seminars and therapy to others were beginning to
whisper that I was less effective. New client referrals were scarce.
People who had participated in my seminars were looking at me
askance and not returning. In the end, the only thing that finally
made me "pay attention" was that my career was threatened. In the
space of a few months, in my late thirties, I literally sat in the ruins
of what I thought was my "perfect" life.

The gross insensitivity in all of this was I finally and only
took personal responsibility when my behavior threatened my
livelihood and reputation, not the well-being of my wife and family.
It was only later I realized I was completely insensitive to the people
I loved. It was through this intense emotional pain I discovered the

power of my aggressive/defensive ego and my adaptive child. At the same time that my life was in a shambles, I realized this child consciousness would eventually prove to be my trusted guide.

*   *

If you recall from earlier chapters, there are two distinct aspects to your child consciousness: (i) the natural child consciousness which is your authentic self, perpetuates a Universe of Love, and can provide meaningful connection to your spiritual consciousness; and (ii), an adaptive child consciousness, formed to survive a childhood experience comprised of circumstances, conditions, and people operating neglectfully or hurtfully (out of their own aggressive/defensive ego consciousnesses). This adaptive child consciousness is designed to accomplish physical and psychological survival. It has learned to be inauthentic and "play the game" rather than be true to its naturally occurring emotional and spiritual processes. This adaptive child is a child shaped by who and what they fear.

This is an unnatural way of being that operates to cope with a rising and eventually overflowing reservoir of emotional pain and fear. This consciousness quickly learns to efficiently use a vast array of strategies and manipulations in an attempt to find the safety, love, and value that it isn't receiving.

Some of these strategies were aggressive such as angry outbursts, bullying others, teasing, or as soon as possible using addictive substances. Others were defensive, like remaining hidden by creating an assortment of contrived public roles — the perfect child, the hero, the comedian, or the family problem. *Being forced to rely on displays of aggression, defensiveness, or inauthentic roles to get its needs met, makes the adaptive child consciousness the earlier and elementary embodiment of what will later become the full-blown aggressive/defensive ego consciousness.*

Running Out of Options

As an adult who has become identified with the aggressive/defensive ego consciousness you will avoid knowing and facing the adaptive child for as long as possible. As a general rule, you have to be in tremendous and usually intolerable emotional pain and crisis to begin this healing work. A direct hit has occurred at the core of your old way of being. One (or more) of your key relationships, career aspirations, physical health, or financial security is usually threatened or ending. Seldom will anything less than disaster motivate you to be as humble, honest, and vulnerable as this healing work requires. This is because until some personal catastrophe occurs, your overriding aggressive/defensive ego consciousness has been able to absorb and dish out an incredible amount of pain and suffering, and still cleverly convince you its ways are still right and the successful attainment of its goals assured.

An often cited aphorism is: "Insanity is doing the same thing over and over again and expecting a different result." And yet, while most ego-identified adults know this intellectually, that is exactly what we continue to do. The stubborn and prideful ego remains convinced that it is just a matter of time before its efforts and actions will be rewarded by a "different" result. So, it plods on, relying only on itself and itself alone, doing the same ineffectual, hurtful, or even destructive things compulsively, rationalizing that this time the end result will be different.

Life, itself, is a powerful and unrelenting teacher. As mentioned earlier, usually the most unwanted and unsavory elements of life (humiliation, heartbreak, failure, loss, betrayal, financial ruin, illness, injury, and death) confront and force the aggressive/defensive ego it to stop in its tracks. It is only when it is confronted with drastic, incontestable evidence that life has become an unmanageable calamity that the ego *might* give way; and even then, it screams and fights. You might say the aggressive/defensive ego consciousness is unhinged and topples first, and then "consents" to collapsing. Like an employee an instant before they hear the boss tell them they are fired, the ego ceremoniously and righteously declares: "I quit!"

Your cunning, baffling, powerful, and patient aggressive/defensive ego needs to be besieged by a life which is a disaster before it will consider any other option. Complete collapse is necessary before the vast majority of adults will move in the direction of the Inner Family member that predates and lies underneath the aggressive/defensive ego—the adaptive child consciousness. Generally speaking, *you will take on the work of reclaiming and healing the adaptive child consciousness only when your life is in ruins and you've run out of options.*

It is an adult that is shaken, humbled, disoriented, and confused who meets the emotional and spiritual requirements for initiation into the realms of the adaptive child consciousness. If this adult can get past the initial fear and disdain of this work, they will discover this Inner Family can guide them to sincere and permanent change.

Losing the Natural Child to the Adaptive Child

When did you lose your natural child/authentic self? Do you ever wonder about life as a spontaneous, loved, innocent being?

It was a time before the strangeness of living with very conditional "love" and acceptance. You were probably very young. Prior to the aggressive/defensive ego was a time when you did not have to live every waking moment protecting yourself. However brief this time was—it was a time when you were not afraid; quite possibly you did not even know how to be afraid. There was absolutely no need to spin, weave, control, or manipulate your way through the mine fields of life. It was a time before you were internally separate and separated.

However imaginary or distant being an authentic, integrated person may seem to you now, you were at birth a naturally spiritual child. You have been away from your spiritual origins for so long, and are so weary from the battle and daily grind of survival, that you have not only forgotten this, but probably doubt it ever existed. You have been forced to abandon your spiritual origins for the competitive and cynical adopted world you have come to believe is natural— the aggressive/defensive ego's Universe of Fear.

Like a soap bubble floating on the wind, living out of your two original consciousnesses—a natural child consciousness/authentic self and a spiritual consciousness—was fragile. Your ability to stay connected to these two Inner Family members probably did not last very long. Rare is the child who experiences this kind of world for any extended period of time. For your natural child and spiritual Inner Family members to remain available to you, the world around you had to be physically, emotionally, and spiritually safe. It wasn't. The adults around you had to know how to mentor your connection to your subjectively felt emotional truths and spirituality. They didn't.

As a result, *you learned to adapt.* If you were underprivileged or grew up in poverty, you learned to adapt. If you were physically violated or abused by others, or knew the threat of being emotionally overpowered or intimidated, you learned to adapt. If you weren't allowed to consistently know, share, or follow your feelings and personal truths, you learned to adapt. If the message coming from your parents, teachers, religious leaders, or culture was that your authentic self was flawed or not enough, you learned to adapt. If you were told (or were covertly expected) to be a more, better, or different version of yourself in order to be approved of, loved or redeemed, you learned to adapt.

The adaptive child has been molded and shaped by the aggressive/defensive egos of its caretakers. The conditions of this child's existence did not support (or actively opposed) identification with their natural child consciousness and spiritual consciousness.

This is a world in which a child is not accorded the right to have feelings, needs, and wants of their own. Or, those feelings, needs, and wants have to be modified or abandoned to fit with the aggressive/defensive egos that surround it. The adaptive child consciousness comes into existence when the natural child consciousness realizes it cannot have its authentic emotional and spiritual self respected or accepted openly, safely, and honestly. *It realizes that it must be indirect, manipulative and false in order to be taken care of.*

The adaptive child consciousness is an artificial, socially constructed accommodation. It is a mask that conceals its authentic emotional and spiritual truths. It is an involuntary state of subservience to the regime of the aggressive/defensive ego consciousnesses that surround it. The adaptive child consciousness is forced to survive this tyranny.

As described in the story that opens this book, the little plug is forced to disconnect from its socket. That connection was its birthright, sustenance, and real identity. It is forced instead to search for "connection" in a world of other disconnected plugs.

The Adaptive Child In Me

It is important to examine in more depth the differences in the traits and features of your adaptive child consciousness (in this chapter) and your natural child consciousness/authentic self (in the next chapter). Use the following questions to see if and how, in your

formative years, you have abandoned your natural child conscious-
ness/authentic self and fashioned an adaptive child consciousness in
its place:

- Did I experience that my simply being alive was a
  cause for celebration and rejoicing for my parents
  and significant others?
- Did I experience that I was beautiful, whole, sufficient, and spiritually perfect exactly the way I was?
- Did I feel unconditionally loved by everyone? anyone? no one?
- Did I start to feel that I needed to be different (or
  better or more or less) than the person I knew I was
  in order to feel safe, loved, and valued?
- Was I allowed to feel what I was feeling, when I was
  feeling it? Could I share uncomfortable, negative, or
  highly charged emotions with others? Was I in-
  structed on what to feel for their benefit not my
  own?
- Could I share my thoughts freely; even thoughts that
  were dark, anti-social, or did not conform to the
  "shoulds, oughts, or musts" of conventional standards?
- Was I encouraged to know, speak, and live my personal truths?
- What did it take to make my caregivers or parents
  pleased with me?
- Was I ever worried about them getting angry or possibly hurting me? What did I have to do to avoid
  this? Could I avoid this?
- What feelings, needs, and wants could I *not* bring to
  my parents?
- What did I have to do to get my caregivers or teachers (or religious authorities) to praise me?
- What did it take for me to avoid public comparison,
  derision, shaming, or being made to feel stupid or
  bad by teachers, religious authorities, parents, other
  authority figures?
- How did I have to be (or *appear* to be) for the religious authorities to indicate that God would approve
  of me—or at least to do my best to make sure that

God would not punish me or disapprove of me?

If you find yourself quickly modifying the answers with thoughts like "Well… yes, but it wasn't *that* bad," or quickly dismissing the questions as irrelevant, these are the responses of an adaptive child consciousness.

Traits and Features of a Person Operating from the Adaptive Child Consciousness

In my experience, most (if not all) adults have come to be overtaken and dominated by their aggressive/defensive ego consciousness, and have a deeply pained, unhealed adaptive child consciousness to deal with. Sadly, these individuals are "adults" in name and age only. They are adults who have reached their full physical stature but who are controlled by an aggressive/defensive ego consciousness and unconsciously identify with their adaptive child consciousness. They have fallen far short of their full emotional and spiritual development.

I will now discuss, at greater depth, the distinguishing features of the adaptive child as it shows itself in an adult body. Please remember that personal healing is an "inside job". If you have an unhealed or unhealthy relationship with yourself, within yourself, then to that degree, *all* of your external relationships are unhealthy. We can only "be" with others as we are with ourselves. If you wish to have healthy, grounded, loving relationships with the people in your life it starts with your inner relationship with yourself. [If you see *any* reflection of yourself in the six points that follow there is work to do in your relationship with yourself.]

1. We Can't Feel

If you are an adult living with an ignored, unhealed adaptive child consciousness within, it will be very difficult for you to experience emotions. Much of the time you will not be aware that you are feeling anything at all. If you are experiencing emotions you do not know what they are or what they mean. At a core level you have a very limited range of emotions for purposes of self-expression.

Everything "emotional" may be exaggerated or defined in

terms of being angry or not-angry; or depressed or not-depressed. Or, it may also be you are not capable of noticing anything subtle about your emotions—you are either exploding or "nothing", or very depressed or "nothing". This is because in your early years you found it unbearable to know or feel your feelings, or you were somehow punished for having feelings that were unacceptable to your caregivers. To "feel" would have made an already lonely or painful time in your life even worse. Numbing your feelings was the solution to an intolerable reality.

Remember: *Feelings have to go somewhere*, even though you (your ego-mind) may have denied them. They may become stored in the body in the form of physical or medical symptoms, weight issues, or sexual behavior (sexual anorexia, compulsiveness, or precociousness). As a youth they may have turned into delinquent behaviors or isolation, and been expressed through aggression or the use of alcohol and drugs. These disowned or denied feelings exist, and may have also turned you into a "straight A" student, or otherwise compulsively driven to fail.

All of these are (often unconscious) strategies to make un-wanted and uncomfortable emotions go away. Ultimately and inevitably, if you are an adult who is unconsciously operating out of your adaptive child consciousness, you will be cut off from your spontaneously occurring feelings. You are thereby bereft of a personal, wise internal information and guidance system that is based on your naturally occurring emotional and spiritual processes.

Being able to know, have, and experience feelings (especially the subtle ones) is the path that will lead you back to the child consciousness within.

2. We Cannot Speak Our Truths

In any family that is run by the aggressive/defensive egos of its power brokers, subjectively known personal truth is frowned upon or actively suppressed. [This is also true about any organization or culture.] This fear-based regime, which is founded on the need for external power and control, is established and maintained by rigidly enforced (often unspoken) laws and punishments. These make certain that no one can have direct access to, nor can they follow, their own internal information system. The inner world of the individual, whether child or adult, and the possibility they will come to trust and follow their internal emotional messages, is a clear and direct threat to the aggressive/defensive ego.

If you are an adult who is operating from an unhealed adaptive child consciousness, you have learned that you cannot trust or follow your very own truths. Instead, you had to become (and are) adept at accepting and abiding by the version of truth put forward by the aggressive/defensive egos around you. You had to "believe" someone else's account of what was real.

Under the conditions of this system, you, as a child of the oppressive family were told what and how you must feel. You were told what to think, what to believe, even what to say. The only personally-derived truths which you could know were "truths" which fit the agendas and vested interests of the more powerful egos that surrounded you. If it wasn't approved of by "them" it could not be a personal truth for you.

Earlier in this book I compared the regime of the aggressive/defensive ego consciousness to that of a cruel dictator. I wasn't exaggerating or sensationalizing. The first order of business for dictators is the abolishment of the process by which an individual is guided by their own authentic emotional and spiritual truths. In the political version of a dictatorship the freedom to hold public meetings, to disagree with the policies of the authorities, or to choose a personal style of worship are prohibited. The counterpart of this in a family run on similar principles is that no one is allowed to know, express, or take a stand for their private, inner personal truths.

3. The Final Authority Is Someone Else

Because you were never considered to be an authority on yourself, there was nowhere else to go but to others as the final authority. As an adaptive child in your family of origin, you learned what others wanted you to be. You figured out how to give them what they wanted, or at least appear to give them what they wanted. You had no choice but to abandon your subjective truths and your own sense of power to the aggressive/defensive egos around you. You progressively lost your connection with your natural and authentic self.

You became brilliant at figuring out *their* rules; agreeing, obeying, appeasing, and conforming to them on one level while tacitly opposing, resisting, and defying them on another. As you adapted to the family (or organization or culture) that you belonged to, you believed that that you could pull it off—give the power brokers the compliance they were demanding, while secretly preserving and protecting your authentic self. However, your secret plan to hide your authentic self until the you could freely and safely bring it back failed.

You got caught in your adaptive self and got lost in your own manipulations. The contrived roles and pretenses that were meant to be nothing more than a temporary emergency measure became second nature to you. You discovered how to please, how to fit in, how to employ a wide array of publicly-approved roles. The intent of many conversations with parents and authority figures was not to become better known to them as an authentic self, but rather to successfully avoid certain topics and personal disclosure which would reveal who you really were, and thereby make them uncomfortable. You played the game. As good a performer as you became, it was the "audience" of more powerful egos who determined your survival. Years later, as an adult operating with an unhealed adaptive child consciousness, other people continued to be the final authority for your life and not yourself.

In your shrewd and desperate maneuverings to defend yourself against the oppressive aggressive/defensive egos that surrounded you, the greatest irony of all was that you turned yourself into another embodiment of that very consciousness. From infancy, as a victim of oppressors, you became the perpetrator of the cycle of oppression. At first their, and then later your own, aggressive/defensive ego remained in charge of your life.

4. Little Ability to Relate to or Empathize with the Subjective Experience of Others

The natural result of the traits noted above is that if you were chronically denied the right to own and express your subjective experience, be they emotions or truths, you will have little (or no) ability to relate to the subjective experience of others. In other words, being able to appreciate and respect someone else's subjective experience is next to impossible for someone who long ago disconnected from their own authentic, subjective experience.

As an adaptive child, in order to survive, you had to detach from the most vulnerable, delicate, and emotional aspects of yourself. You denied your own humanity and became a one-dimensional cardboard cut-out figure: a commodity. This required that others were perceived as one-dimensional cardboard cut-out figures, too. Like pieces of furniture in your home, you saw other people as necessary to serve a valuable but objectifying function: to be aesthetically pleasing and status-enhancing. [This was discussed earlier regarding men and women turning each other into sex objects.]

As an adult operating from an unhealed adaptive child consciousness, you will be inclined to see other people as movable objects that take up space. As long as they cooperate and are aesthetically pleasing and status enhancing you tolerate them. As soon as they disagree, interfere, or clutter things up by getting in the way of what you want, they lose their appeal and are disposed of. This is especially true when they ask for or demand uncomfortable change or are otherwise persistent in wanting you to access anything you have denied or hidden.

The adaptive child consciousness, because it is a rudimentary form of the aggressive/defensive ego, is riddled in contradiction and paradox. This same consciousness that has turned others into the final authority and denies your own truths, and goes to extreme lengths to please others, can also be ruthless in keeping others away, and not bonding or empathizing with anyone. "Please love me, I'll do anything," one moment, and "You can't make me do it! Stay away from me," the next moment. Either of these prohibit the human connection that fosters compassion or empathy.

5. Love Is Unreal/Unavailable

At their deepest emotional and spiritual levels, the adult who is operating from the unhealed adaptive child consciousness emerges from childhood as an ardent *non*-believer in love. Think about this: How could you come to believe that love might be real and steadfast if those who claimed they loved you methodically crushed your authentic self? It stands to reason that (as a child) if "love" was dangerous and oppressive it would never be trusted as an adult.

Considering your *actual* experience of being loved as a child, you will carry the belief, most often unconsciously, that love is unreal. Or if it appears real and sincere, it can be taken away in an instant and become the source of unrivaled hurt and pain making it dangerous. To the Inner Family member known as the adaptive child, love may disguise itself as a friend and ally for a while, but it is only a question of when it will show its real colors as an enemy.

Every adult operating with an unhealed adaptive child consciousness enters any primary love relationship waiting for the bomb to drop; continuously operating a high-alert inner radar screen (developed in childhood) in order to survive the experience of "love". Any blip on the radar screen will be interpreted as a threat and set off alarms and activate suspicion and withdrawal, and attack or defense. The aggressive/defensive ego consciousness will race into action, believing the "enemy" has returned; this time brilliantly disguised as a loving partner or spouse, with the accompanying judgment that they made the mistake of believing in love (again). Behind the agonizing dissolution of marriages and families, unhealed adaptive children are re-living the traumas of their painful past.

Because of the pain from the past, everything is backwards and upside down in matters of love to an adult operating from an unhealed adaptive child consciousness. Instead of love being safe, it is unsafe. Rather than being welcoming, it is threatening. It is not natural and easy, it is unnatural and problematic. Though hard to admit, you will be more comfortable with conflict than peace, aloneness than togetherness, and irreconcilable differences than common ground in your primary relationships

Not only can love not be trusted as good, neither can those emotions or states that are associated with it: trust, closeness, vulnerability, honesty, kindness, caring, concern, and simple generosity of spirit. Compliments, encouragement, even gift giving, for an adaptive inner child are radar blips of danger—nothing but hucksters with sales pitches and angles, wanting only to fleece the customer and move on to the next sucker.

To the adaptive child, love is unreal and something to be feared rather than surrendered to, and all things which resemble it are to be avoided. This world view is no different than the one held by its successor—the aggressive/defensive ego consciousness. It is a world in which love is feared.

6. No Personal Version Or Unique Experience Of Spirituality

The adaptive child is bereft of spirituality. Authentic spirituality requires access to the inner nature of things. It calls for a deep trust and surrendering to realms beyond the five senses; realms which are not only removed from the consensual reality of everyday ego consciousness, but which also challenge that reality. Each traveler into spirituality is unique. They do not and cannot run in packs. They abide in the aloneness of a solitary experience. Following formulas and prescriptions offered by recognized external authorities and religious and political organizations is anathema to a true spiritual pilgrim. External dogma can never replace the necessity of exploring their (our) own emotional and spiritual depths to find our personal God.

However, for a child controlled by the aggressive/defensive egos around them, there is no possibility for a personal exploration or a personal expression of spirituality. *It is these dominating egos which take over the role of that child's spiritual consciousness or Higher Power*; it is they who insist upon the child's complete obedience; they decide for the child which life-paths are to be explored and which paths are forbidden.

Just like so many other aspects of their humanity, the adaptive-child is denied access to an inner awareness and thus to their own divinity. This loss of a personal vision—of a unique experience of spirituality, may be the most devastating consequence of all.

Taking on the Healing of the Adaptive Child Consciousness

If you wish to take the next quantum leap in healing your relationship with yourself, beyond the work you have done so far, the challenge I will present in this section is to parent your adaptive (wounded) child consciousness through their emotional pain and fear. They may then return to the state of the natural child consciousness/authentic self they were by birthright. This helps the little disconnected plug become reconnected to its original socket.

Why do so few of us volunteer for this assignment? Why is it so often the case that we cause ourselves or others such enormous amounts of pain *before* we are prepared to face and heal the emotional pain and fear within ourselves? It is because the aggressive defensive ego, which rules our consciousness, sees any threat to its dominance as a death-knell—because we have developed an unquestioning allegiance to the aggressive/defensive ego consciousness and become almost totally identified with it.

As self-respecting adult people in our culture, we perceive ourselves to be competent, capable, and successful managers of our affairs. We believe our self-reliance provides sufficient resources to face and weather all of life's challenges. We are the captains of our ship; the masters of our soul! What need do we have for an inner child consciousness? How useful would having one of "those" be in conducting our important affairs like making more money, or creating and making a favorable impression, or rising to the top of the heap, or warding off the treachery of adversaries?

To ego-identified adults, a child consciousness (if something like one even exists), would be a huge liability to their survival and a threat to their power and rank in the war games they have become so adept at playing.

As ego-identified adults we resent the child consciousness and see it as an impediment to the execution of life's "more important" requirements. What may be worse, is we sentimentalize that aspect of ourselves. We thereby trivialize and patronize the consciousness that can reveal a great deal about how we have come to be the adults we are.

The Therapeutic Journey Of
Healing The Adaptive Child

I will present a first-hand, experiential account of the process of healing the adaptive child consciousness. Of all the inner work I present in this book, none is more emotionally charged and painful as this. It is hard for anyone to consciously and deliberately face distasteful emotional material from the past. What makes this undertaking so challenging is fierce resistance from the aggressive/defensive ego. Remember that to it, emotional pain is death, so be prepared for it to oppose your efforts at healing practically every step of the way. It is very important to treat the aggressive/defensive ego consciousness like an Inner Family member. When you hear from it, include and embrace it and help it deal with its tremendous fear of emotional pain.

This approach to inner healing is called the Inner Family Model for good reason—both the ego and the adaptive child consciousnesses need to feel like equally respected and loved family members for your individual healing to occur. It takes an independent/aware adult who is strong and courageous (and devoted to healing acute emotional and spiritual pain) to go down this path.

In actuality, the therapeutic process detailed below is not that of any one client. It is a composite profile of many people I have had the privilege of helping. The people depicted here are not make-believe. They are real people who were willing to do whatever it took to save their own lives. Along the way many tests presented themselves and many surprises awaited them. These are their stories.

The Journey Begins

A client sits before me, uneasy, expectant, ambivalent, alert. After a few sessions they are familiar with the concepts of an Inner Family—of an aggressive/defensive ego, a child consciousness, a spiritual consciousness, and an independent/aware adult consciousness. We are about to embark on an intuitive and experiential process in search of an adaptive child consciousness who has been forgotten and left behind; but, at the same time, is influencing present-day behavior patterns in powerful and consequential ways.

I usually recommend to the client that they not attempt to force or manufacture anything. It is possible that the session will not reveal anything substantial. I prepare them by advising they may feel it was a meaningless experience or a complete waste of time (and money). I also mention that it is possible the session might be extremely meaningful and moving; that it might reveal a good deal about perplexing and self-defeating symptoms—it could very well be a benchmark in our work together. Lastly, I suggest that the client relax and just work with any presence, image, or visualization that does appear. I assure clients they can stop the process at any time they choose.

In the search for a long-lost, fear-based adaptive child, the process sometimes begins physically. I may ask the client to close their eyes and pay attention to any areas of pain, discomfort, or any unusual bodily experience that is calling out for attention. If this happens I will ask that they notice and describe anything that is physically happening. If their attention wavers or drifts I will encourage them to go back to their body again and again as an anchor and guide.

With others, the process may begin emotionally. Attentive silence may be the best way for the client to stay with the feelings that arise. Otherwise, I may ask for two or three one-word depictions that identify the feelings they are experiencing. As with the physical sensations, I suggest the client stay with their feelings as long as possible, which provides an anchor and guide in this process of self-awareness.

I may use any of the following questions to promote awareness: "What is happening for you?" "Is there anyone or anything you see?" "Is there anyone or anything you remember?" "Who or what does your adaptive inner child look like?" I will encourage them to not force or fake anything and not to turn away, no matter what shows up.

Then, more often than not, the physical or emotional experience the client is having transforms into a vision or dream-like image. It often happens quickly, easily, and effortlessly. I may encourage them to wait a few moments for the image to stabilize. Then, with consent, we approach it through discussion and disclosure.

Encountering The Grotesque and Gruesome

Though we may be in search of a banished adaptive child, sometimes it is not the image of a child which initially appears. The unwanted and denied psychological and spiritual wounds of a lifetime, combined with the dislike (or even loathing) for the child who experienced them, may manifest in a vision or picture of something that does not take the form of a child, and sometimes not even a human form at all. The client and I may be temporarily catapulted into a dark and hideous underworld. A grotesque entity may appear that represents deformity, depravity, or decay. While going in search of a little child, we may inadvertently have to cope with a "monster" first.

As I write this, I remember an assortment of distasteful and hideous characters and images. These images ranged from piles of fly guts, abandoned and emaciated baby birds, an aborted foetus stuffed in a jar, and a petrified mummy, to a bloated, starving and dying child. Some of the images were very disturbing. As abhorrent as these initial images of misery and wretchedness may be to you (or to the aggressive/defensive ego consciousness), it is important to stay with the process. They invariably prove to be perfect and precise representations of the deepest layers of the client's (your) buried pain and mangled inner self.

In these early images and metaphors clients obtain a glimpse of the severity of their emotional and spiritual childhood wounds. In each case, *at the outset*, their adaptive child manifested itself in sometimes gruesome forms. And, inevitably, later on in the healing process, we could marvel at the brilliance and appropriateness of these originally repugnant images. These images (any image) carries with it an accompanying plea for healing and love.

Images Of Normal Children

Most of the time a client is presented with an image of a seemingly "normal" looking child. What appears is often a snapshot from some memorable point in childhood. For example, sitting alone on the steps in front of a house, or wearing favorite clothes attending a family gathering. These first observations may suggest the child we are looking in on is the natural child consciousness (and this well may be the case); a child who feels safe, loved, and valued for "just being"; accepted for being no more or other than who they are.

Sometimes, however, on closer examination of the emotional messages coming from this child's eyes, manner, presentation or energy, it becomes abundantly clear that the child we are in the presence of is one who has already lost (or is in the process of losing) their connection to their natural and authentic self. This is a little person who has had to forfeit and conceal their deepest feelings, wants, and needs. This child has developed an adapted child consciousness and is an early embodiment of a person with an ego-forged identity, complete with its cover-ups and falsehoods.

The child will often be frozen in mechanical poses or stuck with "pasted on" socially contrived expressions. Closely observing this memory snapshot will almost certainly reveal a hidden reservoir of emotional pain and fear not far from the surface. It will take very little at this point for the adult client to intuit or discern the nature of the child's feelings. Fear, anger, hurt, sadness, shame, insecurity, guilt, shock, loneliness, despondency, depression, despair, or various combinations of these, will be present.

Stepping slightly back from the buried emotional pain of the child, the client may now be able to detect the early origins and makeup of a rudimentary aggressive/defensive ego consciousness. They will be able to discern how this child has already adapted to the aggressive/defensive egos which surround them and is already in a Universe of Fear.

We may notice the child is already manipulative and covert in getting their needs met. It may be possible to sense how far away the natural child consciousness self has already gone and how much of the adaptive child consciousness has developed. An element that will be of critical importance in future healing will start to show itself: How does the present-day adult client feel towards the child appearing in the image? Is there empathy, concern, a desire to protect, anger, judgment, disdain, love, rejection, disgust? All of a client's reactions will be a part of future discussion.

The Aggressive/Defensive Ego Consciousness Returns And Objects

To enter these deeper realms of inner experience, the client has had to become vulnerable and real. As an independent/aware adult they have been willing, if only for a short time, to separate from (and no longer be controlled by) their aggressive/defensive ego consciousness. Not only has the client broken ranks with their "dictating authority", but from the aggressive/defensive ego's point of view, they (the client) have crossed over and aligned themselves with a seemingly opposing force—the child consciousness.

The client's aggressive/defensive ego consciousness will forcefully react to this act of desertion. It will *not* gracefully accept this unilateral act of autonomy; this sudden demand for adult independence and choice.

In most cases it will return quickly and forcefully into the client's consciousness. Its objections will be loud, harsh, and vigorous. For the independent/aware adult consciousness to be opening up to the adaptive child's buried emotional pain and fear is perceived as dangerous and irresponsible to the aggressive/defensive ego. If emotional pain is "death", then for the adult to consciously and deliberately experience that pain is tantamount to "suicide".

By willingly opening their heart to the adaptive child consciousness, the adult is declaring: "Ego, you are not my leader any more. I will not always follow you blindly." The adult consciousness has declared its independence, and the aggressive/defensive ego consciousness is *not* a big fan of independence movements, or anything else that detracts from its authority or diminishes its control.

Even if all the client has actually done is to discover and relate to the adaptive child consciousness, it will have gone much too far for the aggressive/defensive ego. It will attempt to do whatever it has always done to prevent any experience of buried emotional pain and fear. For instance, if historically the client has adopted addictions (food, sex, chaos, busyness, television, alcohol, nicotine, drugs, work, relationships, drama, shopping, greed) to stay away from what the adaptive child really experienced growing up, these might increase as any healing work deepens. If they have been excessively dependent upon the approval of others, the aggressive/defensive ego will attempt to subvert the growth into an independent/aware adult by "arranging" for a cherished significant other to express disapproval in regards to any healing work. This will be the excuse to quit healing work. Or suddenly money is a concern (when it wasn't before), or time considerations, or geographic moves, or physical symptoms and ailments will "unexpectedly" be presented, demand attention, and take the person away when transformative change becomes a real possibility.

Less dramatic but equally challenging, the client will often report being bombarded by demanding, extremely self-critical voices—another gambit the aggressive/defensive ego may employ to register its vehement objections to healing and transformation. These punishing voices may say things like: "This stuff is too weird or flaky for me!" "You're seeing things too darkly!" "You're making mountains out of molehills!" "Maybe you're just making the whole thing up!" Denial of the terrible pain and loneliness of the adaptive child may be very strong. The client may hear: "You had a good childhood! These images are too extreme, too deformed, too ugly. They could not possibly represent your childhood. Our parents always did their best. How dare you insult them or be disloyal to them in this way!"

The aggressive/defensive ego consciousness may implore and beseech a client to stop. It may shout: "Turn back! Turn back now! What in the hell are you doing? Putting your attention on this adaptive child is stupid and risky! Besides how does any of this apply to your present day difficulties and issues? This therapist is probably making a good dollar making up this nonsense and getting gullible clients like you to pay money! Don't be a fool."

These denunciations tend to get louder and harsher the closer a client comes to experiencing the emotional pain and fear which has shaped them. This is often an intense and frightening time as simultaneously they are having to deal with three things: (i) the attacks stemming from the aggressive/defensive ego consciousness; (ii) the waves of emotional pain i.e.: shock, hurt, anger, sadness, or grief stemming from their newly revealed adaptive child consciousness; and (iii), whatever the recent crisis was that motivated or pushed them into healing in the first place.

Their long-employed denial mechanisms are bending, cracking, and breaking. Emotional truths are ever more visible. It is now impossible to deny that these feelings are present and real somewhere deep inside them. Equally so, it is impossible to deny how tyrannical and savage the offended aggressive/defensive ego can be when its domination is threatened.

Continued inner work will be required if a client is to develop and remain living out of their independent/aware adult consciousness. They will need support to keep from buckling under the bullying of the threatened aggressive/defensive ego consciousness. Not unlike floundering on an open sea clinging to a life jacket, *they must hold on to their new ability to see their ego rather than be their ego; observing it, understanding it, hopefully caring for it, but not letting it overtake them as before.*

The aggressive/defensive ego will try to do whatever it has to do to reassert its control and supremacy over the fledgling independent/aware adult consciousness. Sometimes all I can tell a client is to ride the waves it unleashes as it attempts to invalidate the reality and depth of the emotional pain and fear they have carried *and* the legitimacy of the images of emotional and spiritual devastation appearing before them. If the client continues to demonstrate courage, self-discipline, and determination to reduce the influence of their aggressive./defensive ego, *while at the same time* opening up their heart to understand and care for the adaptive child, they can come into a freedom and inner peace the likes of which they may not have ever known.

This is a crucial point in this healing work. Will you abort the struggle and return to your old ego-forged identities and the severe familiarity of your aggressive/defensive ego consciousness? Will you carry on in your desire to heal yourself and transform the quality of your life? Now that you have seen the adaptive child within, will you ignore, abandon or betray it all over again? These choices must be made.

Conversing With The Adaptive Child

Once a client has had the time to stabilize and feel more comfortable with their new connection to their adaptive child, we are ready to take the next step. This is getting to know this child from the inside out rather than from the outside in.

Instead of merely observing the wounded child who has appeared, the client (you) will now start speaking with them. In doing so, a client will often feel some trepidation, intuitively knowing in facing the adaptive child consciousness, they will have to take some responsibility for the condition this child is in. It's not just the significant adults of the past who have mistreated, suppressed, or ignored this child. The client themselves has been a source of neglect or harm unconsciously picking up where the aggressive/defensive egos of early caregivers left off. It is entirely possible, from the adaptive child's point of view, the adult person the client has become may be indistinguishable from its original oppressors.

In facing this wounded child consciousness, the present-day adult will be forced to take inventory on how they have behaved in this relationship. Being held accountable can be painful. This is why so few clients initially embrace the opportunity to come face-to-face with their adaptive inner child.

As painful or humbling as this all may be, the courageous client will stay in relationship with the child that appears before them. In seeing and taking responsibility for the condition of this child, a client may feel a wide range of sensations or emotions, and experience a vast array of unflattering or unpleasant thoughts.

I begin the process by suggesting a client (or you) pay attention to what is happening within them: shock, shame, self-loathing, regret, sadness, terror, fear, anger, aches, pains, headaches, thoughts, ideas, or nausea. Begin a conversation with the adaptive child regarding these. It often comes about that a client will realize that more than the abusive or insensitive people from the past, the client is responsible for the adaptive child consciousnesses' current condition and behavior. This unflinching self-confrontation can make even the brave client shudder.

Yet, as a client acknowledges how badly they have dealt with their inner child, it is also possible they will be flooded by waves of love, compassion, and understanding. This can be a beautiful and moving experience of healing as two previously alienated and conflicted Inner Family members (the newly forming independent/aware adult consciousness and the child consciousness) meet and open up their hearts to each other. A client will sometimes report feeling emotionally and spiritually unified or integrated for the first time in a long time. The previously, incessantly conflicted inner voices are temporarily quieted and reconciled. A profound peace may accompany this experience.

To retain this sense of unity will require additional healing work. Time and again, the client's threatened aggressive/defensive ego consciousness will attempt to reassert its (formerly) unchallenged dominion over the Inner Family. It will try to subvert the healing process.

When trying to reestablish dominance it may blame the child consciousness for its shattered state or embarrassing neediness. Or it may try to convince the client that taking on the caring of this child is far too demanding an assignment and one that, if pursued, may threaten many cherished aspects of life—income, relationships with significant others, living situations, the roles and ego-forged identities that have been used for years. Remember: *the aggressive/defensive ego will try to do whatever it has to do to blame others and reassert its control and supremacy*. It will do whatever it can to distract, overwhelm, or criticize the adult client for getting too close to their adaptive inner child's emotional pain and fear.

The Conversation Between The Independent/ Aware Adult And The Adaptive Child

How this begins varies significantly. It may be a little while before the child is willing to speak. If there are deeper levels of trauma and injury it may take some time before it even *can* speak. This child has been badly affected by the treatment it received at the hands of ego-identified adults (including the client). It has learned only how to survive life and love, not surrender to them. By bringing back the natural or authentic self (by *un*-adapting) it will feel certain that more hurt and harm will come to it.

That an adult person has acknowledged the adaptive child's painful reality in a therapist's office doesn't mean much. Why should a child begin to trust and open up after being mistreated or ignored for a lifetime? Justifiably, this inner consciousness may be leery and cautious. Understandably, they may need to test the adult client's newfound sincerity and devotion. Like any other important relationship, a measured process of slowly getting to know the adaptive child will be required.

Speaking With Your Adaptive Child

Once you have a stable image of your adaptive child, how do you begin a conversation? With the truth, the whole truth and nothing but the truth. Here is an excerpt from how one client alternates between loving and rejecting their adaptive child:

"Little Diane, I can barely look you in the eyes. I am so ashamed of how I have treated you. Somewhere a long, long time ago I decided to get rid of you, to drop you in a dumpster some-where. If I didn't do that, I decided to hide you from public view as if you were someone so hideous that I was sure no one in their right mind would want or accept you. (crying... long silence) I've been that way with you ever since. Even now, as I look at you, I'm afraid that's who I'll find. I'm shaking as I say that.

"But I also know that my life as it is, is not working. That trying to do things my way hasn't worked. As a matter of fact, it's got me very, very lost and confused. But, to tell you the truth, if I let you back into my life, it could get worse. What if it's true? What if there is something so bad or ugly about you that no one will want to stick around us? Besides, I like being free, independent. You look very, very needy to me. If I give you an inch, you might take a mile. I might get completely suffocated. I don't need someone else to be responsi-ble for.

"So, to tell you the truth, a part of me would much rather keep you where you've been all these years... Or maybe just do the job officially once and for all, and kill you... But I guess I've tried that already and look where it's got me.

"Still you look so miserable, so broken, so pathetic. Maybe you're just a figment of my imagination. Your vulnerability and neediness really bother me! I guess I feel for you and I hate you at

the same time. How could that be possible? (smiles and laughs) Come to think of it, that's exactly how I felt Mom felt about you growing up!

"*I don't know what I'm going to do with you. I've got nothing more I want to say right now.*"

Hearing Back from the Adaptive Child

Similar to the work described in <u>Chapter VII</u>, when you gave yourself over to and became the aggressive/defensive ego consciousness of the Inner Family, it is possible to do the same thing as your adaptive child consciousness. How is this done? Just follow your intuitive emotional process and give yourself over to the image or form of your adaptive child which has already been coming to you.

With a client, for example, I would ask them to leave where they are presently sitting (that particular spot henceforth reserved for the independent/aware adult consciousness) and go to a location in the room where the adaptive child has shown itself. Once there, I tell them to just let go as much as possible and become the adapted child they have already perceived.

If you recall, sometimes gruesome images are presented as a first glimpse of the adaptive child. Reading about these, or having such an image yourself, may shock you. However, it may be more shocking for me to suggest that you, or my client, "become" this image, whatever it is. Nevertheless, that is what is most effective. From my experience, a small minority of the initial forays into an awareness of the adaptive child require you to cope with images such as these.

Your own first-glimpse may be more palatable—a lonely, little child sitting on the steps behind your house in the middle of a large family gathering; the class clown pouring over an exam paper in which you will not be getting a single right answer; or a child frequently abused and in trouble. *Whatever the image is that is presented to you, try to become it.*

This is an important exercise in *self*-acceptance; a crucial key in any healing work. Climb into the skin of the adaptive child you have visualized. Let it shape or mold your body in any way it likes as an instrument of self-expression. What happens for you as you become your adaptive inner child?

In sessions, as a client's image of their adaptive child consciousness becomes present, I do very little to direct the process. Rather it is the child who leads us. Perhaps it is not ready to interact with the client or me. Even if it cannot or will not utter a word, just by their chosen location and posture they will be communicating a great deal.

Where has this child placed themselves in the room? Have they chosen a distant corner; under a desk; right beside you; or even on your lap? What is their physical posture expressing? Are they curling up in the fetal position or sitting cross-legged at your knees? Does their posture indicate that they seem comfortable or uncomfortable; trusting or leery; wanting to open up or withdraw? What is all of this telling you? Let the child lead you.

As your child consciousness, perhaps you will not wish to speak to the adult you have become in the present day. Maybe the child just wants to be left alone; that simply letting itself be known and seen is enough of a risk. As the child consciousness, you may feel inclined to just make noises or sounds and nothing more.

The adaptive child may elect to start speaking immediately. If it does, what does it want to say to the now fully-grown adult you have become? Let the conversation go anywhere it wants. The opening statements are often significant indicators of the emotional pain and fear which is still carried. Present-day concerns may be easier to talk about than things which have happened in the past. In order to come to know this consciousness here are some questions which you, the adult, can use:

- "What's it really like to be you in the present day?"
- (If you are taken back in time...) "Why have you taken me back to this age/time/place?" *or* "What happened to you at that age/time/place?"
- "How does this affect you today?"
- "How has this affected me?"
- "How have you felt treated by me (your adult) all these years?"
- "Do you feel that I treat you better/the same/worse than the adults who were a part of that age/time/place?
- "More than anything else in the world, what do you need?"
- "Why are you choosing to situate yourself where you are in the room?" (i.e. underneath a desk, in a far cor-

ner or right beside me, etc.)
- "If you had one message for me today, what would that be?"

As your adaptive child, you may experience an array of emotions as you respond to these questions. Sometimes these may be powerful and strong. If intense feelings become apparent in this process make sure that you stop if you are feeling overwhelmed in any way and return to the child at another time.

Resistance and delays by or from the adaptive child consciousness should always be respected. In sessions, the client and I will use these periods to gently explore what has just happened. Is it too painful? Are there feelings of distrust for you, the present day adult? It's quite possible the child hasn't trusted or shown authentic feelings to an adult and is extremely leery to do so.

The adaptive child consciousness doesn't know if the now-adult client (or the therapist, or you if you do this, or anyone else who may be present if you do this with an observer) will treat them any differently than they were treated in the past. Perhaps "we" will behave and react as other aggressive/defensive egos have. The attention from or by "us" may be a manipulation and short-lived, such that the child could be abused, forgotten, or rejected all over again. And, at the same time, perhaps the resistance and requested delays come from the adult client. This process can be very subtle and it is important to take time to explore, understand, and integrate the experience before you move on.

An Adaptive Inner Child's First Words

Here are examples of the first words spoken by one client's adaptive inner child.

"I am your inner child, Bill. You have wanted to have nothing to do with me for many years. [Long pause] *It's always felt like you've hated me, like you're embarrassed by me. This hurts! It really, really hurts! How could you be so mean? What have I ever done to you?*

"Leave me alone. Leave me alone! Just leave me alone! You're mean!. Go to hell!

(And now referring to his past...)

"Why do I look the way I do? Because Dad has just left Mom and I now live with Mom alone. I feel very sad inside but Mom just wants me to smile and pretend like I am happy. I'm not happy. I hate it here! I hate it! I hate it! I hate it! I'd run away right now if I could. But where would I go? But you don't care. You're just like all the rest of them. You don't listen either."

Statements like these from the adaptive inner child— expressions of anger, hurt, confusion, and deep emotional pain may not be particularly easy for the adult client or you to hear. The client may feel attacked or blamed. It is crucial that this budding relationship not devolve into an argument of who's right and who's wrong.

Having heard words that might sound like accusations from the child, it is important that the adult be given an equal right to voice their reactions. Some typical reactions from clients are:

- *"Who is this and what the hell is happening here?"*
- *"How dare my adaptive child be saying such things! What an ingrate! Who does she think she is?"*
- *"Don't blame me! I didn't know what I was doing. I didn't know any better!"* (which is true)
- *"I don't relish the task of dealing with a withdrawn, furious or hateful child and bringing him into the so called Inner Family! Who needs it?"*

These, and any other reactions are just as important as those of the child. Additional spoken or written dialogue will be necessary to continue the process; it is on-going.

The Written Work

As shown earlier regarding the aggressive/defensive ego consciousness, you can also access the adaptive child consciousness through writing. *In the case of writing the child's words, place your pen or writing instrument in your non-dominant hand.*

Like some of the inner healing work already described in this book, this technique may seem silly or goofy at first. Yet, as with almost all clients, I think you'll be amazed at how this simple practice can circumvent and penetrate through the complex intellectual and conceptual framework of explanations and interpretations "adults" use to hide their emotional pain and fear. This style of writing—that of a young child, with pen or crayon in your non-dominant hand, can support you in accessing levels of vulnerability and simplicity which quickly allow you to get closer to yourself emotionally and spiritually.

Remember that there are two different aspects to the child consciousness: the natural child consciousness and the adaptive child consciousness. It is usually the adaptive child you will come to know first. This is because you have adapted so early in your childhood (in order to survive) that there is little or no memory of ever being wholly and completely yourself. Thus, it will be the adaptive child who will use the writings to first get your attention. However, this is not *always* the case.

On occasion it will be the natural child conscious-ness/authentic self who will be the first to write. If this happens, you are being given a wonderful spiritual gift of immediately being able to meet your "original face". Timeless, wise, free, and loving, this child may appear to physically be quite young, but spiritually it may radiate a wisdom that will amaze you. This vision of the natural child consciousness/authentic self can be a wonderful motivator, holding the promise of what your inner child once was like and could be again.

In some situations there is a serious wrinkle that may appear that you need to be made aware of. Should someone have seriously romanticized or idealized their past (most notably around their parents and childhood), they may not be capable or prepared to admit their romanticized delusion. [Romanticizing childhoods to conceal mistreatment and neglect is extremely common—denial is a *very* powerful dynamic.] When your adaptive child consciousness presents itself it may, on first glance, seem to be an authentic natural child.

Closer examination will often reveal the images the adaptive child presents have been "brush-stroked" to appear happy and natural but actually represent just another form of adaptation. Just as in the past, even in healing, you may still be polishing images of your childhood to survive the aggressive/defensive egos that surround you. This produces a "perfect" memory and must be challenged. Be patient and go slow; this is tricky.

In time you will come to know who is doing the writing—

the adaptive child consciousness or the natural child consciousness/authentic self. Sometimes, as you will see in the examples below, the two will alternate in the same writing. In the early writing exercises try not to be concerned about which child is writing, just write what comes to mind and accept what you get. Try not to force the words. At the same time, no matter how uncomfortable, startling, or seemingly irrelevant the writings may appear, try not to censure anything.

One last reminder: With almost every attempt to connect to the child or the spiritual consciousnesses of your Inner Family, you can expect to hear from the typically loud, critical, and judgmental voice of the aggressive/defensive ego. It will be firmly opposed to this venture. You will hear denunciations or variations of: "This is nuts!" "I feel like such a fool doing this!" "How do I know if any of this is real?" "Maybe I'm just making the whole thing up!" "What if I go off the deep end?" "This is too scary! It may even be danger- ous!" "Who does this therapist think he is?"

This is only your aggressive/defensive ego consciousness be- ing threatened by the new allegiance you are beginning to form with an Inner Family member (other than itself), and the increasing possibility of it losing its influence. *Persevere.*

Samples of Writings From the Adaptive Child Consciousness

Below are client samples of writings from their adaptive child consciousness:

"My name is little Tammy and I am your adaptive inner child. I am a little girl about nine years old and I am seeing and feeling a lot of sad and mad people. My tummy feels sick and hurts when that happens. I like being alone or with animals. Then I don't feel that way.

"I am good at keeping secrets. I can go to my best friend's house to play and not tell her that my Mommy cried when she got pushed down the stairs. I can go to school and no one can tell that my Daddy got mad at me again and my head broke the wall and now they have to fix it. I gave the school my note from home that tells them I had to stay home sick. I'm glad the big bump on my head is going down so no one asks about it. No one can know I've been bad

again.

"*I am to be seen and not heard, my Mommy and Daddy tell me. I've been in trouble with my family for my whole childhood. They are always saying that if I stopped arguing or talking back, that I wouldn't get in trouble and get hurt. But all I want is love, so I go to my parents for whatever I can get. They are always mad and unhappy, so that's what they give me.*

"*I keep going back for whatever I can get. I will be anyone they want me to be. I will do **anything** to feel connected to them. I'll take anything. I don't care anymore what happens afterwards. Because maybe today I'll get a hug.*"

*

"*I am Carl's long forgotten child. When I started school at the age of five, the world terrified me so much that I decided I couldn't be who I am. I needed to create someone else to survive.*

"*My trick worked great and everyone liked the boy I created. The best thing was that I could avoid being bullied if I pretended to be strong. But inside I was even more terrified than ever. Not only was the world just as scary but I had forgotten who I really was...*"

Carl now writes regarding the present: "*I had no idea at age five that my little pretending trick would lead me to where I am at age thirty-eight. Because I have totally lost touch with who I am, I am completely incapable of any type of meaningful relationship with a woman, my family, or friends. I am still that terrified five year old, pretending to be who I think people want me to be.*"

*

"*I want to feel alive. I want to experience child-like curiosity in the wonders of the universe. I want to be loved, and to be able to love unconditionally. I want (you) to bring me back and know me. I am the child who died at boarding school.*"

*

"*I am little Cindy and I live in fear. I am afraid of big people and little people. I am afraid they are going to be mean to me or hurt me. It's what I've always known. I also love to laugh, to jump and sing and I love beautiful things.*

"I desperately want to be beautiful and be loved and to laugh and jump and sing as much as I can."

*

"Who am I? I like animals, trees and the sea. I like to play and read and get big hugs. I like to look out of the back window of a car and see everything going backwards. I like to lie on the floor in front of a big fire with all the lights off and watch the shadows dancing on the ceiling.

"Where have I been? From being loved to being hated to being totally ignored. And the same thing happened to me in my Inner Family. Half a century later, I'm getting some attention again. Most of my life I've been banished, ignored by my ego who thinks he doesn't want to feel my pain. Now ego's losing his grip, so sometimes I get to do what I want.

"I want a nice, big, black cat."

*

"I am the part of Patrick that has been hidden most of his life. I'm the part that is curious and excited about almost everything in the world. I know when I want to laugh and when I need to cry. I'm the part that likes people, looks for a smile, loves a hug and really believes it when someone says 'I love you.'

*"I've been keeping myself out of sight for most of Patrick's life. Everyone in the whole world seems so different than me. I must be wrong. Most of my life I've felt like I have nothing really important to offer the grown-ups. **I don't want to be a burden**.*

"Recently it feels like Patrick has at least noticed me. Sometimes he asks me what I would like to do today, what I really need right now. Some days we spend a whole day hiking or skiing or just walking in the forest. Those are the best days—when every little thing we see is beautiful and amazing."

*

This letter from the child consciousness was written well into the healing process. Notice the details, the advances, and the setbacks that this child feels have been made in her relationship with the independent/aware adult:

"I am Kathy's inner child. This is what it was like before Kathy found me in her healing work.

"I was very, very lonely. I felt like I didn't matter. I wasn't important. I was used to this because I always felt like this. I didn't have a lot of fun because Big Kathy [the ego-controlled consciousness] *wanted us to work and work and work. It was all adult stuff. I didn't have any real playmates and I was very sad.* **I was so afraid.** *I got even more afraid when Big Kathy started seeing Big Ernie all the time* [her future husband].

"When Big Kathy started to do her healing work I was happy because she finally started to pay attention to me. But I still felt bad because I didn't know if she really wanted me in her life and wanted to spend time with me. Big Kathy was very uncomfortable with me starting to be around and so I felt uncomfortable too. I didn't know if things were going to change or not. I got to start to say what I was feeling but I don't think Big Kathy was that happy about it. It still kept feeling like it always had - that Big Kathy just wanted me to be quiet and pretend that everything was O.K. But I was still very scared and lonely and didn't feel O.K.

"Now, I know for sure that Big Kathy wants to know my feelings and spend time with me. Kathy does things with me and she doesn't spend her whole time worrying about adult things. She will let me have almost all my feelings now. This makes me feel safe. Life is easier than it has ever been. I feel important now. And what a thrill for Big Kathy to show me to Big Ernie and for him to like me and take me just the way I am."

*

Here is a two-part letter. Part I is the adult client writing about their present day life. Part II is the adult writing to her adaptive child.

Part I: *"There are times when I don't know anything and all I can do is return to the truth inside my body. I try to run from the pain and truth, pacing, hiding, working, accomplishing until my body can't take it anymore. I find a private place and I rage, I rage, I hate, I hate. I crumble and scream: "No more!" I finally reach the pain. [My knees pull up to my chest, with every sob, drawing the grief out of my body.]*

Part II: *"You tell me what you see and feel. I let you feel all of it. I hold you. You rest and I allow God to wipe your brow. I tell you* [the adaptive child] *no matter what, you are mine and I will love you. Please tell me your truth and I will listen. I tell you that it was never your fault, and you did nothing wrong. There was never anything wrong with you. You are not a mistake. You are deserving of all of the love this world has to offer, and your love is a beautiful gift. Yes, grown ups did abandon you; yes, they turned on you; but it had nothing to do with you. You have always been good. Those adults were hurt and confused.*

"Can you trust me? I will stay very, very, close and listen to everything you tell me.

"I feel your heartbeat. You are open. You are free. You are love. I feel you. Together with the knowledge of this world and its suffering, we will learn to forgive and move away from the illusion. We have a voice. It's a new voice. It speaks from the truth of our being. Journey on, brave child and teach me. I will trust in your heart to guide me."

Letters On Specific Subjects: Differing Points of View & Conflict Between Inner Family Members

Getting conflict between Inner Family members out into the open is a critical part of the work that needs to be done. Letters from the child consciousness (non-dominant hand, one ink color) and from the aggressive/defensive ego consciousness (dominant hand, different ink color), on the same subject, can be extremely illuminating. They will portray the uneasy relationship between these two totally different ways of perceiving and experiencing everything.

Letters between the aggressive/defensive ego and the other Inner Family members will highlight the civil war going on inside you even more. *Healing the conflict and antagonism between members of the Inner Family is where your healing work must inevitably go.*

You can ask any member of your Inner Family to write a letter on any subject. Earlier I presented Amanda's letter from her aggressive/defensive ego consciousness on the theme of "Loving,

Trusting, and Committing to a Man". It is relevant to present it here again so it can be easily compared to a letter from her natural child consciousness/authentic self written on the same subject.

First, the letter from Amanda's aggressive/defensive ego:

"I am the aggressive/defensive ego consciousness in this Inner Family and here's what I have to say about loving, trusting, and committing to a man - NO FUCKING WAY!! Trust is something someone made up to get you where they want you. Love is a fairy tale—no happy ending though. The only person you can depend on completely is yourself. Everyone is in it for themselves and if they tell you otherwise, they are lying!

"Men enjoy you for their own pleasures. Sex, comfort, food—other than that, they can get what they need from their buddies. It is too risky to invest your time and energy on something that will not last and end up feeling lousy. Starts off with excitement, novelty, feelings of euphoria and quickly becomes standard and routine, requiring minimal participation. Love, trust, commitment— BULLSHIT! Give me what I want and I'll tell you that I love you if you want me to. You won't be valued for WHO you are but WHAT you do. Look pretty, smell pretty, deliver the sex on command and do not talk back. Don't challenge any ideas. [Men see...] women as typically foolish creatures, flighty at best. No brain capacity.

"It is ridiculous to think you can actually find someone who is genuinely loving, trusting and committed to you. Only in the movies, baby! You have to give to get and eventually you'll be doing all the giving and getting nothing in return. Don't dare complain about it either or you'll be punished for that."

Here is a second letter from Amanda's natural child consciousness on the same subject.

"I am the inner child consciousness of [Amanda's] Inner Family and here's what I want you to know about what I think about loving, trusting and being committed to a man. I think it would be wonderful! I wouldn't have to be by myself. I would have someone to talk to, laugh with, play with, dream, hug and snuggle with. Someone I would feel protected by. I don't know any man whom my ego will let close to me. I would sure like one just like I said though. I can see me skipping and whistling, dancing and singing if I could have this man.

"It would be so nice to have, just like my dog, Spencer—loving that never stops, that's dependable, no changes, no scares. Constant warmth and calm. Like a sunny day everyday and cozy too, like on a rainy day in your flannel pajamas. I wonder what it would be like to have all this and never have it taken away or leave unexpectedly. I think loving and trusting is easy but ego doesn't. La, la, la! I love lots of attention, hugs, kisses, looking right into the eyes and knowing there's real love in there and the eyes don't move away. They stay and stay."

*

You can easily see how different members of an Inner Family can have differing points of view on the same topic.

The Story of the Adaptive Child Unfolds

Like any other human relationship, the one between the independent/aware adult consciousness and the adaptive child consciousness can continue to heal. It is a process. However, the emotional pain and fear that has built up needs to be satisfactorily brought forward and resolved.

It is in this phase of the healing process that the adaptive child begins to disclose their true story—a story that has never been told; one that no one has ever wanted to hear. The story will be both extraordinarily unique and, at a deeper level, universal to all human beings.

In what way is it unique? No one, other than this child, has gone through the particular experiences and relationships which have formed and forced them to become an unnatural adaptation of themselves in order to survive. When it was occurring, the submergence and loss of the natural child consciousness/authentic self was a deeply private affair. Quite likely, the adult caregivers' aggressive/defensive egos didn't even notice it was happening. Even if someone had noticed it, (and many didn't even want to notice it), none were able to appreciate the process or the pain, much less prevent or resolve it. The emotional pain and fear felt was a misery so deep it severed the connection with the Universe of Love, and precipitated living in the Universe of Fear. As unique a possession as a fingerprint, the child has carried the particulars of its emotional wounds until today.

Yet, on this day, this child is alone no more. An adult has come forward to parent them. Of all the people in this world, it is this newly emerging independent/aware adult consciousness that can come the closest to totally understanding them; an adult no longer completely identified with the aggressive/defensive ego who knows this child's anguish and pain, disappointment and shame, aloneness and grief, firsthand. It is only this particular adult who can heal this adaptive child as they tell their story. Only this adult consciousness can give them what they need so that they may become a natural child/authentic self. This is actually a return to your natural state of being, but for many it will feel like the first time.

In what way is this story universal? The experience of the adaptive child is not just about a particular child or a particular childhood. When anyone sensitizes themselves to their child consciousness the evolving independent/aware adult soon realizes that they are not the only person in the world whose natural emotional and spiritual self has been mangled and forgotten. *You are not the only innocent victim who has become controlled by the aggressive/defensive ego consciousness and its fear-based, survival-oriented ways.* Siblings, friends, spouses, and parents have been victimized to a similar or possibly greater extent. It is easy to appreciate that no one escapes unscathed. This same story was (and is) unfolding for the children living next door, in the next town, or in another country.

A myriad of oppressive family, cultural, religious, and social conditions (poverty, racism, sexism, politics, religion, chronic unemployment, lack of education, arranged marriages, addictions, greed, anger, mental illness) victimize everyone, forcing children and the adults they grow into to twist themselves into adaptive misrepresentations of the natural, authentic selves they once were.

It is important that the client (the emerging independent/aware adult) come to see that the parents, authority figures, politicians, and power brokers who could easily be blamed and viewed as the perpetrators of these damages are themselves victims of yet other/earlier fear-based egos and childhood injustices. Their perceived persecutors have carried the same unacknowledged, unhealed emotional and spiritual wounds which have spilled over onto the next generation. In turn, these psychic wounds have already spilled over from the client onto other innocent bystanders (such as their own children, friends, lovers, co-workers).

Coming to this realization and accepting it is a freeing and liberating experience. Reaching out in love to the adaptive child is the beginning of truly breaking this horrible chain of pain and suffering. This chain links you to everyone. No human being has ever escaped from it. No human being will escape from it any time soon. It is the human condition.

In taking on the responsibility of healing yourself and saving your own life, it is only the newly independent/aware adult who can break this chain. With far greater insight, you know none of the people (past or present) could have acted much differently than they did. Without consciousness and awareness no one had any real choice—no one stood a chance. What may always be the two most important and impressive accomplishments of any healing work are:

- The way you were treated wasn't directed at you "personally". It was what it was and, very probably, everyone just did the best they could. Not blaming and having acceptance of this is crucial; and,

- The recognition that now, today, *you* have a choice. You are free to re-create yourself and put a stop to the oppression that brought you to this point. [And of course, this undertaking is difficult and requires courage and taking responsibility.]

The newly independent/aware adult client can appreciate we are all broken beings and it is yet another ego-based illusion to view the world as if it has clearly defined good guys and bad guys (like an old western movie). In reality there are no clearly distinguishable good guys and bad guys. There is no hard and fast line forever dividing the forces of light and darkness or good and evil. Realize that it is a dangerous and deceptive tactic of the aggressive/defensive ego consciousness to believe that anyone has a monopoly over goodness or truth. *We all carry the potential for kindness and love or cruelty and fear and have acted in these ways towards others*. We are beings who, at any given moment, can choose to be led by our natural child consciousness/authentic self and our spiritual consciousness, or allow ourselves to be dominated by our aggressive/defensive ego and our adaptive child.

The reward for coming to know and embrace your adaptive inner child is that they can lead you to, and help you through, the original, unexamined, and often denied emotional pain and fear of your life. *To the extent that you heal the original emotional wounds of your adaptive child consciousness is the extent that you free yourself to embrace and operate from a loved-based, growth-oriented consciousness.* This allows a return to the natural child consciousness/authentic self and the Universe of Love which surrounds it. Thus, you can more regularly leave behind the Universe of Fear and increasingly reside in the Universe of Love.

Now that you know this, what choice will you make?

Chapter IX

*"The result of a child becoming dulled to pain is that ac-
cess to the truth about himself will be denied him all his
life."*

Alice Miller, from *For Your Own Good:*
Harper Collins Canada, Ltd., 1990.

*"We must have... a place where children can have a whole
group of adults they can trust."*
Margaret Mead

The Child Within: The Link To A
Love-Based Consciousness

The Choice

Our primary focus (to this point) has been to understand and
heal the fear-based aggressive/defensive ego consciousness and its
predecessor the adaptive child consciousness. In taking on the work
of healing I have briefly discussed the creation and development of
an independent/aware adult consciousness. This is an adult
consciousness, hopefully "you" at this stage of your healing journey,
who:

- knows the nature and workings of the aggres-
  sive/defensive ego consciousness;
- is consistently willing to take responsibility for it and the
  consequences of its behavior; and,
- can, by choice and effort, clearly shift to another state of
  consciousness when you are aware that you are being
  controlled by it.

As I have written about, there are two other states of consciousness which are love-based and growth-oriented. These are two Inner
Family members who have so far received little of our attention.
They are: (i) the **natural child consciousness**, which I have also
referred to as your *authentic self;* and (ii), the **spiritual conscious-**

ness. By learning to identify and align yourself with either of these, a new world view (originating from the Universe of Love) will open itself up to you. *The ability to make this shift is the core practice in your continued personal healing and transformation.* It is your natural child consciousness that is the most practical guide into a new, loved-based operating state and way of being.

To the extent that a person experiences sufficient safety and support in their childhood, they will (to the same extent) be able to display their natural emotional and spiritual self as an adult.

This adult, if connected to their full natural child consciousness, would be congruent with their ever-changing natural emotional and spiritual processes. They would not have to worry about having to "fit in" for the sake of pleasing anyone. They would be able to accept and love themselves for their actual, experienced moment-to-moment reality.

For an adult person, their natural child consciousness provides access to a timeless source of emotional wisdom, peace, clarity, and guidance. This is the little plug connected to its socket.

Traits and Features of a Person Operating from Their Natural Child Consciousness/Authentic Self

As you read the eleven aspects notice how often you experience them. Be mindful that the aggressive/defensive ego and the adaptive child consciousness are *brilliant* at maintaining illusions.

1. Feelings Are Guides to Personal Truths

> " It is only with the heart that one can see
> clearly. What is essential is invisible to the eye."
> Claude St. Exubery, from *The Little Prince*

If it can be stated that all of the wisdom you will ever need is within your own heart and soul, the source of a great deal of that wisdom is the natural child consciousness/authentic self. This Inner Family member relies exclusively on feelings as their way of knowing what is real and true (and what isn't). They do not process things intellectually or analytically. [Those ways of information gathering and understanding the world can be extremely useful but do not of themselves lead to wisdom.] The child consciousness penetrates through the matrix of culturally-determined, ego-based status symbols. Un-phased and untouched by the agendas of the aggressive/defensive egos around it—survival through the wielding of external power and position—it can spontaneously and piercingly see through any person or situation to its core emotional and spiritual energy.

If, an as adult, you are operating from your natural child consciousness, you know things clearly, immediately, simply, and directly. These same things are tortuous, mind-numbingly complex, or entirely blocked off when you try to grasp them through your aggressive/defensive ego. The natural child consciousness can be described as possessing an unerring "truth detector" about people, events, and circumstances. Because it has immediate access to its pure and direct feelings, it can quickly read people or situations.

Someone may come dressed in the finest ego trappings, be well-spoken, demonstrate impeccable manners, and convey motives which are seemingly sincere, but the natural child within you may perceive only danger around this person. Consequently, this consciousness will not trust or like this individual. On the other hand, a person may be considered some type of "black sheep"—an eccentric, a failure, or an outcast by the larger ego-based world and the natural child within you may experience safety around them and will like and trust them far more than others do.

As an adult operating from the natural child consciousness/authentic self, you will trust your feelings and experience. None of the "shoulds", "oughts", or "musts" (the codes of convention imparted and enforced by the aggressive/defensive egos around you) will affect you. When you are identified with this Inner Family member, you are blessed with an ability to see through the smoke and mirrors of ego presentations and ploys around you. You trust what you feel and sense to be true.

2. A Born Visionary: No Need for Personal Gain or Advantage

The ability of the natural child/authentic self to understand and holistically discern the true nature of a person (or situation) is possible because this consciousness does not see itself (nor is it) a localized, separated, finite object in space and time. It may be suppressed but cannot be destroyed by the aggressive/defensive ego.

Therefore it does not battle every second of life for survival. Because it sis not a static "thing", it can experience its real identity as a verb (as a *process*) not a noun.

This is rather abstract but important. What I mean by being a verb rather a noun is this consciousness knows its essence to be a part of the process and unfolding of all things; it is an emotional and spiritual process belongs to the unfolding of the universe. Like life, the natural child consciousness is in a state of perpetual flow and not handicapped by a single point of view. It can operate from a higher point of view than anything personal. It does not have to be *right* about anything in order to feel empowered in the world. This allows and promotes the originality and creativity of a visionary. Your natural child consciousness is a part of a universal consciousness.

Freed up from having to use all your available resources to survive, if you are an adult operating from your natural child consciousness/authentic self, you will have little need for personal gain or advantage with any person or in any circumstance. You will not need to use tactics, schemes, or contrived public images of yourself that are calculated to raise your status in the eyes of others.

The competitive games which aggressive/defensive egos play occur in a zone to which you are naturally immune. The prizes heaped upon the successful players of these games hold little appeal for you. And, equally so, the jeers and criticism extended the losers of these ego-based contests don't affect you. All of these ego-based "life-or-death" struggles for external power and control are understood for what they are: illusory and irrelevant.

No longer playing the game to win, the adult who can access their natural child consciousness/authentic self is **not attached to any particular outcome.** They have no vested interests and therefore do not have to push for any desired result. This allows for a peaceful and loving awareness regarding life that passes all understanding; or permits insight that is simply not available to those engaged in the death-struggle for temporary and empty aggressive/defensive ego victories.

3. The Experience Of Complete Sufficiency

The natural child consciousness/authentic self does not experience any kind of "lack" or insufficiency. When, as an adult, you are identified with this consciousness, you have all that you need right now: love. money, health, safety, attractiveness, value, possessions, and peace. *Nothing is missing.* Gone, like a bad dream, are the incessant and merciless operating judgments of the aggressive/defensive ego consciousness: *"I am not good enough,"* or *"I do not have enough."*

You do not have to search for something outside to fill you up, give your life significance, or make you feel temporarily better about yourself (and it is always temporary). You are in touch with the perfection of your creation—not perfect in the ego sense of being a flawless package of socially approved attributes and credentials, but perfect in the spiritual sense of needing to be absolutely nothing other than who you are now: inestimably good and important *without* any package. It is the authentic experience of wholeness and the antithesis of any inadequacy or failure your aggressive/defensive ego has kept you believing.

4. Motionlessness, Stillness, Timelessness—A Conduit to the Eternal Now

With nothing that you have to do or achieve to prove your worth, and no one you have to adapt to in order to "know" you are loved, and no need for an elaborate personal defense system in order to feel safe, there comes with the natural child consciousness/authentic self a quiet motionlessness. This is a stillness; a sense of timelessness that categorically sets it apart from the mad, frantic "doing" energy of the aggressive/defensive ego consciousness. You discover the "still point in a moving circle"; the silence behind the dance of life.

Time is no longer something that inexorably marches you towards death. Strenuous efforts to save, cheat, or rush through time are not a part of this state of consciousness. When you live out of your natural child consciousness time does not exist as a force to be reckoned with. There is just an eternal present forever unfolding. "Being" is all that happens and all that is necessary. When you are an adult operating from your natural child consciousness you are a part of the Eternal Now; a dimension which exists behind the world of your body, your ego, and your actions.

5. Content With The Smallest Pleasures

As opposed to the adaptive child, the natural child/authentic self is not afraid of life. With the Universe of Love as a permanent, full-time residence, there is *nothing* to be afraid of. Knowing the miracle of all things, there is only the experience of the wondrous nature of being alive. The natural child is content with what might be referred to as the smallest, simplest pleasures because it is not what they are that make the tiniest things miraculous, it is *that* they are. The friendly smile of a stranger; the babble of a brook; the scent of the flowers; the tastes of the food you eat; watching kittens play; the glory of your next breath; one small touch from your beloved—these are examples of the small pleasures the natural child can disappear into and enjoy to the fullest. Each of these, and countless other small joys of everyday life, are a universe unto themselves; tiny ways to access a richer dimension of being.

In ways that defy rational understanding, you, as an adult operating from your natural child consciousness, can share the experience of participating in these smallest of pleasures and tiniest of joys. Great magic and wonder become available in ordinary moments.

6. Deep Sensitivity and Vulnerability

The natural child consciousness is the Heart dimension of your Inner Family and, as such, is a deeply "feeling" consciousness. Emotions are the means employed to discern reality and to detect and evaluate the subtle emotional energies of others. As the natural child consciousness, you are capable of and want to feel things deeply— the more you feel, the more you know about your world and who you are in it.

Vulnerability and the willingness to wear your heart on your sleeve is your usual state and your personal ticket into the amusement park of life. Being vulnerable is not something you are afraid of. (As opposed to the aggressive/defensive ego's view that vulnerability is a threat to your survival and should be hidden from yourself and others.) As an adult who operates from your natural child consciousness, you know vulnerability is the bond that allows you to relate meaningfully and deeply to others. All living things share vulnerability, and you know that in vulnerability, everything is revealed. Accessing the natural child consciousness will add a great deal of richness, depth, and a fantastic diversity of inner experiences to your life.

7. The Lack of an Ability to Judge or Harbor Ill Will Towards Others

Feeling things deeply and fully can be an extremely mixed blessing. The capability for experiencing great love is offset by the capability to experience profound grief. An ability to trust absolutely brings the potential for absolute betrayal. The joy of being accepted for who you are will be matched in intensity by the pain of rejection. Being so closely identified with and reliant on emotions to navigate through life, coupled with deep sensitivity, necessitates that the natural child consciousness experience a complete range of feelings.

Yet even in the face of flagrant mistreatment and mean-spiritedness, it is the nature of the natural child consciousness to never retaliate. [On the other hand, the adaptive child and its full-blown aggressive/defensive ego counterpart can (and often will) respond to an offence with the same or another greater offence; but not the natural child.] *The natural child consciousness lacks the requisite amount of ill will necessary to even formulate a negative judgment of others, let alone make enemies or retaliate.*

The very ability to formulate negative judgments, beliefs, and criticisms that is so endemic to the aggressive/defensive ego's strategies for survival is something the natural child consciousness does not possess. It knows only acceptance. Its most defining feature of all may very well be its abject harmlessness; there is simply no malice in this Inner Family member. Completely untouched by the aggressive/defensive ego, it cannot blame, criticize, or attack. There is no build up of negative feelings which then fossilize into harsh judgments, beliefs, and criticisms about oneself or others.

As described above, the natural child can experience a full range of its feelings, including anger; however, without an aggressive/defensive ego consciousness to harbor resentment or blame, the experience of anger will have a beginning, a middle, and an end to it. It cannot harden into prejudice, bitterness, ill will, or become a justification used by the aggressive/defensive ego consciousness for revenge.

The natural child consciousness can feel emotionally hurt and may need to withdraw from someone. Yet by nature, it will whole-heartedly, want nothing more than to restore trust and good will. As an adult operating from your natural child consciousness, this tendency to easily and totally accept people and situations may, on occasion, not serve you well. There are times when it might be wise to realize that certain people will just continue to hurt you and exclude them from your life, but this would be done with kindness and simple acceptance of them being someone you don't want to be with. If you want to discover an earthly embodiment of constant love, acceptance, and understanding, you will need to look no further than your natural child consciousness.

8. Trust

Children are born with total and complete trust. They do not know how to distrust. Distrust is not an aspect in their emotional and spiritual being. As I described in the section on the birth of the ego, it is only when a child is overwhelmed with emotional pain and fear that distrust begins to creep in. There was a time when you had unquestioning trust and faith in others; however, as you plummeted into the Universe of Fear, distrust became the lens through which you looked at people.

No matter how deeply buried the natural child consciousness may be today, it still carries that same enduring, unfaltering trust. No matter how far you may have drifted away from it, if you look deeply within, you will notice a reaction of shock and disappointment whenever anyone fails to act in a trustworthy or ethical manner. It is as if a part of you somehow still can't believe it. It is your natural child consciousness/authentic self who can't and won't believe it.

As the adult you are today, you have probably come to the sensible conclusion that you cannot and should not return to the days when you felt that you could trust *everyone*. Yet it might be a wonderful step forward into healing if you could trust *anyone* the way you once did as a natural child.

9. A Source Of Unconditional Love

This takes us to what might be the most miraculous and awe-inspiring quality of the natural child consciousness—the ability to love totally and unconditionally. No greater love exists in human form than the love offered by a child. In my view, it is the highest and best love that humans are capable of.

I am forever humbled, inspired, and guided by the gentle lessons my sons teach me. They always demonstrate the towering grandness of love. They never judge me or make me bad or wrong, no matter how often my aggressive/defensive ego, with its heavy and dark clouds, rolls in to block the love from their open and willing hearts. I am always forgiven for my faults and gracefully given another chance to get it right. Their trusting eyes show me how steadfast, pure, and unfathomably powerful love can be. Time and time again I experience being healed and redeemed by it. My goal is to be just like them when I grow up.

Such is the love of all children who populate this planet; little angels be they; emissaries of God sent to the lost and confused tall people on planet Earth (adults). Children's love provides opportunities to return to everything that is real and important. In a world pushed to its disastrous limits by the barbarian qualities of the aggressive/defensive ego consciousness, children remind us of the world's potential to be a sane and safe place to live. They are here to show you a higher love, and a better, more peaceful, simple, natural, and harmonious way to live. *"Unless ye be as little children, ye cannot enter the Kingdom of Heaven."*

10. The Experience Of Peace

The natural child consciousness knows peace. With no need for defense, this Inner Family member does not employ any of the rigid armor or war paraphernalia of the aggressive/defensive ego consciousness, which costs you, the adult, the experience of peace. It is not a exaggeration to state that the natural child consciousness *is* peace.

"In our defenselessness our safety lies," was a statement I first came across in *A Course In Miracles*.[6] It shook me up to such an extent that I thought it was a misprint. In the ego's Universe of Fear, to adhere to the tenet that "in my defenselessness my safety lies" is an absurd, irresponsible, dangerous, and even suicidal proposition. However in the Universe Of Love, the permanent home of the natural child consciousness and the spiritual consciousness, this assertion is profoundly wise and makes perfect sense.

It is your need for defense which can only add to your fear. Interpreting it this way, buying a gun or bombing the enemy always adds more fear to the amount (of fear) you carry. Of all the aggressive/defensive egos that you will ever meet, the one which will cause you to be the most afraid will be your own. It therefore bears repeating: *"In my defenselessness my safety lies."*

As an adult operating more frequently from the natural child consciousness you can be shown the experience of perfect and complete peace; a peace which, as described earlier, is beyond understanding.

11. The Knowledge And Experience That God Is Close At Hand

If you are a person who is sincerely attached to a belief in the non-existence of God, or have been abused within the confines of a rigid belief system, this point may offend you or cause you to turn away. I will take this opportunity to remind you that when I speak of "God" I mean in the widest possible terms. If you are an atheist to all organized religions it may be that god is something that represents a deep and abiding psychological peace and harmony. And, at the very minimum, it is a god of your own understanding.

Putting together all of the principle traits and features of the natural child consciousness, you can see that when you are identified with the natural child consciousness/authentic self and not the aggressive/defensive ego (or its earliest form—the adaptive child), you are in an elevated emotional and spiritual state. You are not absorbed in a life and death struggle for physical and psychological survival which demands your unwavering attention and energy. Life is not a battlefield. Beyond the grip of the aggressive/defensive ego, there is peace. There is oneness. There is God.

A Brief Review and Comparison

Because of the importance of understanding the differences within the child consciousness, I have drawn a chart indicating what statements and questions would be prominent for a **natural child** or an **adaptive child**. Notice the adaptive child is figuring out how to be and the natural child is spontaneous.

Natural Child	Adaptive Child
"What am I feeling?" (with a spontaneous and honest answer)	"What do **they** want me to feel?" "What feeling am I supposed to be having now?" "What feeling will get me the attention or acceptance and approval of the people around me?"
"I need..." (or) "I need you to..." (a direct and spontaneous request)	"How can I get them to give me what I need?" "What do I first have to give them or appear to be giving them in order to get what I need?"
"I want..." (or) "I want you to..." (clear statements of desires and preferences)	"What role should I play to give me the best chance of getting what I want?" "How little can I tell them about what's really happening and still get what I want?" "How can I avoid telling them *directly* what I want and still get what I want?"
"I am loved." (this is known and experienced as a subjective truth)	"One way or the other, how can I get them to care about me?" "How can I get their attention?" "Who do they insist I be before they will love me?"

The Way Back:
The Natural Child Consciousness and
The Independent/Aware Adult Consciousness

The abundant spiritual capabilities of your natural child consciousness were present before the birth and domination of your aggressive/defensive ego, and before you began living in the Universe of Fear. As such, reclaiming it is the way to live in the Universe of Love. The path back will take you from the aggressive/defensive ego consciousness to (and through) the adaptive child and home to the natural child consciousness.

Though seemingly insignificant and irrelevant in a world which venerates the power of the ego, if you, as an adult, are both humble and willing enough, this child can lead you in simple and sane ways back to whence you came: a love-based, growth-oriented state of being and a deep and personal relationship with spiritual consciousness. *When you become more identified with your natural child consciousness/authentic self and your spiritual consciousness, than you are with your adaptive child or aggressive/defensive ego consciousness, your personal healing will have taken root.*

To summarize thus far, I am suggesting two separate and ultimately converging paths for the healing of your relationship with yourself:

- FIRST: The development of an **independent/aware adult consciousness**—one who has separated itself from the **aggressive/defensive ego consciousness** and all of its mental, emotional, and behavioral aberrations. This "new" consciousness chooses to be responsible. With it, you will embark upon a discipline of inner healing which can bring forth an entirely new, love-based, growth-oriented set of emotional and spiritual values; and,

- SECOND: The discovery and healing of your **adaptive child consciousness**. This healing process will promote a gradual return to your **natural child consciousness/authentic self** and your **spiritual consciousness**.

Chapter X

"God is the name by which I designate all things which cross my willful path violently and recklessly, all things which upset my subjective views, plans and intentions and change the course of my life for better or worse."

Carl Jung

The Spiritual Consciousness

A Heart-Based, Spiritually-Guided Identity

Let's briefly review your path of self-healing to this point.

* You have become acquainted with an Inner Family comprised of disparate, extremely conflicted consciousnesses operating within you;
* You have identified and taken personal responsibility for the workings of your aggressive/defensive ego consciousness;
* You brought forth a new Inner Family member: the independent/aware adult consciousness;
* Now, with this "new" Inner Family member, you have choice over your fear-based, survival-oriented conditioning;
* You can determine, moment by moment, whether you are operating from the Universe of Fear or the Universe of Love. This requires vigilance and commitment;
* With an emerging adult consciousness that's progressively independent of the aggressive/defensive ego, you have made the choice to help it heal;
* You have done so by following the paths to your greatest emotional pain and fear: responding to the emotional pain and fear of an adaptive child consciousness (the predecessor and earliest embodiment of your aggressive/defensive ego); and,
* By becoming a deeply committed, caring adult (an

inner parent for that adaptive child consciousness), you have helped to slowly return to, and become the natural child/authentic self, you once were. The little plug is reconnected to its original socket.

As I wrote at the beginning of the book, any system of therapy or self-healing which wants to offer you more than temporary relief from your physical, mental, or emotional symptoms, must guide you to examine and transform your core identity. You must come to know that you are not whatever the aggressive/defensive ego consciousness has decided you are.

This fear-based, survival-oriented consciousness has only allowed you to see constantly changing, elusive, and ultimately never-satisfying pictures of yourself. Over and over again, throughout the course of your lifetime, you have tried to "feel good" about those pictures. Regardless of whether you have been admiring and pleased or repelled and put off by them, you have been riveted and consumed by them.

Yet, there has been, and will be again, occasions in the course of your journey through life when your aggressive/defensive ego gets shaken and toppled from its position of being the ultimate source of "self"-knowledge. Experiences of pain, loss, failure, disappointment, betrayal, setback, illness, and sometimes success (as Carl Jung stated, *"all things which cross my willful path violently and recklessly, all things which upset my subjective views, plans and intentions"*) can affect the ego's world.

It is in times such as these that the aggressive/defensive ego (and its cast of diverse identities) may be dislodged from its role as the undisputed head of your Inner Family. At these times, your eyes are torn away from the ego-produced show which had previously enthralled you, and you can no longer find your old identity. You may feel temporarily lost but you are also freed up to rediscover and live from your original identity — a heart and spirit-led consciousness which is yours by birthright.

As the Aggressive/Defensive Ego Diminishes, the Spiritual Consciousness Rises

The aggressive/defensive ego consciousness can have its influence reduced because of major external events and circumstances which have compelled you to challenge it, or by conscious, directed, inner work such as this model of personal healing (or by the combination of the two). In these ways, room is made in the Inner Family for the heart dimension of the natural child consciousness/authentic self to increase its presence. This, in turn, allows for the reemergence of the last member of the Inner Family—the spiritual consciousness.

Who or What is The Spiritual Consciousness of Your Inner Family?

This "spiritual consciousness" is *not* necessarily God or Jesus Christ or Allah or Buddha or YHWH or Krishna or any other formal deity. These are various names for specific "Higher Powers". What I am referring to as the spiritual consciousness of the Inner Family is an innate, organic, inwardly-felt, and individualized spirituality. It is a highly personalized guide, presence, teacher, and source of direction and love that, in your experience of it, is unique to you. It may or may not attach itself to any formal deity or symbol.

As you open up to the spiritual consciousness of your Inner Family, your relationship with your own higher power will deepen and expand. If a metaphor is helpful here, perhaps see the spiritual consciousness as an old, wise loving friend or guardian angel; one who has been there all along and has a compassion for *all* Inner Family members which can help them heal beyond anything they can give themselves.

Perhaps a law that governs the make-up of any individual consciousness or Inner Family would be as follows: *The more you have become attached to and identified with your aggressive/defensive ego consciousness, the smaller is your ability to live through a heart-based and spiritually-led consciousness. The less you are attached to and controlled by the aggressive/defensive ego consciousness of your Inner Family, the greater is your ability to live as a heart-based, spiritually-led consciousness.*

I believe the intended flow of every human consciousness is from an identification with the aggressive/defensive ego consciousness to an identification with the spiritual consciousness. As such, it is only a question of time and detail but, with most people, sooner or later, voluntarily or involuntarily, they will be forced to shed all identification with the ego consciousness as their primary identity. If they (you) choose a "voluntary option", like a path of healing, this process will happen consciously and deliberately while they are alive. For those who choose the "involuntary option", this process happens, frequently, with tremendous accompanying resistance, emotional pain, and fear while they are physically dying. When it comes to abandoning the ego consciousness as a primary identity and identifying with a heart-based and spiritual consciousness, the old adage: "You can pay me now or you can pay me later," will largely apply.

The aggressive/defensive ego consciousness is the last member of your Inner Family to be born and will need to be the first Inner Family member to be abandoned. If a personal catastrophe of some kind is what is usually required for this to happen, dying is often perceived as the *ultimate* personal catastrophe. Dying is generally accompanied by large measures of invasive pain, hardship, and helplessness, to such a real degree that the ego cannot maintain any control.

As such, the occasion of a life-threatening illness or the actual dying process might be said to be the final opportunity for the adult consciousness to dis-identify from the overriding ego consciousness. During this time, dramatic "psychological" healing can occur for the dying person as well as for individuals connected to them. This, of course, does not necessarily promote physical healing—the body may die—yet, a healing of conflict and antagonism can occur within the dying person or between the dying person and others.

When our identification with the aggressive/defensive ego consciousness is gone, what is left? Harmony and peace, and for some, the presence of God.

Admissions Which Support the Spiritual Consciousness to Rise

Whether it be in life or in the process of dying, it frequently appears that the adult who has become identified with the aggressive/defensive ego consciousness will be brought to a point where they are prepared to acknowledge that the person they see themselves as (an "ego") cannot take them any further. Their inherent human limits and complete and utter inability to overcome those limits by relying on their own resources becomes blatantly obvious. At that point, they are forced to concede certain truths in regard to these fundamental limitations. To the ego-controlled adult, these admissions are at the same time devastating and liberating, embarrassing and empowering, shaming and healing. However, making these admissions, if sincere and deeply felt, is a step forward in personal healing. They are an opening for the spiritual conscious-ness to enter their life more fully.

I'll examine some of the key confessions an ego-identified adult might need to make before the spiritual consciousness can take its full place in the Inner Family.

EGO ADMISSION #1: "I am good at many things, but I have not found nor do I know how to find the experience of real love and peace."

> *"There's no taste quite like the taste of humble pie;*
> *no meal quite as memorable as eating crow."*
> A client.

It can't be emphasized enough that the aggressive/defensive ego consciousness is not the villain of the inner world. This Inner Family member has been essential for your survival. It has done and will continue to do whatever it perceives necessary to preserve your physical and psychological protection. Remember also, that to it, the experience of emotional pain is equivalent to the experience of death. Consequently, it is a useful ally in keeping the emotional pain and fear you carry from flooding and incapacitating you. Because there has been no independent/aware adult consciousness present to moderate, soothe, and heal it, it is true that, in your *un*conscious state, it can slip beyond the pale into viciousness and savagery. And, as cited earlier, this possibility must be stopped.

Yet, it is also the case, if the ego consciousness can be guided by the same independent/aware adult to become a healthy ego (an ego-in-service), it can prominently and meaningfully contribute to the betterment of yourself and others. Ego characteristics like endurance, ambition, stubbornness, willfulness, tenacity, single-mindedness, boldness, outspokenness, and toughness combined with ego-based skills like planning, strategizing, and devising the methodology needed for completing any difficult, long-term projects, have enabled you to achieve many worthwhile things in your life. Completing your education, finding and holding your job, establishing yourself in a profession or career, the acquiring of your home and possessions, and achieving some financial security, are all directly connected to ego strengths and talents.

No other Inner Family member knows the ways of the "real" world quite like the ego, including how hard, competitive, and manipulative it can be. It knows the angles, deals with adversaries, has plenty of "street smarts", and can certainly be a catalyst to action. As an ego-controlled adult, you have become extremely skilled at how to navigate successfully through the external world and obtain many of its more impressive rewards.

Furthermore, your ego consciousness has also allowed you to endure and overcome innumerable emotional and psychological hits and setbacks. It is thick-skinned and to a large extent self-absorbed. It can be an enormously strong and useful Inner Family member in the face of the rejection, criticism, and hurt that may come your way in the very efforts required to realize your most cherished dreams.

However, in matters of deep and sustainable love and inner peace the aggressive/defensive ego consciousness fails miserably. Built and designed only for survival out of the emotional pain of the adaptive child consciousness, and generating a Universe of Fear, and comprised of tried and tested attack/defend mechanisms, it cannot be the Inner Family member to bring forth any kind of inner peace nor can it produce happy, healthy and mutually beneficial love relationships. Not only does it know nothing about the true experience of love or peace, but it perceives these experiences as fearful and threatening. To the ego, love is a dangerous word. If the experience of enduring love and peace is something you want, following the ego consciousness will *never* get you there.

EGO ADMISSION #2: "I admit that I am powerless over _____ and my life has become unmanageable."

This is the brilliant first step of twelve-step programs; bar none, the most effective program ever devised for recovery from addictions of any and every kind. No matter what form, activity, or substance any addiction takes, the twelve-step approach requires an admission of powerlessness and unmanageability. Similarly, bringing harmony and peace to your Inner Family begins with some kind of an admission of powerlessness regarding being controlled by an aggressive/defensive ego. I have referred to this as a shift from an ego-based consciousness to a spiritually-based one.

As an ego-identified (ego-controlled) adult, you must come to the realization, at deeper and deeper levels of your being, that you *alone* are ultimately incapable of achieving the most important things in life. Powerless over obtaining or preserving anything you want— you can do your best; you can do all that you can do; but ultimately, *you cannot really control anything.*

- Will you live a long and healthy life or will your heart just stop beating in the very next moment?
- Will you forever remain employed by the company or organization you work for today?
- Will you ever get that promotion you hope for, even with diligent efforts and extraordinary dedication?
- Will the economy of your province, state, country, or continent be robust or stumble? Will your money be worth anything if it falters or crashes?
- Will the one(s) you love, love you in return? Will they continue to love you?
- What will truly become of your sons and daughters, no matter how much you plan or care or try to wisely guide them?
- Will you get hit by a vehicle driven by a negligent driver at the next intersection?
- Will the very planet you call home survive the many forces which threaten to annihilate it?

Over all of these situations (and any others you can name) the Inner Family member known as the ego consciousness has no control. For all intents and purposes, it really is powerless. Yes, it may continue to insist that "it" is the captain of your ship and the master of your fate; but how much is *really* in your hands anyway?

There is a saying: "Man makes plans and God laughs," and perhaps this is true; or perhaps God may not be laughing so much as

not agreeing or blessing your plans. Perhaps the spiritual consciousness of your Inner Family has other plans for you; other successes
and lessons of the heart and soul variety, that it sees as more
important than what you thought you needed.

EGO ADMISSION #3: "I know very little."

The mind or intellect of an ego-based adult can know a great
many things about any given subject. It can also know a few details
about a great many things. It can employ reason, logic, and argument
in many brilliant and useful ways. Even with that, what does it know
about anything for sure, really? Does it know where you came from
before you were born? Does it know where you are going after this
life is over? Does it know, more than anything else, what you are
here to give, receive, learn, rectify, or heal? Does it know what
constitutes a life well spent? How much can knowledge, so
pragmatic and essential in understanding how things work, tell you
about ultimate things? Not very much.

Very often the knowledge you possess has been modified,
enhanced, or rejected over time. There are probably things about
which you were completely clear and definite at one point in your
life that today you're not so sure about. There are people you once
admired and now don't, and others you formerly rejected and now
admire. Whatever you know, at any given time, is very often
extremely changeable and limited.

The changeable nature of what you're sure you know does
not mean however that you live foolishly or that somehow you are
deficient. On the contrary; your deeper emotional and spiritual
"knowing" (the natural child consciousness/ authentic self and the
spiritual consciousness of your Inner Family) will teach you that life
is a learning process; that you are here to make mistakes; that you are
even supposed to make mistakes.

> "*Living is an art, it's not bookkeeping. It takes an awful lot
> of practice for a man to be himself.*"
> James Cagney, actor

A clear awareness, which comes from the spiritual consciousness, tells you that an authentic, honorable and well-used life
is a work of art; a work which is constantly in progress, constantly
beautified, and constantly improved upon. It knows that sometimes

large and painful blunders are required to get your attention, to motivate you to learn extremely valuable soulful lessons. It knows that life is sometimes a deeply disturbing, confusing, embarrassing, and humbling experience of refining the truths by which you live. Your heart-led and spiritually-guided consciousness knows that each and every one of us must worship many, many false truths so as to find our way to the ones we experience as lastingly real.

The ego consciousness, however, does not know any of this. Taught by other egos how to operate and what to value, it knows and uses only external, consensus-based, culturally-established standards of evaluating progress. It defines the "good life" by comparison and consensus. The ego will always say: *"Success is always good and failure is always bad. Making more money this year than last is always good and earning less money this year than last is always bad. Being active and busy is always good and being idle and slow is always bad."*

To qualify as a "success", your life must show you, and more importantly show others, tangible, observable, and measurable indications that you are on an ever-ascending positive spiral: more acquisitions, more power, more sex, more money, more friends, more status. If this isn't the case at year end then, in ego terms, the year has been a write off.

For the most part, what people know is restricted by cultural mores, their five senses, and by conditioning. Our knowledge is always distorted by what the aggressive/defensive ego consciousness perceives it needs in order to survive. Thus, the adult who has become identified with it, in order to allow the spiritual consciousness to more fully enter their life, must admit they know very little. "I know very little," is a *necessary* personal admission. Yet, paradoxically, as a result of this admission, more can be known than the ego could ever imagine or conceive.

EGO ADMISSION #4: "I do not know emotional and spiritual advances from retreats. I do not truly know what is in my best interests."

> *"Put yourself not in charge of this, for you cannot distinguish between advance and retreat. Some of your greatest advances you have judged as failures, and some of your*

greatest failures you have evaluated as success."
A Course In Miracles

With only external, worldly measuring systems to guide it, the ego consciousness does not have any way of knowing the difference between inner victories and defeats. It does not know how to discern if what you are doing, saying, thinking, or feeling is truly something that is advancing you emotionally and spiritually or is not. As an ego-controlled adult, you believe you know the obvious differences between personal successes and failures; you're certain that you can differentiate between progressing or regressing in any action or project you undertake. You're convinced that you know the things which are in your best interest from those which are not. But do you?

Is getting that job promotion a personal success, even if it requires more sleepless nights and less time spent with loved ones? Is making more money a sign that you are progressing, even if money is on your mind and you worry about losing it more than ever? Losing the championship game could never be in your best interests, even though the experience of "losing" may take you into a life-enhancing process of self-examination, a greater ability to actually feel rather than hide your emotional pain, and a truer, more personal relationship with a timeless and changeless spiritual presence in your life. Is it possible what you perceived at one time to be "failures" in love or business prepared and directed you to your life's *real* mate or work? It is also possible through "failures" you realized you didn't need who or what you were convinced you did.

It was a female client of mine who shared the most beautiful illustration I have ever heard about the marked differences between how the aggressive/defensive ego and the spiritual consciousness view the circumstances and events of life. She described her ego consciousness as being able to see only the back of a magnificently woven tapestry. From that perspective, the tapestry was comprised of gnarled blotches of thread, unattractively presented in clashing colors, chaotically leading nowhere, which altogether demonstrated no symmetry or larger meaning in its composition. Seeing only this side of the tapestry, her ego consciousness had all of the evidence it needed to confirm that life is disordered and senseless. Her spiritual consciousness, on the other hand, has the ability and wisdom to view the tapestry from its other side. Revealed is a picture of spectacular beauty, woven by a master, with craft and skill, following perfect patterns of workmanship. Only from the spiritual consciousnesses' perspective is it unquestionably clear that there is a brilliant and perfect Grand Design to everything; a creative pattern wherein each and every thread is woven with intelligence and crystal clear intent.

The isolated, fear-based, survival-oriented aggressive/ defensive ego consciousness can never see the full picture. Given its habitually conflicted relationship with the spiritual consciousness, it does not credit the spiritual consciousness with making sense or having purpose, much less being able to see things through its eyes.

If the ego consciousness cannot (or refuses to) see the Grand Design, how can it know forwards from backwards, success from failure, or inner victory from defeat in the fulfillment of that design? As an adult who is identified with (controlled by) your ego consciousness you can greatly benefit by admitting that you do not know what developments are for the best and highest good of your soul or, for that matter, anybody else's soul.

EGO ADMISSION #5: "Nothing I obtain alone or by overriding my natural child and spiritual consciousness can ever satisfy or nourish me for long."

As an ego-identified adult you will generally try to force things to go certain ways to have them conform to your personal design for your (and often others') life. Overriding the Grand Design, which is like the flow of a great river, you will try to "push the river", rather than let it flow and follow it *wherever* it might lead. Decisions will be made and actions taken that will lack balance, integration, clarity, and wisdom. These will generally be reactive and impulsive in nature—limited and short-term solutions, often harmful, that seem in the moment to get you to where you insist you need to go.

When it is your ego's decision alone (without including or consulting the independent/aware adult consciousness, the natural child consciousness/authentic self, or the spiritual consciousness) that is determining your agenda for your life, you will never be satisfied or nourished for long. Even if you achieve goals and ambitions which are primarily ego-based, you will soon feel empty, hungry, and unfulfilled.

This is because as an ego-controlled adult, you are identified with a false self. The images of yourself that you use to try to affirm who you are by achieving aggressive/defensive ego-based goals and ambitions are illusions. *No matter what you feed a false self, no matter how you enhance or adorn it, no matter what you accomplish to "prove it", it remains a false self.* Whatever you do to feel better when you are living an aggressive/defensive ego-controlled life will never be enough.

To illustrate just what the ego consciousness (operating alone) can and can't get you, I recall working with Lionel. He was a businessman who had made and subsequently lost, then made and lost again enormous amounts of money. Lionel arrived at my door at the bottom of this extremely frustrating and painfully debilitating cycle with a straight forward therapeutic agenda: "Tell me what I have to do to get back in the saddle and make money again, and this time keep it!"

His misery and anguish were so overwhelming, his exhaustion and burnout so acute, that he realized early in our sessions that he just couldn't pick himself up and get on with the business of making money again. Fortunately this exhaustion gave us the time to get to a deeper set of therapeutic questions like: What's *really* going on here? What's going on in my relationship with myself? How must I be seeing and feeling about myself such that I keep putting myself through this bizarre and punishing emotional and financial cycle? Eventually we landed on what was to become the most important therapeutic question of all: Why do I spend so much of my life obsessing about money?

Lionel's healing work took him to the discovery of an aggressive/defensive ego consciousness that, long ago, had taken over from a natural child consciousness that did not experience being sufficiently safe, loved, or valued. Power and the making of money became ways to feed that unloved and long-forgotten little boy. It had been his steady diet. Lionel came to understand that he might as well have tried eating hundred dollar bills to provide him with the emotional and spiritual nutrients he was missing.

This is an example of an aggressive/defensive ego consciousness, by itself wanting something so badly (in this case money) that it overrides or crushes the rest of the Inner Family in the singular pursuit of its goal. In his healing work, Lionel came to see that he was relying upon a false self in order to feel better. But there was never enough "better" to satisfy or nourish him for long. His way of feeling better about himself was not only impossible but insane. He could finally understand his personal and financial catastrophes.

A tremendous toll will be taken on anyone who has become identified with the ego consciousness *before* they can come to the deeply felt realization that if this consciousness alone is directing their goals and ambitions, they will never be satisfied or fulfilled for long. Much wasted effort, repetitive frustration, and emotional pain may have to be endured before this subtle yet powerful lesson can be learned.

Ego Admission #6: "I am here for a short time and will die. I am not the centre of the universe."

The adult who has come to be identified with the aggressive/defensive ego consciousness lives much like they are the all-knowing and invincible centre of the universe. Denied is the reality that they are not their own creation. Denied is the awareness that physical life is extremely fragile, and life on planet Earth is but a miniscule fraction of a second on the clock of the universe. Denied is the unalterable truth that one day we will die.

The inevitability of death terrifies the ego. If we ask this Inner Family member for its beliefs about death, it will tell us something like this: Death is a complete and merciless annihilation and an eternal obliteration of consciousness. It may further declare that death is a sick and cruel travesty perpetrated upon us by an utterly dispassionate and malicious God. Authors like Ernest Becker (*The Denial of Death*), have convincingly argued that a great deal of how human beings live is an attempt to avoid the immanence of our own deaths.

The "impending" event of your own physical death may send chills down the spine of your ego consciousness. However, for the purposes of your personal healing (and to support the shift to a more heart-based and spiritually-guided consciousness), confronting this fear and this reality is necessary. If done with guidance from the spiritual consciousness it can amount to a liberating and transformative experience. Unless you, as an ego-identified adult, embrace your transitory, fragile, and temporary nature, you will, *on some level*, continue to operate as if you are the centre of the universe.

The aggressive/defensive ego believes that there is no power mightier than itself. As such, it must be gently but firmly dethroned. Embracing the inevitable reality of your own death acts as a quiet revolutionary force which can contribute to toppling the ego consciousness' self-appointed dictatorship. The deeply-accepted truth that you will die is a necessary and valuable, if hard-nosed, teacher helping you to step aside from an Inner Family member which sees itself as indomitable, invincible, and omnipotent.

There are innumerable other forms of death in life. These "mini-deaths", though generally unnoticed by the ego consciousness, can be seen as smaller versions of your physical death. They provide emotional and spiritual openings and alternatives to the ego's unfeeling impermeability. Leaving behind the innocent days of childhood, the care-freeness of youth, or the experimentation and adventure of young adulthood; saying good-bye to a cherished home, a favorite school, a once-loved mate, a dear friend, or a valued career; a crunching financial setback, an illness, the discovery of a significant character flaw, or the inability to accomplish a dream—all of these events bring you closer to the experience of death.

If you can acknowledge and go through the emotional pain and fear of these events; events which are perceived by the ego consciousness to be horrible and unwanted, you can challenge its hold over you and move towards Inner Family members like the natural child consciousness/authentic self and spiritual conscious-ness. In this shift to a heart-based life you will find solace and a glimpse into your eternal nature. In this way the admission "**I will die and I am not the centre of the universe**" can be both healing and life-giving. When this admission is authentic and sincere it can lead to an embracing of humanity and finding a compassion you never knew you had.

Ego Admission #7: "I cannot heal myself, no matter how hard I try. I am completely dependent on other Inner Family members to save me from myself."

As an ego-controlled adult you cannot heal yourself—even if your ego desired this, it couldn't by itself. Why?

As I've described earlier, the aggressive/defensive ego exists in its own universe, diligently excluding everything except itself and its own views and beliefs. It creates and lives by a mission statement of "all-powerful, independent/alone, and constantly right". However, by our spiritual and child consciousnesses' true natures, human beings exist and live *in* relationship, which is more the nature of our being. Healing occurs in relationship not in isolation.

Most often, you have become so absolutely controlled by your aggressive/defensive ego, and entrenched in its beliefs, there is no authentic, intimate relationship with yourself or others. At the start of your personal healing journey there is likely (a) no separate independent/aware adult consciousness to guide the process; and (b), no other "outside person" you will trust or look to for guidance.

Initially, as addressed earlier, *you are not an adult who possesses an aggressive/defensive ego consciousness; rather you are an aggressive/defensive ego consciousness who possesses an adult.* As such, at any early stage of healing, you are much more a part of the problem than the solution. More accurately, it is the state of ego consciousness from which you are operating that is the problem.

You cannot heal yourself by relying upon the same consciousness that has made your personal healing necessary in the first place. If you want to escape from the prison house of an ego-based life and be set free, do you wait for the judge who convicted you to initiate an appeal on your behalf? No. Do you request that the warden whose job it is to keep you locked up to show you the way out? No, you don't. You must go elsewhere for your help; you must go outside the aggressive/defensive ego's entire system.

The first step of a twelve-step program asks you to make this admission: *"I admit that I am powerless over _____ and that my life has become unmanageable."* Only after wrestling with the denial and resistance that arises in regards to this admission, and only after letting its meaning become clear, is a person ready to take the second step: *"I came to believe that a Power greater than myself could restore me to sanity."* This second step contains a somewhat obvious caveat that is seldom recognized: It requires a "relationship".

Put in the terms of the Inner Family Model of healing, this implies the acknowledgment that the person has become so identified with their aggressive/defensive ego consciousness, and has been so inextricably entwined with it for so long that, left to their own devices, *they can not navigate out or around or through it alone.* The person begins to see that all of their future attempts to change or remove themselves from the tyranny of the aggressive/defensive ego will be futile. Without outside help the ego will cleverly control and manipulate so that everything is a disguised version of the same way of living and thinking. Because of this, the same problems which have ensnared them will inevitably resurrect themselves and lead into another vicious cycle.

An oft-cited maxim of twelve-step recovery work is: "My best thinking has got me here." Implied in this is the understanding that it will never be your best thinking that will get you out. Stated in terms of relationship: It won't be you or your thinking that will get you out. If you are to be freed from the emotional and psychological ego-penitentiary of your ways of living, you will need to depend upon other consciousnesses and guides to get you out. By yourself, you're not going anywhere!

Ego Admission # 8: "There is a child and a spiritual consciousness that can help me heal. I must let go and see if they can lead me home. "

For healing to occur, in the end, we must all let go. After we have coerced, manipulated, cajoled, planned, strategized, hoped, raged, impressed, seduced, bargained, threatened, wished, bought, competed, deceived, demanded, lied, betrayed, pouted, and employed every ego-maneuver to ensure that we get our own way, we lose again. After another knock'em out bang'em up fight with the universe, we lose again.

When we either cannot or will not use the aggressive/defensive ego consciousness to fight another day, the remaining option is grieving and letting go. Grieving what we never had; grieving what we never found; grieving that our best efforts weren't enough; grieving that we have been so misguided; grieving how shamelessly we have acted. We will grieve about people we have hurt or harmed; people with whom we couldn't be bothered or simply did not see; people on whom we have passed judgment; people from whom we have withdrawn our love in a misguided effort to survive. Perhaps, most of all, we will grieve how very long, oh how long it has taken us to wake up to the error of our ways.

Chapter XI

*"What lies behind us and what lies before us are
small matters compared to what lies within us."*
Ralph Waldo Emerson

Opening To The Spiritual Consciousness

As you, a new-born independent/aware adult, step away
from your aggressive/defensive ego consciousness, you are stepping
away from everything the ego has used until now. The ego
consciousness has given you almost all of your identity.

It has shown you who you are in this world. It has directed
how you live and how you are and what you live for. From early in
your life, when it became the dominant Inner Family member, it has
had extremely well-defined purposes, priorities, and goals and a very
rigid set of perceptions and values. Though fear-based and survival-
oriented, those have been the equivalent of internal commandments—the unalterable personal rules by which you should be living.
Furthermore, the aggressive/defensive ego has provided you with a
myriad of public roles, scripts, and faces through which you live out
these commandments.

As your principle compass in life, the aggressive/defensive
ego has created the games to play in life. How do you step away
from a consciousness that has structured so much of your life? How
do you let yourself be led by the spiritual consciousness, which
comes with new ways of how to live and be; with new values of
what to live for? Your spiritual consciousness comes with equally
well-defined, but very different purposes, priorities and goals.

Practices For Moving From The Aggressive/Defensive Ego Towards The Spiritual Consciousness

Changing the Ego's Formula For Survival

Recall that everything, *absolutely everything* which your aggressive/defensive ego does has, at its base, the preservation and enhancement of your survival. Over the course of your lifetime, and right up to this present moment, it has tested, polished, and perfected a formula for success in Life. And, it must be stated that, right up to this moment, the ego's formula for successful survival has been an unqualified success! How do I know? You're here. You're alive. You've made it to this point. You have survived!

Now, if you are to listen to your aggressive/defensive ego's views on this unmitigated success story, it's quite a simple explanation: You survived because single-handedly, it has saved you. You would have been dead long ago without it! Not only that, but it will tell you that you must continue to do exactly and precisely what it has demanded of you in the past to ensure your survival in the future. *The formula for your survival cannot be changed or compromised one little bit!* Like the recipe for a special cake created by a gourmet baker—not one single ingredient can be adjusted, omitted, or added if you are to expect the cake to come out just right the second time. In your ego's thinking, you must keep repeating everything you have done to this point in life to ensure your survival.

Though an over-simplification let's, for example, say that your aggressive/defensive ego consciousness has helped you make it to this point by creating and following this "exact" recipe for survival:

15 %	Being too busy
41%	Controlling others
12%	Refusal to experience uncomfortable emotions
15%	Using alcohol and sex
17%	Attachment to external identity and power
100%	The "me" I have been until now

If you listen to your ego's directives, it will maintain that you must, *absolutely must,* follow this recipe unerringly and forever if you want to survive. *No* deviation is acceptable. After all, it has worked to this point, hasn't it? Any changes to the recipe for life, any improvisation, according to this consciousness, will result in disaster (meaning more calamity, the experience of more pain, or death).

All spiritual practices that make a difference, including the ones I will be speaking to here, challenge and slowly change the aggressive/defensive ego's recipe for survival. Any change in the recipe will feel uncomfortable and threatening. The more you have become identified with it, the more uncomfortable it will be for you.

As you go deeper into any effective or authentic inner spiritual work, there will be occasions when you will necessarily feel lost, vulnerable, and off-balance. You might even feel unhinged for a spell, like you're really losing your grip on reality. You might begin to fear that if you persist with your spiritual practice, then personal disintegration, craziness, or even death, might be the result.

Generally speaking, these are the fear-based, survival-oriented, aggressive/defensive ego's reactions to giving up control. It will strenuously object to any changes to its life-long recipe for survival. It will do all that is within its power to counter or undermine your decision to place your allegiance elsewhere (like with your spiritual consciousness). If you persevere, it *will* attempt to coax you to return to isolating and self-defeating behaviors like being busy, controlling/dominating others, being angry or petulant, using alcohol or sex, using food, shopping, etc., more compulsively and dependently than ever before. This is its effort to stem this tide of healing change. Expect it to do whatever it deems necessary to force your return to the "safe", known and time-tested recipe for your survival: the ego's agenda.

With your newly-formed independent/aware adult consciousness, *you need to remain firm, resolved, and courageous in resisting the aggressive/defensive ego's tactics to relapse.* Persevering in steps that are neither too big or fast that the ego becomes paralyzed with fear, nor too small and slow that its recipe for survival remains unchallenged, you move skillfully in the direction where. at least according to this consciousness, personal disaster and annihilation await you. Yet, if you choose to open up to the path of personal healing, and open up to the spiritual consciousness within you, *you must challenge and change the ego's recipe.* You must go into awareness and emotions that you, an adult who has become identified with the aggressive/defensive ego consciousness, have not gone before.

Many of the events and experiences you will go through as you change your behaviors and experiment with a new recipe, will be unique to you. What you can count on, in a more general way, is that you will immediately be approaching or entering the unknown stillness; the silence. In these uncharted and unfathomable places, you will be asked to do your best to remain open, trusting, and reachable; and you wait. You wait to see who or what shows up. You wait to see if there really is a spiritual consciousness; a spiritual Inner Family member. You wait to see how this spiritual consciousness will slowly introduce you to a new recipe for living rather than continuing to merely survive life.

Entering the Silence, Entering The Void

There are many spiritual practices which have as their aim the observing of the ego mind. This is often called developing the Observer or the Witness; developing the practice of non-identified awareness. Any of these disciplines can be highly effective means of moving away from your allegiance and identification with (or lessening the control of) the aggressive/defensive ego consciousness. These are designed to develop a stronger allegiance and identification with the spiritual consciousness.

Becoming quiet, entering the stillness or the silence, stepping into an *apparent* void, challenges the ego mind and its recipe for survival. A meditation practice as simple as the methodical and diligent focusing of your consciousness on your breathing i.e. placing all your attention on the in-breath and the out-breath, and the empty space in between them, is another way by which the aggressive/defensive ego consciousness can be gently and persistently set aside. Practices such as this invite the ego to relax its grip on the perceptions, beliefs, and behaviors which it has generated.

You, the (now) independent/aware adult consciousness will discover time and again that your "survival" continues without the aggressive/defensive ego consciousness being in charge. You will realize this Inner Family member, at least temporarily, can be put on a shelf. Guidance, safety, and comfort will come from the spiritual consciousness and the natural child consciousness/authentic self.

Spiritual practice that is approached sincerely and with discipline, and done over time, is not limited to the previous example of breathing meditation. It may be (for you) regular and consistent prayer to a higher power of your choice, or concentrating on offering kindness to others in all circumstances (not just when they are being kind to you), or offering compassion when your aggressive/defensive ego tells you not to, or being resolutely determined to be gently honest *all* the time, or forcing yourself to find goodness in someone you are "convinced" is a horrible person. If done sincerely these will all qualify as aspects of spiritual practice. Practices such as these allow you, and more significantly your ego consciousness, to discover that survival can be maintained and even *enhanced* by allowing other Inner Family members to influence you.

You can enter the stillness within, the *apparent* void, beyond anything the ego consciousness knows, in many creative ways. However, what is always required and always most challenging *and* most effective is that *you must consciously and deliberately change the behavior patterns that comprise your ego's recipe for survival.* Bringing harmony and peace to your Inner Family is never accidental. It *always* requires a focused and consistent effort over a long time. It certainly gets easier, but it requires a determined effort.

Bringing Forth the Spiritual Consciousness Through Behavior Change

Let's use, for example, the ego-recipe for survival I gave earlier. Yours will be different. By making specific, concrete changes in your behavior, you can move towards a more heart-based, spiritually-guided state of consciousness. Here's the example again:

15 %	Being too busy
41%	Controlling others
12%	Refusal to experience uncomfortable emotions
15%	Using alcohol and sex
17%	Attachment to external identity and power
100%	The "me" I have been until now

Each time you deliberately slow down the pace of your life, even a little, you will be entering your version of the stillness and the void. Mentally step back and watch yourself (be a self-witness) during the course of a typical day. Notice the choices you make, which keep your life excessively busy and over stimulated. This is one way of slightly altering the recipe. If you could get to a point where you were committed to spend, say, one evening each week at home, alone, in quiet, introspective activities like reading, listening to music, or journaling (perhaps to other Inner Family members), you would be experimenting with changing the old ego recipe for survival. Learning to meditate to see if you could slow down, or simply watching the unending mental material of the ego-mind, would be other ways of creating more inner space for the spiritual consciousness to occupy.

When you have the need to control others (the second ingredient in the ego's recipe for survival), you are always operating from the fear-based, survival-oriented aggressive/defensive ego consciousness. Changing this behavior in yourself in a real and substantive way would amount to taking on the inner work of helping this consciousness to heal. A great many suggestions and exercises for this purpose have already been offered in this book. Here is another one that will help you reduce the subtle ways your ego attempts to control others.

When communicating with words, aggressive/defensive egos really don't like to *listen*. Egos hear the words but mostly they wait for the other person to finish so they can make a point to impress or win. In conflicts and misunderstandings especially, they rarely listen and simply wait for another opportunity to talk, or "listen" for loopholes and formulate another argument.

This exercise will sound difficult, and maybe foolish, but it works to slow your ego down. For you, while someone is talking to you, silently repeat in your own mind each word the other person says to you. Silently repeat *exactly* what the other person says. This forces your mind to slow down; it creates a space for hearing with compassion; it demonstrates respect for them; it prevents your ego from rushing off creating arguments. People who speak with you will feel respected and cared for. When they are done it only takes a moment for you to decide what to say. [This exercise was developed by Richard Clark, a Vancouver therapist/author who designed various programs to stop violence.]

Further to these, participating in any personal therapeutic relationship or program wherein you can openly and authentically address the emotional pain and fear you carry (that underlies behaviors such as the need to control others) will contribute to opening the spiritual consciousness in your Inner Family. The underlying dynamic here is "relationship" not isolation, as I discussed earlier.

A way to challenge the third ingredient in the ego's recipe for survival—the refusal to experience uncomfortable emotions, is to admit them and move towards experiencing them. An excellent way to begin would be to get to know and tune in to your body. Become aware of all the physical and emotional information it can provide.

- In what circumstances throughout your day is your body tense and uncomfortable?
- When and with whom is your body comfortable and relaxed (or tense)?
- Can you identify what emotions or physical sensations you are experiencing?
- Are you willing to pay close attention to unwanted, uncomfortable, or painful feelings like fear, anxiety, loneliness, depression, sadness, anger, and allow yourself to experience these states?
- Do you notice you sometimes feel satisfied or subtly "enjoy" being depressed, angry, or righteous?
- Do you notice you repeatedly talk about how bad things are going or your sadness or unhappiness, and what happens in your body when you do this?
- Do you notice how much you criticize yourself or others, and what happens in your body when you do this?
- When you have the opportunity, could you write sincerely about these experiences and observations in a personal journal?
- Are you willing to discuss any of this honestly with someone?
- Do you notice you are willing or reluctant to challenge any of these?

Regarding the fourth ingredient in the ego's recipe for survival: If you have developed a dependency on alcohol or drugs to bolster the ego-forged identities you have presented to the world, making the decision to abstain would decidedly break the grip of the aggressive/defensive ego consciousness. This will allow you to step towards the spiritual consciousness of your Inner Family. Giving up alcohol however, as people who have done so can attest, involves much more than remaining "clean and sober". It requires the voluntary renouncing of the many external references by which you have defined your self. Giving up a social network of friends and acquaintances, changing leisure activities, or possibly ending important relationships, and introducing new ways of having fun, can be extremely disorienting. Nothing less than a complete change in lifestyle may be necessary. Yet all of these voluntary losses are spiritual advances; advances which can transform the ego's old recipe for survival in ways which allow the spiritual consciousness to assume a much greater place in your life.

Coming to recognize the many ways you use sex for something other than an expression of emotional and spiritual intimacy and connection with another, will modify your ego's recipe for control. Each time you become conscious of how you use sex in unhealthy or manipulative ways *and resist doing this*, allows you to follow a path leading to a more heart-led, spiritually-guided life.

Regarding the last ingredient in the ego's recipe for survival (the attachment to external identity and power): Notice in the course of your interactions with others when you use professional image, credentials, social rank or position, quick wit or sarcasm, or power to get your way. [Power can be expressed as anger, depression, wealth, volume (loudest shouter), self-injury, etc.]

This is your aggressive/defensive ego's attachment to external power and control. When you find yourself doing this, stop. Force yourself to "shift" so you can speak from the natural child consciousness/authentic self so as to influence, rather than dominate others. This allows you to open yourself to the spiritual consciousness of your Inner Family.

Patience, Kindness and Understanding for the Aggressive/Defensive Ego Will Be Key In Moving Towards the Spiritual Consciousness

Throughout the course of your healing work, you will always have to show the aggressive/defensive ego consciousness that you, the independent/aware adult (and the rest of the Inner Family) can survive life in new ways. You must demonstrate the recipe for survival which it has devised, and rigorously enforced (it believes, for your own good), can be beneficially altered for the enhanced good of everyone in your Inner Family and *everyone* in your life.

You will have to demonstrate to your ego that these changes will *not* result in physical or psychological death; no one in the Inner Family will get hurt or die if these changes are made. Though it has been stated several times throughout this book it cannot be emphasized enough: ***personal healing and real and lasting change*** *can never occur by trying to shove a new way of operating down the throat of the aggressive/defensive ego.*

At every stage of your transformation; every time you challenge the aggressive/defensive ego's old recipe for survival, you must treat it with patience, kindness, and understanding. If it is to be disarmed it will not be through any coercive means. If this is to occur, it will only be disarmed with love and acceptance from the rest of the Inner Family.

Wise and authentic spiritual work will provoke objections from the aggressive/defensive ego consciousness. As the connection with spiritual consciousness is deepened it will rebel. In the Inner Family Model of Self-Healing this is not to be perceived as the return of the "bad guy" or problem. The aggressive/defensive ego is fear-based and survival-oriented, but it is still a full-fledged, legitimate and valuable member of the Inner Family. It is just as important and appealing as any other Family member, and just as deserving of patience, kindness, and understanding as any of the others.

When it returns, I urge you to view it the same way you would a child who is threatened by the lavish attention given to a new baby sibling. True, the family dynamics change and already established members (like the aggressive/defensive ego) appear to be getting less attention. In truth, for a while, they may well be getting less, but in a healthy and functional family there is enough love, patience, kindness, and understanding for everyone. Compassion is not scarce. Giving these to a new family member does not require that they be taken away from someone else.

Becoming The Spiritual Consciousness

Becoming the spiritual consciousness is a very direct way of opening up to it. Doing so is similar in approach to the healing work described on two earlier occasions—firstly, when you allowed yourself to become the aggressive/defensive ego consciousness of your Inner Family, and secondly when you gave yourself over to the adaptive or natural child consciousness. The following exercise, like the others, can be done alone, however much more value tends to be gained from it when you can "go public" and have it witnessed by a non-judgmental person with whom you feel safe.

Be seated in a chair or place in the room as the independent/aware adult consciousness. Go inward. Invite the aggressive/defensive ego consciousness to come into the room. See what you see; sense what you sense; and visualize what you visualize. Accept whatever is presented—any presence, image, or form which this consciousness takes on. Is it a savage warrior, an Attila The Hun like figure? Is it a self-confident lecturer pacing back and forth pontificating in front of its captive audience? Is it a business executive with an attaché case in hand? Whatever you get, that's what it is.

Perhaps, because of the healing work you have already done, it might surprise you as now being more humble, cooperative, or vulnerable than you had expected. Maybe it is willing to show itself to be an exhausted, weary warrior or, some powerful figure that would be happy to leave the power-tripping behind if only they could feel truly loved by somebody. It may certainly be less aggressive and wish to be still and quiet. Accept what you get. Let the aggressive/defensive ego consciousness occupy a place in the room. In the process of receiving the image, let it be in the room however it wants. Perhaps it will want to stand in front of the others or, conversely, sit in a corner of the room preferring to be left alone. Again—accept what you get.

Go inward again. Invite your child consciousness to come into the room and pay you a visit. *Be open and receptive; don't force or fake anything.* See what you see; sense what you sense; and visualize what you visualize. By accepting what you "get", regardless of how confusing, embarrassing, or outrageous it may seem, it will be impossible to make a mistake.

- Notice what form the child consciousness takes on. Is it two weeks, two years, or twelve years old?
- Is it over-weight? Sickly appearing? How is it dressed?
- Is it concealing real feelings and projecting appearances? Is it desperately trying to please others? (i.e. the adaptive child);
- Does the child consciousness appear to be real, relaxed, free (a natural child consciousness/authentic self)?
- Does it appear to feel safe or frightened, open or

closed, loved or unloved?

- Does it emanate a real sense of belonging to this Inner Family or does it seem to be disconnected, isolated and alone?
- Where does it wish to position itself in the room—in relation to you (the independent/aware adult) and in relation to the aggressive/defensive ego? Let the child consciousness choose any location or position it wants (of course, with the exception of those spaces already occupied by the other two Inner Family members). Having said that, it is also important to notice if this child consciousness wishes to "sit" on anyone's lap or is particularly adamant about wanting a place already occupied.

As the independent/aware adult consciousness, accept and work with what you get.

Lastly, invite your spiritual consciousness into the room. Here again, don't try too hard; *don't force or fake anything*. See what you see; sense what you sense; and visualize what you visualize. Just take what you get. Is your spiritual consciousness present in the room? If so, what form (if any) is it taking? Where in the room would it like to locate itself? Perhaps it will choose to be standing in the sunlight or prefer to be sitting inconspicuously to the side. Make certain that your spiritual consciousness has a place of its own. You now have your whole and complete Inner Family meeting each other.

As much as all of this may sound silly, the benefits from this exercise can be quite amazing. With all your Inner Family members present, take a few moments to let them see and appreciate each other. It may be the first time they have been together, and for some, it may be the first time they knew they had a family.

When you are ready, get up out of the seat you are occupying as the independent/aware adult and give yourself over to the spiritual consciousness. Go sit or stand as the spiritual consciousness of your Inner Family and give your body over to this spiritual presence. Let your body be enclosed by it. Do your best to be enveloped by it. Notice any subtle physical changes that come over you. It's not uncommon for the mind to become quiet, the shoulders to loosen and lower, other tension to dissipate, a soft smile to come over your lips, and the timber and tone of your voice to soften. At the same time you may not notice any physical changes whatsoever. One more time—don't force or fake anything, just accept what you get.

As you move more deeply into this slightly altered state, the first and loudest voice you hear may come from your aggressive/defensive ego consciousness. It may say things like: "This is completely ridiculous! How stupid! This is *very* dangerous. You could really lose control here! This is really silly! There is no higher or spiritual consciousness!" etc., etc. By now you should be able to recognize these rants as the predictable expressions of this consciousness when it is threatened and afraid. Try not to take them too seriously.

These are the ways the ego attempts to re-subjugate you to it and invalidate the existence of any other Inner Family members. Try not to fight its judgments and criticisms. Don't argue with them. In fact, it is wise to honor them and to respond kindly: "Thank you, Ego; thank you for the caution. I just want to try this for a few minutes. You will have your chance to express your views." Gently and firmly set these objections aside for the time being. Respect that the aggressive/defensive ego consciousness has a right to its beliefs and opinions.

You may, however, be overwhelmed by harsh voices of judgment and criticism. In this case, you cannot become the spiritual consciousness or remain with it. You may temporarily need to abandon becoming it and instead devote this time to the aggressive/defensive ego and the exercises designed to heal it (described in Chapter VII). Listen to its reservations and concerns. Respect that it is angry and terrified (but won't admit it). See if you can allay some of the fears. This is also healing time well spent. Try again soon to make a connection with your spiritual consciousness. Trust that it is patient and graceful, and will continue to love all of you no matter how long this takes.

If you can remain as the spiritual consciousness of your Inner Family, continue to give yourself over to it. Then allow it to speak through you. One very useful opening statement that generally gets things going is: *"My name is Spiritual Consciousness (or Higher Self, Higher Power, Loving Consciousness, Spirit, or Soul) and I have been with you, my Inner Family, all your lifetime. This is what I'd like to say to you today."*

As the spiritual consciousness, don't think you need to be deep, poetic, cryptic, profound, or all-knowing. These are usually ego-based versions of what your ego thinks a spiritual consciousness must be like. Remember, you are not attempting to be "God" or the Highest Power here; this is not about receiving a direct transmission from Jesus, Buddha, Moses, Allah, YHWH, or the Atman-Brahmin. Rather, just allow yourself to hear a few words from an old, wise, loving friend of this Inner Family; one who knows everyone well and is dropping in to see how everyone is doing. (Yes, it may sound silly or pretentious, but it is very effective.)

It is probably best to be ordinary and to speak in an everyday way, as if in a conversation with very good friends. Then see what happens. Maybe nothing will happen. Perhaps words, sentiments, and guidance will come through you. If you hear more than one voice from within (the aggressive/defensive ego may become belligerent), try to stay with the most loving voice you hear. This voice will most likely be that of your spiritual consciousness.

If you are doing this exercise with a trusted friend or therapist, have the other person prompt you with open-ended questions from the list below. These will help keep you in the spiritual consciousness. If you are doing this work alone, read these questions and respond to them as your spiritual consciousness.

- "Spiritual consciousness, what's it been like to be you in this Inner Family?"
- "What is your role or purpose in this Inner Family?"
- "From your vantage point, how do you view this Inner Family and what they are going through?"
- "Do you have any counsel or loving suggestions for the aggressive/defensive ego?"
- "Do you have any counsel or loving suggestions for the inner child?"
- "Do you have any counsel or loving suggestions for the new independent/aware adult?"
- "Is there anything else you would like us to know at this time?"

As the spiritual consciousness reveals itself, see if you can naturally and spontaneously invent other open-ended questions that are of interest to you.

When you become aware that your spiritual consciousness has completed what it wanted to say (or you have lost the connection with it) return to the chair or position in the room that you occupied as the independent/aware adult consciousness. Journal or talk about what just happened and how you felt; note what stood out as most valuable for you.

The Written Work:
Using Writing To Become The Spiritual Consciousness

As already illustrated in earlier chapters on healing the aggressive/defensive ego consciousness and the adaptive child consciousness, it is possible in much the same way to get to know your spiritual consciousness by writing in the first person *as* this Inner Family member. In giving yourself permission to write as the spiritual consciousness, you may encounter a good deal of resistance from your aggressive/defensive ego consciousness. It may attack, telling you that what you are doing is the equivalent of blasphemy; that you are acting sacrilegiously by attempting to play God. *Again please know that having access to (and hearing from) a spiritual side of yourself does not mean that you are usurping the place of God.* Having a non-physical guide or teacher is the same as being in the presence and receiving guidance from a highly respected, experienced mentor. This mentor has a wisdom, love, patience, and vast perspective on your life that is unlike anything you can know by yourself.

Why is this the case? This consciousness is not in the least bit concerned with survival, be it physical or psychological. Consequently, it can concentrate on much bigger things. Things like what constitutes a good and beautiful life; or, rather than living for self-advancement alone, how to live in ways that are congruent with the highest and best good for all. If consulted, it can help you to know what you are here to give, to receive, and to learn in this lifetime.

Using the technique of different color pens that you have used before, choose a different color from what you have already used in earlier written work (different from the aggressive/defensive ego and child consciousness) and assign it to the spiritual consciousness. Using your dominant hand, start writing as this Inner Family member. Be spontaneous in writing messages from your spiritual consciousness and see what happens.

Many people begin this experience with a little bit of trepidation and uncertainty. However, once they allow themselves to be spiritual in an ordinary kind of way, what often comes forward is a higher wisdom which effortlessly delivers relevant and powerful messages to them.

Here are some examples of writings these individuals have received:

"I am the part of you that has always trusted your journey. I trust that it will lead you to the place that is right for you—it is unique to you.

"When you really get to the end of your rope, and (recently) this has happened, then you come to me. Our relationship is growing. It's the start of a real friendship. I'm like the river that runs through your life. Lately the path has not seemed clear to you - and that's when you are most open to a reminder from me.

"I am the river that will always keep flowing; I know where I am going. You just need to step in and let the current take you. Wherever you end up will be the right place for you in this lifetime. You must make the choice to step in, however. I cannot make that commitment for you. I can only guide you, once you have taken this step.

"Seemingly impossible obstacles—big boulders in the stream—will always be there. I am the water which always finds a way around them to a calm spot on the other side. All the little calm pools would not be there if there were no big boulders just a little upstream.

"For most of your life you have not believed that I am real and that I have valuable advice to offer. That is gradually changing over the past two years. You are beginning to trust the advice I offer.

"I share your inner child's sense of wonder of nature. I have empathy for ego's fear of where and when the next big boulder will suddenly appear along the path. And I have more patience for letting trust grow than you, the adult, realize."

*

"I, Higher Power, help you see that life is full of those "a-hah" moments. I show you the beauty of life, its paradoxes, its clever, ironic twists of experience and reassure you that pain is a necessary part of living. I also tell you that it is not necessary for

your survival to put yourself down and that you are good regardless of your shortcomings.

"Sometimes, though, the aggressive/defensive ego is so in control that I seem to be non-existent to you. This is when you feel most lost and feel the most full of despair.

"Your goal now should be to remember that I exist and that I accept you and your Inner Family, no matter how the inner child is hurting, no matter how aggressive/defensive ego retaliates and no matter how often you feel that you don't measure up."

*

"I am your spiritual consciousness and this is what I want you to know about me: It is through me that you escape the destructive side of the ego. By accessing the strength and healing I provide for you, you are able to pick yourself up off the mat and move away from aggressive/defensive ego's vicious onslaughts."

*

"I am Spirit. I am oneness becoming awareness by being present. I am the joy which is always there but is usually masked by aggressive/defensive ego's addiction to thinking. When thinking stops, I am there. Thinking and pain self-create each other. When you have had enough pain and thinking, you will find me, always present.

"Ego consciousness is the tool I use to experience duality and pain and pleasure until I exist fully aware. My source has no self-awareness. Ego lets me learn self-awareness. Ego will mask my presence until it has had enough pain and pleasure. When it lets go, my joy will be resplendent."

*

"I am the essence of what you have learned and much more. I am a sort of spiritual consciousness—a mentor of sorts to you. I can be called upon to give wise and sage advice and you have found life to be infinitely better and easier when you follow that advice.

"I was formally recognized about three years ago but I have been around you all of your life. I am always there for you, and willing to respond whenever asked. It's easy to be me. I am always

here and always ready to help. I bear no ill will to anyone, no judgments, and my words have no conditions—only love. I understand a lot.

"*I am now being accessed a lot and can give guidance to you that occasionally stops you right in your tracks. To you my responses seem to come from a higher understanding than you have yourself. I am unlike any other member of this Inner Family and my ideas and suggestions are often totally different than you expect. My words seem to come from an "otherworldly" place, somewhere close to God or from a Universal Higher Consciousness. I live on a plane other than what the rest of my Inner Family experiences and so I am able to speak from a point of view that reflects the Universe. I have been back as far as many past lives and out to the future, beyond the edge of the Universe. I bring a feeling of peace, harmony and tranquility into your life.*"

*

"*I am the spiritual power of Bernie's Inner Family. I am a constant, un-judgmental witness to the insanity of his life. When he turns to me for guidance I am usually able to offer him a brief reprieve from the madness. But most of the time he chooses to be run by his aggressive/defensive ego and is lost in the chaos that ego creates. I am not called upon often because ego consciousness does not count me among his friends. He refuses to believe that he needs a friend. But I have always been and always will be within easy reach should Bernie ever choose to change his ways and look to someone other than his ego to help guide him through life.*"

Chapter XII

"Childhood is a nightmare. But it is so very hard to be an on-your-own-take-care-of-yourself-because-there-is-no-one-else-to-do-it-for-you-grown up."
Sheldon Kopp
From: *If You Meet the Buddha on the Road, Kill Him!*

The Independent/Aware Adult

The Emergence of the Independent/Aware Adult Consciousness

Who and what are you when you have largely completed the personal healing work suggested in the pages of this book? Well, in short, you have become aware of, taken responsibility for, and stopped the aggressive/defensive ego consciousness from being your primary operating state of consciousness. You have gone a step further and helped that fear-based, survival-oriented Inner Family member to heal. You have returned to the adaptive or broken child and heard its story; a story fashioned by emotional pain so overwhelming that it was unbearable until now, when you acknowledged and released some of it. This helps the adaptive child to begin to return to the natural child/authentic self it was by birthright. You created an opening for the spiritual consciousness to inform and guide you. You have established the beginnings of a truly understanding and harmonious Inner Family.

Who or what do you find beyond the ways you have thus far used to survive life and love? The aggressive/defensive ego consciousness most assuredly will say: "Death. Annihilation. Catastrophe. Loneliness. Eternal nothingness." The natural child consciousness /authentic self may whisper: "Peace. Safety. Love. Harmony. Home." The spiritual consciousness may simply be there as a quiet, receptive, wise and supportive presence; or it might quietly say: "I am here. Come to me." The fledgling independent/aware adult now established in the Inner Family may say: "I don't know who *or what* I may find or what lies ahead. Maybe you're right, ego; however, I sense that you're wrong. Either way, we can't go back to what we were or who we used to be. We can't and won't go back to the old aggressive/defensive ways and the Universe of Fear that we lived in.

Who and what you find yourself to be is a "new" adult, one born out of your healing work. This is the independent/aware adult.

Having survived the voluntary dismantling and collapse of the building in which you lived for as long as you can remember, as this "new" adult, you are likely to feel quite naked and wobbly for a while. You might need to cough and wheeze from the dust and debris of your former "home". Yet, at the same time, you find yourself in a space of new beginnings and virtually unlimited possibilities.

You are a newly-born adult who is finally and at last freed up from the fear consciousness that long ago overwhelmed and defined you. You are liberated from having to endlessly endure the clashing armies and endless darkness of the Universe of Fear. You have made a transition to the Universe of Love and can now be defined by, and belong to, "a love that passes all understanding".

In healing your relationship with yourself (which means creating harmony in your Inner Family), you have become an adult who is no longer forced to take your marching orders from a tyrannical, inner dictator. You can govern yourself out of love rather than fear and make appropriate choices. Amongst these truly fresh options none will be more important than having a choice over the single most influential factor determining the entire quality of your life: the state of consciousness from which you operate. Having a choice, and taking responsibility for your choices, may be the most important result of all your hard work. Now, regardless of how you have been in the past, or whatever your present circumstances are, be they wanted or unwanted, or how others around you might be treating you—*you get to choose moment by moment how you want to be.*

Here are some of those choices:

- Do you choose to operate from your aggressive/defensive ego with its limited emotional repertoire (varying from mild defensiveness to destructive viciousness)?

- Do you choose to blame and attack others for your emotional pain and fear, or take it on as your own responsibility?

- Do you choose to transform your pain and fear into judgments, criticisms, and generalizations about others? Will you remain stubbornly and tenaciously righteous?—right to cast your spouse out of your heart? Right to justify screaming at your children for not doing what you want them to do? Right to curse at or give the finger to another driver for cutting you off in traffic? Right to drop bombs on that other group or religion or nation because they aren't doing what you want?

- Do you choose to try and dominate others or only exert influence over yourself?

- Do you choose to cling to your ego-forged identities and remain isolated or to expand your unlimited potential for beauty, peace and happiness through your natural child and spiritual consciousness?

All of these choices are determined by the state of consciousness from which you choose to operate. With newfound access to the natural child consciousness/authentic self and the spiritual consciousness, it is the adult you have brought forth in the course of your personal healing—the newly-created independent/aware adult, that has both the awareness and the ability to make these radically different, life-affirming choices. The coming into being of this "new" Inner Family member, this "new" adult, is the quintessential indicator that your personal healing is occurring.

Who Is The Independent/Aware Adult Consciousness?—A Tale of Two Inner Families

Perhaps the easiest and clearest way of describing the independent/aware adult consciousness is to compare and contrast two Inner Families—firstly the Inner Family of an unhealed adult and the Inner Family of an adult healing.

The unhealed adult is an individual who unconsciously remains almost completely identified with the aggressive/defensive ego consciousness. Almost all of their thoughts, feelings, and actions derive from a fear-based and survival-oriented mentality. They perceive the world to be a place in which they must constantly attack or defend themselves in order to preserve what they assume is the precarious position they hold in it.

Because they never feel truly and totally safe, loved, or valued they are in constant need of more of whatever their ego thinks will give them security (meaning control), like money and "power". Again, because they rely exclusively on the external world for that security, they are enslaved by the world's constantly changing patterns of approval and disapproval or success and failure. Operating as the aggressive/defensive ego and the adaptive child, more than as an independent/aware adult, they are an adult only in the sense that they have physically grown to "adult size", or reached some chronological age at which they are accorded the status and privileges of an "adult" member of society.

As to whether psychologically, emotionally, and spiritually they have become an adult; their own adult; one who has a real choice over their operating state of consciousness and the quality of their life is another matter entirely. For in an Inner Family (thoroughly dominated by the aggressive/defensive ego and adaptive child consciousness) there is, for all intents and purposes, no adult present to make such a choice. Access to the life-affirming and love-enhancing possibilities of the natural child consciousness/authentic self and the spiritual consciousness are extremely limited.

The Inner Family of such an individual is characterized by conflict and divisiveness—the state of civil war described earlier. Typically, the aggressive/defensive ego consciousness has had to defend the front lines of the war for survival. Consequently, it attacks and harshly judges the unhealed adult whom the person has grown into. This "adult", prior to healing, for their part, perceives the ego consciousness to be an irredeemable enemy and oppressor whom they must both fight and hide. They fight for any measure of freedom and relief from its constant barrage of judgments, criticisms, and negative beliefs; they hide so that no one will know they have such a dark aspect of themselves.

Usually the lonely and embattled aggressive/defensive ego is in extreme conflict with the natural child consciousness/authentic self and the spiritual consciousness. Granting any influence or leadership to these softer, less defended, less conflicted Inner Family members appears suicidal to the hard-bitten warrior the ego has become.

The Inner Family of an individual on the path of healing is quite different. The adult consciousness in this Inner Family is demonstrating the courage to institute a paradigm shift in their inner world. They are extricating themselves from complete subjugation to the ways of the aggressive/defensive ego consciousness. Determined to free themselves from the automatic, conditioned, fear-based reactions they have employed (likely since childhood) to make it through life, they are giving birth to an entirely new consciousness. Within their Inner Family, there is now the independent/aware adult who is increasingly determining the state of consciousness and the quality of life.

Thought by thought, feeling by feeling, spoken word by spoken word, action by action, and moment by moment this consciousness is an accountable ambassador of fear or love, conflict or peace, external power and control or internal self-empowerment and integrity. As opposed to a civil war raging within, like any healthy nuclear family, they are characterized by the principle of inclusion, support, and understanding between all of its members. In such a family, everyone is welcomed and treated as equally important. There is great acceptance for and appreciation of each person's unique, authentic self. Individual differences are understood and honored. Everyone experiences that the acceptance and love they experience from other family members will always be secure and abundant.

Similarly, in the Inner Family of an adult healing, each consciousness is included at all times. Each consciousness is welcomed and treated as equally important. There is great acceptance and appreciation for the unique nature and contribution of each Inner Family member. Individual differences are understood and honored. Each member knows and trusts that understanding and acceptance of themselves by the other Inner Family members is secure and steadfast. There is no need for a competition for scarce resources because there are no scarce resources, and therefore, no need for divisive alliances between members of the family. Excluding or dominating any consciousness for the "betterment" and peace of the others is unthinkable.

The individual committed to this healing is really a tale of twin births—the birth of the independent/aware adult consciousness and the birth of an Inner Family. The new independent/aware adult consciousness can now become the head of the Inner Family. The new Inner Family is circular and egalitarian in its power distribution, not hierarchical. It is not elitist and totalitarian. It is consensual in its decision making process, not unilateral.

The Independent/Aware Adult Replaces the Aggressive/Defensive Ego as Head of the Inner Family

As a new adult consciousness—the independent/aware adult, you are no longer almost totally identified with and dominated by the aggressive/defensive ego (and its predecessor the adaptive child consciousness). Instead, you emerge as the new head of your Inner Family. In making your decisions and representing yourself in the world you are able to receive input and guidance from all your Inner Family members. You are a far different type of leader than your Inner Family has ever known; a leader who has no difficulty being led by the wisdom of others.

Not needing or wanting external power and control over others, you, the independent/aware adult, are a part of an egalitarian family experience. Your desire is to facilitate the free flow of information between the various Inner Family members. And though the final say on any decision rests with you, you know that the process of making any decision has incorporated every facet of who you are (the four consciousnesses).

As the new leader of a unified Inner Family, you, acting as an independent/aware adult are interested in:

(i)   Recognizing and appreciating the many gifts and resources of each Inner Family member, and tapping into the unique expertise of each member;

(ii) promoting a unified, harmonious Inner Family in which members respect, understand, and support each other in working together for the common good;

(iii) collaborative, consensual decision making; and,

(iv) having the way things get done be more important

than what gets done (meaning being aware of the state of consciousness that is operating and harmony in the process is more important than achieving some end result).

Depending upon what the circumstances and events call for, you can surrender the leadership of your Inner Family to the simplicity, vulnerability, and emotional clarity of the natural child consciousness/authentic self, or to the wisdom and higher perspective of the spiritual consciousness; and even, when necessary, to the fierce protection afforded by the aggressive/defensive ego consciousness. You are able to be extremely flexible and adjustable in the delegation of influence. For example:

- If you are feeling in physical danger, or if your feelings or needs are being repeatedly violated, you may choose *for a short time* to call upon the expertise and forcefulness of the aggressive/defensive ego for your protection and defense. [I stress *for a short time* because, once you have fended off any immediate threat, you will always be more effective dealing with situations as the independent/aware adult.]

- When wanting to communicate important and tender matters of the heart to your primary partner, family members, or friends, you might elect to call upon the expertise and leadership of your natural child consciousness/authentic self.

- If you are feeling lost, alone, or confused, or at a significant crossroads in your life, you may fall back on the expertise and leadership of your spiritual consciousness to show you the way.

Forever a member of something larger than yourself, as the independent/aware adult you know that you are never alone. You know that you are always in the company of a loving Inner Family which supports you and wants the best for everyone. No matter what challenges lie ahead, you can rest comfortably in the knowledge that you do not have to face them exclusively on your own. Within you are wonderful and reliable resources. On a moment's notice, a small team of wise, individual experts, each uniquely gifted in particular aspects of living, may be summoned for assistance. With regard to any decision, issue, or course of action, or any relationship, you are not forced to act alone. This is remarkably different from those days when you were dominated by the aggressive/defensive ego. On *any* matter, you know that you will produce wiser, more grounded and beneficial outcomes for yourself and others *after* having heard from your entire Inner Family.

As the independent/aware adult you are no longer unconsciously and automatically run by the dictates of a fear-based, survival-oriented consciousness. You can reclaim your life and live it in a way which is your own unique creation. Perhaps for the first time since being forced to become an adaptive child you can become *self*-determined. It is now possible to live your life and nobody else's; you can live *for yourself* and not the people around you. After all, it's your life isn't it? Your life is a gift from the universe to you. No one else. Now, as an authentic steward of this gift, you can do or not do whatever you want; taking responsibility for your state of consciousness; making choices that befit you. The more you live from your independent/aware adult consciousness the more your life is your own.

You will trust that other Inner Family members, albeit in very different ways, will look out for each other—protect you and enhance your life in this world. Mere "survival" is a thing of the past. Your entire Inner Family, as an egalitarian team, will take you unimaginably beyond survival.

This team (*a healed you*) can look out for and protect other people too, showing them a way to live beyond the need to survive. With the natural child consciousness/authentic self and the spiritual consciousness playing leading roles, life will be about much more than just surviving. It can become an experience of real beauty wherein opportunities to deeply connect with yourself and with others in love, peace, and happiness become exponentially greater.

Harry, a client and seminar participant, eloquently captured the growth and awareness he experienced as a newly forming independent/aware adult, and the transformative "changing of the guard" which was occurring within him. His writing below speaks to how he, and no longer the old aggressive/defensive ego consciousness, was emerging as the head of his Inner Family.

"I awoke this morning feeling peaceful and relaxed. But like all mornings, the peacefulness gradually began to slip away as thoughts began to take over. Most mornings I awake already immersed in the chaos, and am much less aware of it. I could feel the familiar tension start to take root in my body and I started to question what was happening. Instead of allowing the thoughts to take me over, I became an observer of them, and realized that they consisted of an almost uninterrupted stream of worries and concerns.

"For the first few precious minutes of the day I was able to be present in the moment, but quickly moved into the future as fearful thoughts began to take me over. Even as I write these words, I am more concerned about how they will be received by others in the group than I am about the possible learning they hold for me. As I am observing these thoughts, I am becoming aware that who I actually am is separate from them. It only seems as though the thoughts are who I am because I give them all my power.

"Last month I did a very powerful exercise with Joel where I told the aggressive/defensive ego that I was no longer willing to give it my power. I told it that its time as ruler was over, and that I was taking control of my life. (At the same time, Joel asked me to acknowledge it for everything it had done for me over the course of my life and I told it that I would assist it any way I could during this period of change.) It gradually shrank from its menacing self with each word I spoke, until it melted into the floor. I left the office that day feeling stronger than I had in a long time.

"Since then, it has tried everything it could to grab back the reigns of my life. But with observing my thoughts this morning and actually becoming the independent/aware adult, I see the truth that **the only way the aggressive/defensive ego survives is through thought***.*

"It exists by me allowing it to use my thoughts to create fear, confusion, and exhaustion. By keeping me weak, it remains strong and ensures its survival.

*"But who is **it**? It has no real identity. It has no physical form. Although when I have allowed it to take over, it certainly feels as though it owns every cell of my being. The answer is suddenly clear—it is completely mind-generated! It does not exist in any way, shape or form without thought.*

"It is actually just thought. It started out as a single thought many years ago, and I have given it the power to grow into almost

every thought I have. The power I continue to give it is the almost exclusive use of my mind. That which is only a thought itself uses the mind I have given it to create an almost uninterrupted stream of negative thought. It needs the fear and confusion to keep the illusion that it really is something to be strongly reckoned with.

  *"As I write these words, it just occurred to me that because I am identified almost exclusively with the aggressive/defensive ego, **I AM AN ILLUSION**. The man that people know me as does not really exist. He has been created. He has been created in my mind.*

  "There is sometimes a small representation of the authentic me, depending on how safe the ego feels at the time. But mostly I am the projected image of what the ego wants the world to see at the time. I am doing this self-awareness work because I am no longer willing to be represented by the collection of illusions it needs to create for any given situation.

  "I have allowed [my ego] free reign with my thoughts, and it has used that power to turn my mind into a movie projector, and I become the unwilling and resentful actor in the very movie that I gave it the power it needed to make!

  "When I am doing this healing work the aggressive/defensive ego sees my attempts at coming into my own as an independent/aware adult as my hand reaching to unplug the power cord to its projector. It resists this with all its might because there can be no illusion without the projector.

  "The aggressive/defensive ego is going to need an immense amount of support, patience, love and guidance to allow this to happen. But I want to do that for this terrified part of me and so does the rest of my Inner Family. Actually I don't know who's doing it for whom. Just that we are wanting a better way to live than the one we've known."

Chapter XIII

The Work In Action:
The Relationships Workshop

Several times I have referred to clients and seminar participants. The seminars I lead are entitled *The Work of Love*. Just recently I led another one. I asked six of the participants to answer three questions for inclusion as the last chapter of this book.

1. As a single person attending by yourself, why did you attend? (or) As "one half" of a couple attending with your partner, why did you attend?

2. What was the value of identifying your aggressive/defensive ego and how it has operated in your intimate relationships to this point?

3. What change did you notice in yourself by taking on the work of actually healing your part of a particular relationship (as you did by going through the Intensive Communication Exercise at the end of the seminar)?

I hope the responses these people offer, and my observations that immediately follow each of them, show the practical and real value of doing this work. The responses are unedited.

*

From a woman who attended with her husband (her husband's response follows hers):

"My husband and I agreed that the next time we got into a major "donny brook" with each other we would go back to see Joel to revisit the "Work of Love". The next argument arrived about six months later and was a difficult one. We were unable to resolve it ourselves so off we went to Joel's office. My husband had been with me once before to the Relationship workshop just before we were

married and we determined that we needed to revisit what we had learned.

"I have attended three Relationship workshops over the course of eight years. The first time I attended this seminar I was still reeling from a divorce. The second time was with my husband before we were married and the third time, most recently, together again with my husband after being married for five years. It was interesting to notice how my ego operated under each of these circumstances. Even though I am very aware of my ego' function and presence it was interesting to notice how cleverly and skillfully my ego keeps love well away from me.

"In the most recent seminar with my husband, I noticed that my ego has become more powerful than ever—of course—I am in a relationship with someone who I want to love and loves me back. My ego signals, "No go!" when the going gets tough. He [my ego] *reminds me that men are not to be trusted, are users, and don't and can't love so give it up. The advantage of having been to three seminars, all with similar design, is to see how my ego has progressed over time and under differing circumstances. Because I know the work of love and Joel's teachings, it is faster and easier to see a masterful ego at work.*

"The change I noticed by taking on the work of actually healing my part of my relationship is that I notice how quickly it can become forgotten if not attended to at all times. I had become complacent over the course of my marriage and allowed my ego to run free with no regard for the effects that it might be having on my husband. It was necessary to ask for forgiveness for my part in the mess and the way I had been behaving. As soon as I moved into the vulnerable place of asking for forgiveness and moving my ego aside the feeling of love for me and my husband was present and that was a new feeling in itself. I also felt his love for me and that was scary but at the same time easier than allowing my ego to fight it off. It's new territory that I am treading but it beats fighting and feeling alone and disconnected. We are able to work with each other better now and can more easily see when our egos are running us and what choices we have instead."

The aggressive/defensive ego in this woman (and in everyone of us) is constantly reinventing itself and, in different circumstances and for different reasons, always wants to distrust love. However, in this woman's case, over eight years and three relationship workshops, her independent/aware adult has caught on to her aggressive/defensive ego's tricks and remains at least "one step ahead". She teaches us that the inner work is constant as is the need for self-scrutiny, personal responsibility, honesty, and humility.

*

From a man who attended with his wife (his wife's response is immediately above):

"I attended the seminar in hopes of improving my relationship with my wife.

"I have realized my ego has a greater impact on others than I originally thought. It's operating mostly when I don't realize it. The seminar taught me to take notice of when it is operating.

"I am more conscious of my wife's feelings now but I am still learning to listen to her with patience. I have a tendency to minimize them but I must realize that her feelings are not a matter of "right" and "wrong". They are what they are and as such worth tending to. I'm still working on it."

The aggressive/defensive ego just loves to be right. For this man to get beyond right/wrong in his relationship with his wife, and to grant that her feelings just "are", or as he put it *"are what they are and as such worth tending to"*, was a terrific new opening for him. New and substantial intimacy and closeness now becomes a possibility for him to experience.

*

From a man who attended with his wife (his wife's response follows his):

"I attended the seminar to develop a more authentic deeper relationship with my wife.

"I found my aggressive/defensive ego would make things difficult for my wife to stay open and safe. My work is to curb this behavior.

"I found myself impatient with my wife's need to dramatize her view and I kept cutting her off and interrupting her."

This man sounds like he is just starting to see his aggressive/defensive ego in action. On the one hand, he is seeing and taking new responsibility for his part of the conflict i.e.: *"I found my aggressive/defensive ego would make things difficult for my wife to stay open and safe..."*.

On the other hand, on paper at least, his statement: *"I found myself impatient with my wife's need to dramatize her view..."* points to the accumulated private judgments, criticisms, and interpretations he has been carrying regarding the (according to him) legitimacy and sincerity of his wife's manner of communicating. Privately held judgments, criticisms, and beliefs about your significant other are the death-knell for consistently joining them in the Universe of Love.

*

From a woman who attended with her husband (her husband's response is immediately above):

"I attended the seminar to <u>continue</u> the inner work that I've been doing on my own and with Joel which has been primarily focused on my own individual issues. The timing seemed right to extend this inner work on me to include the issues that I've been having in my marriage.

"The value of identifying my aggressive/defensive ego was to give this <u>very</u> <u>real</u> part of myself a <u>voice</u> and allow my feelings— expressible perhaps <u>only</u> through my ego to be revealed for the first time.

"The advantage of this REVELATION has been to understand the depth of my emotions—anger, frustration, lack of faith, disappointment, hopelessness, isolation, despair, etc., and how <u>denying</u> them as a part of myself—the DARK side—has kept me from living a truly authentic life.

"The aggressive/defensive ego identified in the seminar was a new version of my previous ego which was very CONFIDENT, HAPPY—FREE OF DESPAIR: NEGATIVITY, etc.

"Having "dropped" that previous ego in my individual work with Joel, a whole new level of aggressive/defensive ego seemed to emerge from and through the seminar.

"Both egos have served to keep me from being 100% intimate with my husband in the 22 years we've been together.

"Unfortunately, because the trust of the seminar weekend (that was created throughout the exercises facilitated by Joel) was broken by my husband during the last exercise—the intensive communication work, I seem to have been stuck in this newly emerged aggressive/defensive ego ever since."

This woman recognized she had shifted from an old version of her aggressive/defensive ego to a newer one. Falling into an updated version of her aggressive/defensive ego indicates there is more individual healing ahead. This woman's honest self-appraisal of how she has remained stuck in her inability to present her authentic self to her husband augers well for the further shedding of her ego. She is realizing this is her future work, and hers alone, to do.

*

From a woman attending by herself:

"I attended the Relationship Seminar because I needed to ensure I had looked thoroughly at my responsibility in why I was choosing to leave my marriage. I resisted attending this seminar for the very reasons I knew I needed to go. It was likely I would have to not only logically look at my part in my marriage—but I had a sense the seminar would force the issue of feeling my responsibility. In my life, and especially in my marriage, feeling was not on the agenda! I have discovered I do almost anything to avoid facing how I feel.

"The value of identifying my aggressive/defensive ego has been gaining an understanding of the motivation of this ego in my life. My aggressive/defensive ego operates to protect me—it's all about protection. When my ego is operating I can be in my marriage because I have no expectations, if you don't expect love—you will not be hurt. My ego allowed me an external existence with my husband. It all looks good on the surface, but there is nothing going on below, no emotional connection. Through the years of my marriage I had concluded certain things on a logical level... as to why this marriage wasn't full of the stuff my fantasy world was, passion, depth, truth, vulnerability—but even that knowledge was not enough to bring about any change, or even any desire to change, just a vague notion that something wasn't quite right.

"Understanding my aggressive/defensive ego brings an awareness into my life that is helping me heal and know the

authentic Me—even when the picture/truth is not too flattering. When my ego is on I am the woman who doesn't feel anything in a relationship—there is too much risk involved in that prospect. Do not feel and there will be no pain, sadly though, there is also no deep joy or love connectedness in this arrangement either.

"Day two of the Relationship Seminar, I thought I had it all under control—I was going to get through this without coming apart... (feeling) and in spite of knowing that was the work I needed to do, my ego has been working many years in my life to keep me away from the feelings this seminar/process was trying to get me to face, I was being protected by my ego and was even feeling a little smug—I was in control and feeling good.

"However, the day wasn't over yet—the exercise of going through the Intensive Communication work with a partner forced me to gently push aside my ego and feel what was going on. I had known it in my head, but never experienced the feeling part of my separation.

"In the process of leaving my husband I had been unable to communicate to him the truth about my discovery of how I actually felt and have for many years—hardly a surprise considering we rarely, if ever, discussed how we truly felt... not something we did. This part of the seminar gave me an opportunity to speak and feel what the truth was about leaving my partner of 29 years. Lots of feelings going on here!!!!

"The result of this was confirmation for me of the truth of how I feel about the relationship I have been in most of my adult life, or as I have been taught, I have not been in a relationship but an arrangement. An arrangement between two people unaware that being in a relationship is risky and requires a willingness to be honest and vulnerable to experience the brilliance of what love can be. I believe only when you understand and feel the truth can you be free to make a choice. The Seminar gave me the gift of choice—I am now free to make a choice.

"Thank you as always! The words never seem to be enough"

The aggressive/defensive ego can fight for a lifetime to deny the admission and moreover, the experience of, our emotional pain and fear. This woman eloquently describes the stranglehold it had over her (and apparently her former mate) over twenty-nine years of marriage.

Her willingness to begin to feel, especially to feel the full extent of her own emotional pain and fear, is the deepest, most significant work in healing. Her adaptive child consciousness has been running from real relationships into fantasy, no doubt ever since she was little. If this woman will continue to help heal the devastating wounds of her adaptive child, a world in which she can both give and receive real love awaits her.

*

From a man attending by himself

"*I had worked with Joel about twelve years previously. I had attended several seminars and been in private therapy with him. Back then it was a curious and profitable relationship—a combination of personal therapy and supervision; certainly friendship and mutual respect. I was (and still am) a therapist in private practice. And, in my own work, I use a slightly different, but similar approach regarding inner work, so I am frequently working with my own ego. So, why would "I", a successful and veteran therapist wish to invest the emotional energy, time, and money, in an intense weekend workshop that I had already taken?*

"*As I write this now, two weeks after the workshop. I will tell you I am seeking and will soon embark on a new intimate, committed, and monogamous relationship; and my career is undergoing wonderful change. I know my ego is forever crafty in trying to re-establish itself. I needed the review. I admire the work of love and wished to connect with Joel again. Re-establishing myself firmly in the work of love, so that I can love myself properly, and then offer this to my partner and friends and my clients is the most important thing I can do. To me, it is the work of Life that underlies everything else.*

"*Up to 1997 or so, I thought I was a committed partner in all my relationships but I never really was; never really completely inside the circle of commitment. I was either an over-committed relationship addict, which to me is a more appropriate term for co-dependent, 'killing myself doing everything for love'; or I was preparing to exit because she wasn't doing... or was doing... 'whatever'. It had nothing to do with her.*

"*This changed. A couple of years later I was in a loving relationship and felt (and still do) that I was completely committed in a healthy way. This relationship ended shockingly because of a* crime. *Within weeks I was left shattered. My years of personal work stood me in good stead but still, I began to fragment and I hid emotionally from the world. In a three year period: my lover was shot; I lost my entire life savings; I lost my home; I moved to a new city; my best friend died; I had to declare bankruptcy; I almost lost my career. I was terrified to love again. My ego re-established itself and allowed me to survive a brutal time.*

"Since about 2003 I began to heal and recreate myself and heal my inner world. I am now seeking a new love and I am determined that from my side of the relationship, I will not impose my insecurities on her. I mean, I know I will (after all my ego is determined and I am human), but I will at least do it less often, with less intensity.

"For me, reviewing the work of love is re-committing myself to Life. It is another way of demonstrating rather than just talking about my commitment to a more compassionate and spiritual life. Life is good, and doing this work makes it beautiful."

"Our 'homework' on the first night was to allow our aggressive/defensive ego a voice. This was to meet it and get to know it (for me to know it again). The Homework: I was to let my ego tell me about ten things. I was surprised to see how deeply entrenched its beliefs were. In view of what I have been through I can see the 'logic' of this; however this does not serve me or my Life. This is my ego's point of view on ten topics:

<u>*Love*</u>*: For Love you have to do everything in the relationship or else no one will love you. Protect them, care for them, drive them everywhere, hold open every door, never be sick, never be needy, cook all the meals... do everything. Generally, love is real for everyone else but not you. You haven't earned it; you're not worth it, and you're not that attractive, anyway.*

<u>*Trust*</u>*: Generally a foolish thing to do. Trust is dangerous— remember everything and everyone you ever trusted has let you down.*

<u>*Men*</u>*: Be wary, they are not trustworthy. They will try and manipulate you with shaming and aggression so be tough. And... they'll hit on your girlfriend or wife.*

<u>*Women*</u>*: Be wary; they are needy and weak so they use men. They use sex to manipulate you. Certainly the more beautiful they are, the more risky the investment of trust. The beautiful women <u>always</u> have men hitting on them. (So don't trust men!) But... a*

beautiful woman that's with you may say 'No' for a while, but sooner or later along comes some richer, more handsome, more dynamic, not-so-screwed-up guy, and she'll leave you. Absolutely. Of course, there are beautiful women who would never cave in, there are a few that are *trustworthy, but they're all taken. So, you've got to marry 'ugly' and be safe (in which case you'll never want sex) or marry 'beautiful' and live at risk. It's better to give up. Just quit trying.*

<u>*Vulnerability*</u>*: This is a pretty good manipulation tactic to use on women to get laid; otherwise, it's pretty dangerous.*

<u>*Commitment*</u>*: Nice if you can get it but don't hold your breath.*

<u>*Monogamy*</u>*: Nice if you can get it, but don't hold your breath. You pretty well have to buy it.*

<u>*Intimacy*</u>*: I can't afford it—too dangerous.*

<u>*Surrendering*</u>*: If you do that you're stupid!*

<u>*How should I be in life in order to survive?*</u>*: Just remain isolated and completely independent. That's the safest 'foreign policy'. Do everything yourself.*

"The advantages of this meet-your-ego exercise were many. It allowed me to gently unmask my ego. It's important for me to do this. I have to know what we (my inner family) are up against. We are <u>not</u> up against my ego, we are 'against' it's rigid and fear-based rules. I have to know what these rules are if I am to have love and spiritual success in my world and in my relationships. The exercise allowed me to develop more patience with myself. It's like taming a vicious junk-yard guard-dog—love and patience are the keys.

"The exercise also (in a back-handed way) allowed me to see how my ego's rigid beliefs have in many cases kept me safe and actually saved my life on more than one occasion. [I was in law enforcement for fourteen years. If my ego was not so suspicious and cynical, I would be dead.] I have more respect for myself now; for the dangerous and violent situations I faced and how my ego got me through all the difficult times of my life. I realized this quite clearly and became grateful for my ego's power, intuition, and clarity. Alone, in my apartment, I thanked myself for it. And, of course, it was also clear that this continued high-grade suspicion would not serve me at all in my life today.

"I also realized that I was now capable of more compassion for others. By seeing 'my ego' in me, I sensed more clearly that everyone I encounter has their own version of my ego; maybe not

quite so aggressive as mine (and in some cases maybe more aggressive), but certainly for them, a force to contend with. I looked with kinder eyes at other people.

"This will be especially true for my intimate relationship. My lover will receive more compassion and kindness from me; not because she is entitled to more kindness, but because she is the person I am closest to. Or – she is the person I wish to be closest to and to whom I have committed myself."

"The seminar's Intensive Communication Exercise I did on Sunday evening was born out of my earlier written homework from Saturday night about my ego's views of women.

"I was surprised. After 28 years of 'healing' in one form or another; including 15 years of therapy as both a client and in supervision, and 23 years as a therapist, I realized I had <u>never</u> closely examined my relationship with my mother. As I went through the ten questions of the exercise and acted as though I was talking to her (she died over 20 years ago), I uncovered a lot of disappointment and innocent anger. What I mean by 'innocent' anger is, it was the anger of a small child that felt abandoned.

"It was an anger replete with loneliness and confusion; I was puzzled about my egos' view of women and how they acted; what they did; that they were (supposedly) largely untrustworthy. This was all through the heart of a child under seven. All of my life I have lived with this angry, lonely confusion. I married (and divorced) three times to try and fix this. Of course it never worked.

"It was quite astonishing to me (as the adult participating in the seminar). My ego had kept this pain from my consciousness. It had hidden it. In my ego's view this was protecting me from 'women'; but it was also allowing my suspicions, confusion, and loneliness to go on unchecked. As long as this was concealed from me my ego had a free rein over my attitude in relationships with women. Now, having completed the exercise, and with the resulting awareness, it has significantly less power over me. I noticed a difference in the following days, and view myself, women, and our relationship to the world, differently."

"I know I live with a vicious junk-yard guard-dog—my 'ego'. Considering my history, I understand this; I am glad, for this has allowed me to survive some pretty tough and violent times; I know, probably more than most people experience. Without it I could not have survived my childhood and the 1960's, let alone a military

and police career, and those three years. Everything inside me is calming down. Peace is present most of the time.

"As I end this now, it is late at night. I listen to quiet jazz and I feel safe and sad. The seminar reminded me of the important work that I do in my own life and career and the important work that Joel does in his. It is the work of love. I reflect on how few people will sincerely attempt to heal. Even with the sadness born of love, I also feel integrated and whole; for the first time in years."

Continuing to be deep, true, vulnerable, and honest with himself, the life-long healing this man has undertaken is clearly evident in his words and his being. Here is the story of a man's naked and courageous emergence from the Universe of Fear, which he fell into as a boy and lived out of for a substantial part of his adult life. Yet, now, one can tell he has done the healing work he has needed to do to set himself free. I believe he will continue to do whatever healing work is demanded of him in the future. He sounds quite firmly grounded in the Universe of Love and this, for him, seems to be the greatest accomplishment of his life. He is determined to offer this to himself and to others.

*

Epilogue

*"The wolf will live with the lamb,
the leopard will lie down with the goat,
the calf and the lion and the yearling together;
and a little child will lead them.*

Isaiah 11:6

A Heart and Spirit Led Consciousness and an Ego-In-Service

The personal healing work described in this book is a work occupying a lifetime; and perhaps many lifetimes. Everyone I have known who has taken it on (including myself) does not finish it. There is always more buried or denied emotional pain and fear to discover. A friend who undertakes to live a sincerely spiritual life from a heart-led consciousness often says the more aware he becomes, the more subtle his ego gets. There is always work, and always more subtle ways the aggressive/defensive ego consciousness will attempt to project its pain and fear onto others.

As I come to the end of this book I know that I, for one, still carry fear. There are people and situations in my world to which I respond with a fear that is significantly out of proportion to the threat they pose. You see, I still possess an aggressive/defensive ego consciousness. Though my own Inner Family has come a long, long way in abdicating our old ways, my ego still takes me over. Every so often it will explode like a grenade in the relationships with those people with whom I am most vulnerable. More regularly and stealthily, it will take the form of private, unshared, judgments and criticisms—an accumulation of negative opinions and beliefs about someone or something that I do not even know I'm formulating. Instantly I find myself thrust back into the Universe of Fear where there is no possibility for inner peace, love, or safety. At this point I know that I have to return to the basics: heal my aggressive/defensive ego; work with my other inner consciousnesses, and return to the Universe of Love. Sometimes I may have to apologize. I take responsibility.

I have come to know there is a Universe of Love to which I

can always return. I know that it is real, always present, and extremely close by. Its embrace is eternally available to me. No matter how mired I become in emotional pain and fear (which I project onto others) the work of healing my relationship with myself has shown me that the experience of inner peace and love is *never more than a choice away.* Even if I, as an adult controlled by my aggressive/defensive ego, cannot or will not make the choice to return to love, I know that I have other Inner Family members within me who will make that choice for me. I can reliably call on my natural child consciousness/authentic self and my spiritual consciousness to take my hand and lead me back.

As a flawed and wounded human being, I know that I have fallen from the Universe of Love I once naturally and effortlessly lived in as a child. It is likely I will never again have effortless, unchanging, "full-time" residency there. I will always have to work at it, going back to the fundamentals of this inner-healing work to earn my return fare home. I accept this. With a united and mutually supportive Inner Family I know I can visit the Universe of Love more and more often and stay there longer when I choose to. This is incentive enough for me.

As you step away from the aggressive/defensive ego as your primary identity, what opens up is the glorious opportunity to live from heart- and spirit-led consciousnesses. This dramatically enhances the experience and perception of unity not divisiveness; sameness not separation; love not fear; equality not dominance; harmony and wholeness not inner civil war or outer conflict.

Using a metaphor of clothes: Instead of being told how to dress to impress by the aggressive/defensive ego consciousness, you claim the right to dress yourself. Your new clothing will feel and look just right; an easy, natural expression of who you are. In the pockets of your new garments, there will be a place for your aggressive/defensive ego consciousness (which you can take out and use if you sense that you absolutely must). This is the critical difference: *You now have an aggressive/defensive ego consciousness you can use when necessary. The aggressive/defensive ego consciousness no longer dominates you.*

Yet in the process of healing your Inner Family even your aggressive/defensive ego will be different; very different. It will not be the same one you have unknowingly carried with you from childhood or adolescence—the fearsome, edgy, quick-to-attack dictator who took control of your Inner Family. You have by this point worked through a good deal of the emotional pain and fear that forced it to operate the way it did (and you to live the way you lived). No longer needing to be singularly responsible and constantly on alert in order to merely survive (meaning to fend off life, love, and other people), it can emerge from your healing work as a courageous, devoted, and cooperative force to be usefully relied on when needed. It will now operate for more than its own narrow, self interests. This means it has transformed into an **ego-in-service.**

What Is an Ego-in-Service?

This is the ego consciousness that emerges from the healing work described in this book. You have given your former aggressive/defensive ego the necessary attention, acceptance, understanding, time, and healing it needed in order to release a substantial portion of the emotional pain and fear it has carried (and perpetuated). Through your efforts, it is now genuinely included, respected, and appreciated by you, the now independent/aware adult, and the rest of the Inner Family. It is now treated as an esteemed family member and no longer perceived as an unwanted, dark and hostile force; nor shunned as a social pariah. The Inner Family now relies on it to make a significant contribution to the family's future well-being.

The former aggressive/defensive ego consciousness will need your continued help making this transition. To become and remain an ego-in-service, it will likely need your assurances that you are not going to use your healing work as a charade to overthrow it (or kill it off altogether) in the equivalent of a secret revolution. And, as the new head of the Inner Family, *you* must reassure it you are not intending to give it the proverbial "golden handshake" and ignominiously put it out to pasture. Instead, it will be accorded a new, vital, and valued role to play in the ongoing welfare of you and the Inner Family.

Its old position of unequivocal, unassailable Ruler of the Inner Family will have to be relinquished *and* its old aggressive and defensive ways reduced as much as possible. It must be given unlimited support in the transition from its old enforcer-dictator role to becoming an equal amongst equals in a collaborative Inner Family. No longer completely and singularly faced with the onerous responsibility of physical and psychological survival, it is lovingly shown that it belongs to something far greater than itself—your Inner Family.

The Family of which it is a part is comprised of four out-standing and skilled members who, in their own unique ways, can also do an effective job of protecting everyone if the need arises. However, they can additionally foster cooperation, harmony, and peace (which the aggressive/defensive ego never could deliver).

Far from being threatened by the discovery of these new pro-tectors and guides, this "new" ego-in-service welcomes their arrival into the ranks of leadership. It has been shown that the world is a safer and friendlier place than it was long ago (when it originally had to take matters into its own hands). It has been shown that the only two approaches it had available (variations of attack and defend), are simply not needed nearly as much in this new world.

A key element in the transformation from an aggres-sive/defensive ego consciousness to an ego-in-service is the realization it no longer has to aggressively protect the Inner Family from outside enemies twenty-four hours a day *every* day. You, the independent/aware adult have located the most dangerous enemy you will ever meet (the old former ego) and you have found it to be within. It has been *your own* fear and aggression that has been the enemy. You have now been able to help the (former) aggres-sive/defensive ego appreciate that it can relax a little; take some time off; even go on vacation! Most importantly, you have shown it that aggression and defense are no longer crucial to survival.

I can't really describe the relief, exhilaration and joy I have seen in demeanor of those whom I have accompanied on this healing journey. When the aggressive/defensive ego consciousness lets go and realizes it can now depend on others the calmness that appears is startling. I can see their bodies and souls laying down an enormously heavy, life-long burden; a load so cumbersome and deadly that it robbed them almost entirely of their energy, optimism, and happiness.

Somewhere, from an emotional and spiritual place deep in-side, they come to the almost inexpressible and tangible knowledge that their survival is somehow guaranteed. This is not guaranteed by themselves (or the former aggressive/defensive ego consciousness to which they had become identified) but by the spiritual consciousness and its clearest representative here on earth, the natural child consciousness/authentic self.

With the crushing, life-long responsibility for sheer survival off its shoulders, this "new" ego-in-service can enjoy its liberation by serving the highest and best interests of all of the members of the Inner Family. It will embrace the other Inner Family members as it has itself been embraced. It is open to new ways of contributing to everyone's protection and well-being, *for that is all it ever wanted from the beginning.*

An ego-in-service is committed to a win/win situation for everyone. Every significant decision made, every goal or ambition sought, and every course of action taken, will be orchestrated to be a win for the independent/aware adult; a win for the natural child/authentic self; a win for the spiritual consciousness; and a win for the ego-in-service. This makes all decisions lastingly beneficial and worthwhile. Rather than a dictator of the Inner Family, it has become accountable to the Inner Family, specifically to *you*, the independent/aware adult (who is committed to collaborative and inclusive decision making).

The Wolf Will Live with the Lamb

When the wolf (as your aggressive/defensive ego) is no more, it will have the ability, the motivation, and the desire to lie down with the lamb (your natural child consciousness). Though it had been forced to be a fighter, and sometimes even a killer, the fundamental and essential needs of your former aggressive/defensive ego consciousness for safety, love, and value have always been indistinguishable from the needs of every other member of your Inner Family.

You have shown yourself, first-hand, that the needs and desires of the wolf and the lamb are exactly the same. You are one with what you have feared. All is one within. All is one without. The deeper you know these truths, the more regularly will you leave behind the Universe of Fear and reside in the Universe of Love.

This work won't make you perfect. There will always be some manner of trail and tribulation; after all, it's Life and we all know life is ever-changing and unpredictable. However, once you have firmly established yourself on this path of personal healing, you will have (to a noticeable extent) transformed your aggressive/defensive ego.

Members of your Inner Family will be generally united in support of each other. The inner civil war that turned you into a frightening and frightened warrior on the battlefield of life can give way to an expanding experience of peace, balance, and harmony. as much within as without. The unity and peace that you have created in your relationship with yourself will be manifested more naturally and effortlessly in your relationship with others.

It is apparent that as humans we are created in, born into, and must live "in" relationship with everyone and everything on the planet and in the universe. It is never a question of whether we are in relationship or not, it is only and ever a question of how we as individuals define the relationship. By doing this inner work the universe may not change much, but your relationship to everything *will* change. This is regardless of whether the relationship is your loved ones, strangers, plants, animals, or nature itself. The inner harmony you experience will manifest in the world *you* inhabit. I promise you this is true.

A Final Word

Two of the more influential people in my life have been Gandhi and my university professor, Ed Allen. I leave you with quotes from them:

> *"Any change you want to see in the world you must begin within yourself."*
> Gandhi (1869 – 1948)

> *"All human beings are angels in armor. It is your job to only see the angel."*
> Ed Allen (1945 – 2002)

About The Author

Joel Brass was born in 1951 in Winnipeg, Manitoba. He holds a Bachelor of Arts (Honours) degree from the University of Winnipeg (Winnipeg, Manitoba) and a Masters of Applied Science degree (M.A.Sc.) from the University of Waterloo (Kitchener/Waterloo, Ontario).

In the course of his career he has worked in Ontario, Alberta, and British Columbia. He has been a psychotherapist in private practice and seminar leader for twenty-four years. For different, extended periods he has been a successful radio talk-show host with CJOC (Lethbridge, AB), and KISS-FM and CFUN, (Vancouver, BC). Joel is a full member of the British Columbia Association of Registered Clinical Counsellors. His passion and specialization is the healing and growth of individuals and love relationships.

At present he lives in White Rock, British Columbia, with his wife Marim, his sons Adam and Simon, and their dogs Harmony and Herschel.

To contact Joel for presentations, seminars, or for information about therapy or his book, please use his website: www.joelbrass.com

To purchase copies of this book please go to the publisher's website: www.trafford.com

---

[1] I believe this is a quote of Werner Erhard but I have not been able to verify this.
[2] *"There will be time, there will be time / To prepare a face to meet the faces that you meet; / There will be time to murder and create…"* from The Love Song of J. Alfred Prufrock, by T.S. Eliot.
[3] This was explained well in Ekhart Tolle's books, *Power of Now* and *The New Earth*.
[4] Richard Clark is a Vancouver therapist and energy-psychology practitioner. He combines ego and Inner Family work with traditional talk therapy, spirituality, and body energy work (energy psychology). He is the author of *Addictions and Spiritual Transformation* (Trafford Publishing). He can be reached through his website: <**www.richardwclark.com**>
[5] *A Course In Miracles,* published by The Foundation for Inner Peace©1975-1992.
[6] Ibid.

ISBN 1425185559-2

9 781425 185596